In the Time of Sky-Rhyming

In the Time of Sky-Rhyming

How Hip Hop Resonated in Brown Los Angeles

JONATHAN E. CALVILLO

OXFORD
UNIVERSITY PRESS

Oxford University Press is a department of the University of Oxford. It furthers
the University's objective of excellence in research, scholarship, and education
by publishing worldwide. Oxford is a registered trade mark of Oxford University
Press in the UK and certain other countries.

Published in the United States of America by Oxford University Press
198 Madison Avenue, New York, NY 10016, United States of America.

© Oxford University Press 2024

All rights reserved. No part of this publication may be reproduced, stored in
a retrieval system, or transmitted, in any form or by any means, without the
prior permission in writing of Oxford University Press, or as expressly permitted
by law, by license, or under terms agreed with the appropriate reproduction
rights organization. Inquiries concerning reproduction outside the scope of the
above should be sent to the Rights Department, Oxford University Press, at the
address above.

You must not circulate this work in any other form
and you must impose this same condition on any acquirer.

Library of Congress Cataloging-in-Publication Data
Names: Calvillo, Jonathan E., author.
Title: In the time of sky-rhyming : how hip hop resonated in brown Los Angeles / Jonathan E. Calvillo.
Description: [1.] | New York : Oxford University Press, 2024. |
Includes bibliographical references and index.
Identifiers: LCCN 2024032007 (print) | LCCN 2024032008 (ebook) |
ISBN 9780197762486 (paperback) | ISBN 9780197762479 (hardback) |
ISBN 9780197762509 (epub)
Subjects: LCSH: Rap (Music)—California—Los Angeles—History and criticism. |
Hispanic Americans—California—Los Angeles—Music—History and criticism. |
Hip-hop—California—Los Angeles—History.
Classification: LCC ML3531 .C415 2024 (print) | LCC ML3531 (ebook) |
DDC 782.42164909794/94—dc23/eng/20240726
LC record available at https://lccn.loc.gov/2024032007
LC ebook record available at https://lccn.loc.gov/2024032008

DOI: 10.1093/oso/9780197762479.001.0001

Paperback printed by Marquis Book Printing, Canada
Hardback printed by Bridgeport National Bindery, Inc., United States of America

*To my familia, Puanani, Kalea, Mahalia, and Jonathan.
May we continue to build resonant worlds together.*

Contents

Acknowledgments — ix

Introduction: Caught in the Resonance — 1

PART I. CHANNELS OF RESONANCE: FOUNDATIONAL MOVEMENTS

1. Caribbean Currents — 25
2. Borderland Blends — 47
3. The Funk Frequency — 72

PART II. CYPHERS OF RESONANCE: SITES OF PROLIFERATION

4. Translating Elementary Knowledge — 95
5. Game Recognize Game — 115
6. Radiotronic Waves — 134

PART III. CHARTING THE RESONANCE: EBBS AND FLOWS

7. Crossing Freeways with Flyways — 157
8. The Stage and the Crossfade — 173
9. Sustaining the Resonance — 194

Conclusion: Rebirths — 210

Appendix: Samples and Sampling — 219
References — 225
Index — 237

Acknowledgments

I am grateful to all those who entered the circle as collaborators or cheered on from the outer edges, propelling this project forward. To my familias, thank you for your constant support: Alvaro, Lydia, David, Ernesto; Pua, May, Simon, Alex, Kielu, Shannon, Mishael. To our Boston family, we could not have made it this far without you: The Johnsons, the Daniels-Lindseys, the Tinglofs, the Papias, the entire FHCC family, and my children's schoolteachers, who infused my household with invaluable joy, knowledge, and curiosity. To those who were conversation partners at various points in the project's journey, I am ever grateful for your insights and wisdom. Mark Villegas, thank you for your friendship and expansive perspectives. Carlos Aguilar, thank you for sharing your grounded knowledge. Travis Harris and Erika Gault, thank you for the opportunity to reignite this project through your edited volume and for inspiring the work through the scholarship each of you continues to produce. Dan White Hodge, thank you for your continued camaraderie in the academy and for laying important groundwork in this field. Jon Gill, thank you for sharing your creativity alongside and through your scholarship. James Diego Vigil, thank you for helping me to develop an early version of this project in your Street Ethnography course in 2012. Rafik Wahbi, Leo Esclamad, Tasha Iglesias, Ryon Cobb, Lloyd Barba, Erica Ramirez, Tony Lin, Matt Rafalow, Patrick Reyes, Aida Ramos, Daniel Ramirez, Leah Payne, Yader Lanuza, Gabe Veas, David Jaimes, Gerardo Martí, Farris Blount, Raul Perez, Stefano Bloch, Jasmin Figueroa, Arnold Sullivan, Marcos Rubio, and Stan Bailey, you have all added to this project in unique ways.

To my colleagues present and past who interacted with me in relation to this project, thank you for your continued encouragement. From Emory University and Candler School of Theology: Arun Jones, Alison Greene, Amy Barker, Brett Opalinski, Danielle Tumminio Hansen, Deanna Womack, Ellen Ott Marshall, Gabrielle Thomas, Greg Ellison, Helen Jin Kim, Ish Ruiz, Ian McFarland, Joanne Solis-Walker, Joel Kemp, Joel Lemon, Khalia Williams, Kyle Lambelet, Kyra Daniels, Letitia Campbell, Maria Carreón, Marla Frederick, Nicole Phillips, Roger Nam, Sarah Bogue, Steffen Losel, Susan Hylen, Susan Reynolds, Ted Smith, Teresa Fry Brown, Tony Alonso, Walter Fluker, Yohanny Olacklin. From Boston University School of Theology: Anastacia Kidd, Andrew Shenton, Bryan Stone, Charlene Zuill, Christopher Brown, Christopher Evans, Daryl Ireland, David Jacobsen, Dana Robert, Filipe Maia, Hee An Choi, Karen Westerfield Tucker, Luis Menendez Antuña, Mary Elizabeth Moore, Nicolette

Manglos-Weber, Rady Roldan Figueroa, Cristian De la Rosa, Courtney Goto, Sujin Pak, Yara Gonzalez-Justiniano, and Shively Smith.

To the many creatives that stepped into the cypher, thank you for sharing your journeys with me. I received not only information but much inspiration: Carmelo Alvarez, Danny Rivera, Hex, Cesar Rivas, David Guzman, Gerard Meraz, Hec Si, J-vibe, Dave Storrs, David Portillo, Click, IceMan, Koolski, Pebo Rodriguez, Ace Rock, BBoy Don, Bobby Duran, Lil Luis, Peps, Manny Villasenor, Markski, Wilpower, Mellow Man, Michael Mata, Tasha Iglesias, Zender, Ruben Guevara, Carlos Hernandez, Danny Lara, Zulu Gremlin, Zane, Orko, Dino Mayorga, Fao Satele, Teleso Satele, Alice Bag, Andre Henderson, Dax Reynosa, Hen Gee, Trudie Arguelles, OG Chino, Lilah, Neecee, Ronek, Gilbert Rocha, Ruben Molina, Charlie Pellecer, ManOne, Ruben Funkahuatl Guevara, Vicente Mercado, and Peaches Rodriguez. Finally, thank you to the organizations that have supported this work: SSSR, The Center for the Study of Religion and the City, Candler School of Theology, Boston University School of Theology, BU Initiative on Cities, AAR Critical Approaches to Hip-Hop and Religion Unit, Libro Mobile.

Introduction

Caught in the Resonance

"We called it Sky-rhyming.[1] We started rapping but at the time we didn't know you could write raps. We were pulling words from the sky" (see Gault and Harris 2019). This is how Dax Reynosa remembers his beginnings as an emcee, prior to even having a name for Hip Hop. The year was 1982. Dax was twelve years old and rhyming was novel among his peers. Rap music had hit the airwaves a few years prior, but according to Dax, in Los Angeles, "nobody was rapping at the time," at least not in the neighborhoods he knew of.[2] Neither had dreams of making it big in Hip Hop materialized for a young, brown Mexican American kid like Dax. Still, paradoxically, to Dax and his crew, the sky was the limit. Under the heavens of Shadow Oak Park in West Covina, California, Dax, and his cousins Albert and Vincent, known collectively as Cousins Three, watched words materialize. They snatched these words from the sky and strung them together, painting word pictures that transported them to worlds beyond their working-class neighborhood (see Gill 2019). The cousins, like many of their peers, circulated through the arteries of urban Los Angeles, on bikes and buses, to the beat of a movement resonating around them and within them. As the movement grew, they battled others, through dance and rhyme, on sidewalks, at community centers, and at church carnivals. At first, they hardly knew they were shaping their futures through these acts. Yet, they were articulating themselves into a nascent Hip Hop scene, birthed from the ground up—or better yet, from the underground up. With time, they committed themselves to upholding this movement and this moment.

This book is about how Hip Hop resonated in revolutionary ways in Brown Los Angeles; it is about a time period, the time of sky-rhyming, when Hip Hop was first received and interpreted in the greater Los Angeles area. During this time, relationships forged between creative migrants, many with Caribbean and Central American roots, and California-born innovators, many of Mexican

---

[1] Some variantly use the term "sky-rapping."
[2] In 1981, Disco Daddy and Captain Rapp released "Gigolo Rapp" (Abrams 2023). Disco Daddy, a New York City transplant to Los Angeles, was a rhyming DJ since the late 1970s and cemented his place in Hip Hop history, battling Ice-T at the Carolina West night club in 1981.

ancestry, helped build alternative lifeworlds sprouting from the concrete of urban containment. Hip Hop, a creative arts movement fueled by Black American cultural streams coalesced within the Afrodiasporic communities of the Bronx, New York, to become a transportable and translatable cultural package of four expressive elements: DJing, breaking–labeled as breakdancing by outsiders, emceeing–often called rapping, and graffiti writing. These elements took Los Angeles by storm, as they were transposed on the existing artistries and aesthetics of the Southern California landscape. Hip Hop's reception within Brown Los Angeles was an important dimension of the movement's expansion; key adaptations took place there, drawing on local contexts to generate a homegrown version of the movement.[3]

While there are multiple conceptions of Brown Los Angeles,[4] I focus on Hip Hop's resonance within a particular configuration of Brown Los Angeles; this Brown Los Angeles is composed of the social-spatial convergences of Latin American diasporas, and descendants of those who survived colonial incursions in the Southwest, within primarily working-class neighborhoods in Los Angeles. The soul of Brown Los Angeles absorbs resonances from the vestiges of California's colonial past, retains native-born and migrant resources, and navigates the perils of containment and surveillance, sometimes living into and sometimes subverting societal expectations of brown life. This Brown Los Angeles shares significant space with Black American diasporas and with brown southeast Asian and Pacific Islander diasporas (Magaña 2022). A critical mass of people identify as brown within this imagined community. Some who have made important contributions to notions of Brown Los Angeles do not identify as brown, yet may find belonging here. Brown Los Angeles is a place, population, and social imaginary—an expectation of how to be, in order to belong, to survive, and to flourish.

During the time of sky-rhyming, distinct diasporic groups were converging upon Brown Los Angeles, and many young, creative minds therein were finding a home in Hip Hop. Central American refugees were settling in the urban corridors of the region, young Chicanos were coming of age in the post–civil rights era (see del Barco 1996), Caribbean migrants carried resources from east to west, and South American immigrants established networks across cities. Creatives[5] from these groups were interacting with other minoritized populations such as Black

---

[3] This echoes Pennycook's (2007) conception of "transcultural flows," typically applied to Hip Hop's adaptation within new cultural contexts across national borders, but also within intranational contexts such as Brown Los Angeles in the 1980s.

[4] Likewise, there are multiple conceptions of brown. See Sharma (2010) for an in-depth look at the intersection of South Asian American identity, often referred to as Brown, and Hip Hop.

[5] I use "creative/s" to denote individuals engaged in artistic production as a way of life, though not necessarily as employment. Erika Gault (2022) presents a helpful discussion of how Black creatives construct a sense of self through networking.

Americans, ethnic Samoans, Filipinos, and Koreans, building and blurring the very boundaries of Brown Los Angeles. These resonant interactions shaped creatives' Hip Hop identities and offered them resources for resistance, survival, and flourishing in the face of imperialistic legacies and urban inequalities. Many of these early participants who identified as brown largely understood they were part of a movement that would not exist without the Black American legacies that grounded it, the Afrodiasporic communities that nurtured it (Rose 1994), and the critical mass of Black American artists who continued to animate it. Bringing their own sensibilities and experiences to the scene, many brown creatives experienced life-giving transformations in this West Coast scene. It was not through a homogenizing mestizaje experience, but rather through distinct channels of resonance operating sometimes in consonance, sometimes in dissonance, that Hip Hop became firmly grounded within Brown Los Angeles.

Dax Reynosa's story reveals Hip Hop's extensive grassroots resonance in Brown Los Angeles. The son of a Chicano Vietnam veteran named David Reynosa, Dax founded the Tunnel Rats, a multiracial Hip Hop collective; taking its name from his father's combat unit, the collective was known for fighting battles in the underground (Borha 2013; Nibokun 2013, 2014). Since David Reynosa was a Pentecostal pastor, much of Dax's creative vision was nurtured in the church, drawing on gospel music, the preacher's cadence, and a penchant for captivating an audience. The Tunnel Rats became part of the creative fabric of Los Angeles's underground Hip Hop scene. Dax would go on to perform and record with highly lauded Hip Hop acts such as Freestyle Fellowship and KRS1, acts especially invested in preserving Hip Hop authenticity. Though, as underground artists, they did not unlock a life of luxury with their music, the Tunnel Rats developed a loyal following, inspiring a wide array of artists and fans.

Much transpired leading up to the Tunnel Rats' founding in 1993. In the preceding decade, members navigated the landscapes of a burgeoning Los Angeles scene. There, they contributed to a movement that, whether consciously or not, challenged colonial legacies of racism, the carceral state, gang violence, the crack epidemic, and migrant surveillance. Many brown creatives, as they navigated the sites and sounds of underground Los Angeles, interfaced with circles of creative resonance energized by historic Black American and Afrodiasporic creative movements. In the 1980s, as many brown creatives made sense of their racialized experiences, often alongside Black American peers, they helped build Los Angeles Hip Hop. This is a story of how creatives within Brown Los Angeles, including over fifty collaborators I spoke with, received the *movement*, and continue to work to preserve the *moment*.

A Resonant Movement

The story of how Hip Hop took root in Brown Los Angeles is a story of *resonance*. Resonance is an experience of meaningful connection in the world; it is to encounter the world as authentically responsive (Rosa 2019), and to react to this connection generatively, creatively even. Resonance is both model and metaphor, drawing from physics, describing how multiple entities experience covibration. In its social manifestation, as Hartmut Rosa posits, resonance allows beings to express themselves in their own voices, physically and figuratively, even as these voices find harmony. In recent scholarship, Rosa has furthered the concept of resonance as central to the "good life," that is, a life wherein human beings are fulfilled in relationally and ecologically sustainable ways. Resonance, I argue, is not only synchronic, experienced at shared moments in time, but also diachronic, experienced from sources originating at different points in time (Khabeer 2016:60).[6] Echoing scholarship on resonance, the collaborators who informed this book spoke of the life-giving, resonant capacities of the early Hip Hop scene. They spoke of the ways that it illuminated their social locations and provided a means to respond to their life conditions. They spoke of how it provided a basis for building resonant relationships, often cross-racial, and often driven by creative expression. Furthermore, they spoke of how their personal identities were shaped and affirmed through participation in the early scene. These connections, as many of my collaborators explained, were often built on existing cultural knowledge that heightened Hip Hop's intelligibility; this was a diachronic resonance that registered across time and across generations.

In relation to Hip Hop, the body of work consonant with Rosa's concept of resonance is best mediated by the school of thought emerging from Tricia Rose's landmark contributions to Hip Hop studies. Rose expounds on the sociopolitical factors giving rise to Hip Hop within its primarily Black American and Caribbean context. Rose (1994:23) shows how "technology and economics contribute to cultural forms." She documents the dissonant and consonant factors that shaped the movement's emergence, with particular attention given to the technologies and creative practices that became embedded in the movement. Attention to styles and aesthetics is important, as these function as modes of "identity formation" involving both "appropriation and critique" to challenge "structures of domination" (Rose 1994:36; see also Hernandez 2020). Likewise, Rose highlights the "lyrical bridges between Chicano and black styles," indicating an important stream of Black and brown resonance, as well as signaling broader possibilities of cross-racial resonance. Finally, Rose (1994:59) makes a key

---

[6] Khabeer argues that knowledge of time, both synchronic and diachronic, was central to the construction of Muslim Cool through Hip Hop, as a component of knowledge of self.

observation that is consonant with my collaborators' experiences of diachronic resonance: Hip Hop is "an experimental and collective space where contemporary issues and ancestral forces are worked through simultaneously." Su'ad Abdul Khabeer (2016:8) further elucidates this phenomenon through her concept of "loops," explaining how the construction of Muslim Cool draws on Hip Hop to provide "a site of continuity and change" similar to practices of sampling. In such creative scenes, resonances of the past, including histories of oppression and cultural resources, are brought into the present, indeed, resonate with the present, and are addressed in creative fashion. Thus, I situate Rosa in conversation with Rose, tracing the technologies and sociopolitical factors that shaped Hip Hop's resonance in Brown Los Angeles.

In the emerging West Coast scene, distinct scales of resonance were at play: At the cross-regional level, Hip Hop as a broad social movement was being translated into new contexts, often through expansive technological means and popular figures in the field, but also through channels of cultural transmission and migratory populations. At the local level, Hip Hop was being experienced as a scene, often energized by relational configurations such as crews, cyphers—circular gatherings of ritualized, artistic exchange (Khabeer 2016; Johnson 2022; Alim 2008)—and ongoing spaces of collaborative creative production. At the personal level, individuals identified with Hip Hop in intimate ways, fashioning their aesthetic and artistic proclivities in line with the broader movement. Across multiple levels, creatives drew on past cultural histories to situate themselves within the movement (Flores 2000; Villegas 2021).

I am especially attentive to how Hip Hop was transmitted, interpreted, and adapted to new contexts in embodied ways (Kitwana 2002; Reznowski 2014). Toward that end, I examine how the movement's transmission and adaptation took place through *channels of resonance*. Channels of resonance are the interpersonal and technological means by which a cultural movement becomes accessible and intelligible to a new category of people. These are pathways through which culture moves between masses.[7] Channels of resonance may involve direct human contact and technological means but are more than modes of data transfer. "The medium is the message," or in the very least is inextricable from it (McLuhan 1964); how Hip Hop was adapted on the West Coast is inextricable from how it was transmitted to the West Coast. The transmission took place via cultural bundles of aesthetics, styles, performative scripts, and social locations, alongside media of communication, including mass communication. The transmission and reception had both aesthetic and existential implications.

---

[7] Channels of resonance share commonality with Khabeer's (2016) model of "loops," cultural expressions and forms of knowledge sampled and reconfigured in Muslim Cool; through "channels of resonance," I emphasize the social structures that transmit culture.

A critical aspect of the emergence of West Coast Hip Hop was the spurring of community-building through resonant experiences. Through the "acoustic and affective production of sociality" (Abe 2018:133), beings have "sympathetic" responses to natural, social, and creative aspects of the world (Lordi 2013:6). In creative resonance, participants collectively catch, create, and/or amplify a vibration, which stabilizes collective frequencies of understanding. Entities, both human and nonhuman, experience resonance as a covibration of aesthetic, existential, effervescent consciousness, with potential for encompassing others (Prinz 2012). In this book I explore how resonance drew brown creatives toward community in the Hip Hop scene, and how they in turn amplified the movement's resonance for others. The relationship between Hip Hop as a movement and Hip Hop as a scene is an important one, as often the deep identification with the movement, the salience and persistence of identification, took place at the scene level and through relational interactions.

Many of my collaborators spoke of moments in which they experienced a powerful individual connection to Hip Hop. That is, these were moments in which Hip Hop resonated within them, by speaking to their life experiences and capturing their creative imaginations. Through technological means, many experienced Hip Hop in an actual vibrational sense, absorbing waves of basslines and kicks corporeally, or taking in the sights of films and moving with the images. Some recalled moments of first-time encounters on the streets in which someone performed the Hip Hop elements. Yet, "Resonance, while primarily a sonic designation, just like music, spills over into other realms of experience, perception, meaning, and significance" (Porter 2020:8). Moreover, the meaning-making aspects of resonance were central in Hip Hop's adoption. Many West Coast creatives experienced a sense of calling in Hip Hop (Armstrong 2019; Reznowski 2014), as if the movement gave them purpose. They had visceral reactions to what they visually and aesthetically encountered in Hip Hop, which often triggered creative visions of their own. The convergence of these personal factors, within social settings, fortified by the plausibility structures of mainstream media and insider channels of resonance, made for a forceful reception of the movement, one my collaborators often drew from to enact change in their social settings.

Hip Hop's resonance was especially central to how many creatives, including myself, negotiated their racialized identities. As a Mexican American starting my teen years in 1991, Hip Hop offered a sense of belonging—a sense of identity—because of how it resonated with my racialized identity. Hip Hop presented an epistemology rooted in the histories and creative legacies of Black Americans (Khabeer 2016; Pinn 2003). I understood that without the sociocultural histories and creative contributions of Black Americans there would be no Hip Hop. As a brown-skinned, working-class young person racialized as nonwhite,

I found wisdom in Hip Hop's racialized history (Fernandes 2011, 2018). When I experienced unjust treatment at the hands of police, experienced gang violence firsthand, or bore the brunt of stereotypes, Hip Hop provided insight into these realities and a platform for processing them. As I dug into the history, I found that many peoples of Caribbean and meso-American descent had found a place in the movement and had long been contributing to it, even in its early stages.

The peoples I descended from, particularly my indigenous ancestors and their brown racialized descendants, faced struggles both in Latin America and in the United States. At a young age, through Hip Hop, I began to envision how parallel and intersecting struggles across minoritized peoples could be addressed collaboratively. This included intentional allyship to the liberatory work of African-descended peoples in the Americas, and Black Americans in particular. Hip Hop epistemology, I came to realize, was most cultivated through collaborative creation within spaces of cross-racial resonance. These spaces were ongoing sites of creative synergy—extended cyphers—where creatives vibed off of each other and built community in the process (Johnson 2022). Los Angeles was dotted with Hip Hop–oriented creative communities, and in some cases I helped build spaces that offered this for others, where embodied knowledge was shared along channels of resonance.

Dax and his crew early on embodied this resonance, which soon manifested as a vision for community transformation. The cousins were not strangers to neighborhood violence stemming from school, territorial, and racialized rivalries, but Hip Hop allowed them to envision and position themselves along a different frequency, as transformational agents in their community. The emcee crew soon took to writing rhymes opposing the violence they witnessed in their surroundings. In our conversation, Dax reached back nearly four decades to recite the lyrics from "Just Schoolin," one of the first songs he wrote in response to neighborhood violence:

> I am not a preacher/ I'm an artist/
> that will stop the violence movement so yo, let's stop this/
> pro-gram/ I am/ ready and willing to fight,
> but wouldn't you think it be better if I only picked up the mic/
> and got stupid/ and let my opinion be heard
> Cuz I am now a pro at this trade—Word!

In this time of sky-rhyming, Hip Hop was resistance against violence—a move to create rather than to kill and destroy, a call to life (Reyes 2016). It was a movement of placemaking and worldmaking among those at risk of being left behind in postindustrial Los Angeles. Hip Hop would take various twists and turns, but some brown creatives participated in building underground spaces to sustain what they saw as the creative, life-giving essence of a cultural movement that forever altered their lifeworlds.

Resonance Channels

While the role of technology was of critical importance in the transmission of Hip Hop, I am especially interested in how experiences of interpersonal resonance helped establish a West Coast scene that was intelligible to Brown Los Angeles. Many of my collaborators located themselves within relational channels of resonance, creative family trees of sorts, through which they traced their artistic development. Such ties emerged from relational interactions or observations in which creatives gained skills and capacities and developed aesthetic affinities. One such lineage is evident in the accounts of Dax and his sister Zane. Zane Reynosa grew up around Hip Hop in large part because of Dax and her cousins' involvement in the culture. Zane was inclined toward writing poetry, and spent time penning verses in her notebook. In her own words, "I loved English class, and I wrote poetry on my own." This love of poetry transferred readily into her eventual commitment to emceeing. First, her inclination toward emceeing grew at the time that her brother and cousins began to perform and develop their craft. Zane explains, "I started to write my own rhymes. Dax started to help me. He wrote some of those first rhymes for me. Dax was very technical. They taught me from jump how to get on, how to record, how to have breath control, how to hold the mic." Dax and his crew, who already had several years of experience, began passing on the knowledge they had to Zane.

Zane's first lyrical incursion began as an experiment. Dax and his cousin Albert, known as Jurny, were recording several songs and wanted a woman's voice on one of their tracks. Dax decided to coach Zane through the process. Zane recalls her brother's disciplined approach: "You know my brother was not soft on me at all, it was like okay, 'we're in the studio, we only have this time frame. You have to get it done, this is the way it's going to be.' So, my cousin was a little bit more understanding, but as far as getting started it was definitely them that got me into it." Zane became one of the few women on the mic in her scene, especially one of the few Chicanas. She recorded several tracks in the late 1980s. She herself would later mentor other emcees, including other women, thus furthering a creative lineage. Today, she continues to move audiences, releasing music and performing at shows throughout Los Angeles, alongside some of the most decorated artists from Los Angeles's legendary underground scene. Her lyrical innovation and delivery continue to press forward, indicating that the early scene resonates in her current work, even as she continues to evolve creatively.

My own story links with Dax and Zane's creative lineage. In November of 1991, I sat alongside over a hundred Los Angeles–area teens at a church camp, listening intently to a young Dax Reynosa: "Pastors expected us to perform in silk suits, but that's not really who we were. How could we reach the streets in silk suits?" Dax was speaking about his experience as a rapper who sometimes performed at church functions. As artists, he and his partner, his cousin, Albert "Jurny" Holguin, consistently dealt with criticism from religious leaders that expected them to convey respectability, while they remained true to the streets that shaped them. Dax was committed to authenticity. Soon after his exposition, a New Jack Swing beat reverberated through the chapel, and Dax's vocals burst forth: "Get raw, so fight the power, you know it's time to get raw!" Dax demonstrated his multiple talents, as he alternated between versatile R&B vocal runs and precise rhyme deliveries. Soon, Jurny marched down the middle aisle, took the mic with might, and rocked the crowd as well.

The sound of these emcees, and what they represented, hooked me in. I had already seen Hip Hop in a church setting (Gault and Harris 2019; Zanfagna 2017), but there was something unique about Dax and Jurny, the group then known as LPG. There was a veteran-like quality to their style, speech, and demeanor. Dax's testimonies conveyed years of creative toil. Their name, LPG, the Lord's Personal Gangsters, was a bold moniker in the heyday of gangsta rap (Image I.1). What street credibility did these artists have toward brandishing such a name?

Image I.1 LPG Posse, album cover, 1990. (Reproduced courtesy of Raphael Henley)

It turns out they had plenty (Borha 2013). Hip Hop had captivated me for years, but when I saw LPG perform up close, I understood the alternative possibilities of Hip Hop belonging. These two cousins were grounded in a spirituality that I was familiar with. Furthermore, they functioned as organic intellectuals, a term that Delgado (1998:109) uses, drawing on the work of Antonio Gramsci, to describe artists "willing and able to rearticulate the cultural affirmation of identity, to provide a critique of the dominant social order (and institutions), and to issue calls to action." Through LPG, I caught a glimpse of what it was to identify with this movement.

LAtino Hip Hop

Much has been written on Hip Hop, Latines,[8] and Los Angeles. Most writings that explore Hip Hop's embrace by Brown Los Angeles focus on commercially lauded artists identified with "Latino hip hop." In the early 1990s, "Latino hip-hop" in Los Angeles (Hochman 1991) increasingly drew the fascination of media outlets (Gold 1990; Hochman 1990a; Lannert 1990; Ali 1993). The likes of Kid Frost, Mellow Man Ace, a Lighter Shade of Brown, Cypress Hill, Spanish FLY, and others, were on the crest of a rising wave of Latino Hip Hop artists. Los Angeles, as journalists and academics noted, was a key site of development for this creative wave, despite being on the opposite coast from Hip Hop's epicenter. Scholars Juan Flores (2000) and Raquel Rivera (2002) note that some Los Angeles artists in the subgenre achieved media notoriety even before many of their New York City counterparts, who had long been on the cusp of the movement.

Los Angeles–area Latino Hip Hop, which I identify as *LAtino Hip Hop*, with "LA" capitalized, functioned as a "zone" of cultural production (Rivera 2003). This zone largely fulfilled Tinajero's description (2016:18) as "Hip Hop produced by those of Latino/a/Hispanic origins and/or by those who self-identify, either fully or partially, with that ethnolinguistic group." Artistic representations often included "rhetorical references to specific experiences, food, dress, Latino/a popular culture, and so forth" (Tinajero 2016:19). Amid a creative boom, some of the Hip Hop styles that Los Angeles became known for were linked to local expressions of Latinidad. Lowrider culture, pachuco and cholo aesthetics, stoner archetypes, Afro-Cuban sonic blends, Latin lover stereotypes, and meso-American motifs, became associated with West Coast Hip Hop.

---

[8] I use various panethnic terms to speak of people of Latin American descent broadly. I retain terms used by my collaborators, and terms reflecting the particular time periods I am writing about. I use the modern term, Latine, when making observations about the panethnic population currently or across expansive time periods.

Latinidad, a sense of commonality and collective belonging purportedly shared by peoples of Latin American descent, held currency within LAtino Hip Hop.[9] The panethnic Hip Hop collective Latin Alliance, for example, trumpeted the possibilities of a Los Angeles–based LAtino Hip Hop identity. Many Latines identified as members of this West Coast wave, this "new funky nation" of Hip Hop, hailed by famed West Coast artists Boo-Yaa Tribe (see Forman 2002). Soon, this scene became a zone of scholarly analysis, with academics analyzing the interplay of three particular dimensions:

1. Context: The sociocultural ethos of Brown Los Angeles that shapes its connection to Hip Hop.
2. Content: The themes present in the music of brown Hip Hop artists, especially forms of protest and empowerment contained in these articulations.
3. Crossings: The ways that Hip Hop facilitates the crossing of social boundaries, especially racial boundaries, by brown creatives.

This body of work offers various insights into how Hip Hop resonated in Brown Los Angeles.

Context

Raegan Kelly's (1993) "Hip Hop Chicano" is foundational, both in chronology and contribution, examining the context for the emergence of LAtino Hip Hop. Kelly posits a Chicano scene distinct from that of Black Americans, with artists such as Arturo Molina, aka Frost, furthering a sense of Chicano Pride. Offering rare glimpses of Chicano participation in the 1980s scene, Kelly's chapter originally appeared in Brian Cross's (1993) volume *It's Not about a Salary: Rap, Race, and Resistance in Los Angeles* and demonstrates how Latino artists such as Frost, Mellow Man Ace, Cypress Hill, Skatemaster Tate, and others were integral to the West Coast scene. Likewise, Cross's volume legitimizes the presence of Latinos in the West Coast Hip Hop scene. Kelly, along with L. Alvarez (2007) and McFarland (2013), highlight the centrality of the pachuco movement in the development of Chicano Hip Hop, noting its zoot suit fashion, musical swing, and a bebop infused verbal exchange popular among Los Angeles Chicanos of the World War II generation. Caló slang and lowrider cars remain influential expressions of Chicano culture. The lowrider car scene, showcasing luxuriously accessorized vehicles, especially, funneled resources toward Chicano Hip Hop.

---

[9] See Castillo-Garsow and Nichols (2016) for a helpful "undefining" of Latinidad in relation to Hip Hop.

Some scholars emphasize the importance of Los Angeles's spatial context in producing the sounds of LAtino Hip Hop. Kelly (2004) and Viesca (2004), for example, identify East Los Angeles as center stage for Los Angeles Chicano creativity. Viesca (2004) and Kelly (2004) highlight the cultural wealth of East Los Angeles and its influence on Brown Los Angeles. The eastside music scene drew crowds from diverse backgrounds and temporarily brought Chicanos into the spotlight. Likewise, the emergence of the Chicano dance party scene, particularly the house party scene on the East Side, and dance clubs, were foundational for Chicano Hip Hop. Jimenez (2011) notes how this dance scene in general, and the role of Chicano DJ crews in particular, influenced the DJ crews that would form the backbone of the West Coast Hip Hop scene. Through this East Side party scene, Kelly (2004) notes, a young Kid Frost was making a name for himself as a rapper.

Content

LAtino Hip Hop is often a platform of creative resistance, as noted in Pancho McFarland's (2006, 2008, 2013, 2018) extensive analysis of Chicano rappers. McFarland details how postindustrial and neocolonial realities shape Chicano rap and how Chicano rappers express angst toward a system designed to exploit them. On the one hand, McFarland's work highlights how Chicano rappers mirror negative influences in their environments, such as misogyny and patriarchy (see also R Rodríguez 2009), often facing physical and cultural violence themselves. On the other hand, McFarland indicates how Hip Hop provides survival strategies for young Chicanos (see also Osuna 2019 and Mausfeld 2019). Writing about Hip Hop group Psycho Realm, Osuna (2019:79) notes how Hip Hop, in blues-like fashion, centers the voice of youth on "the margins of the postindustrial city under conditions of rampant exclusion, discrimination, and abandonment."[10] Hip Hop, after all, emerged in response to urban neoliberal restructuring. Mausfeld, furthermore, argues for the legitimacy of Chicano rap as a text of scholarly analysis for understanding Mexican Americans' struggles with politics, transnational neoliberal economics, policing, and ethnic consciousness. Mausfeld's approach is particularly insightful when tracing personal and political intersections in Kid Frost's artistic evolution. These observations complement Rivera's (2003) argument that the "ghettoization" of Hip Hop provided credibility for Chicanos in Los Angeles to speak authoritatively from their social

---

[10] See also Tricia Rose (1994:22), who argues for "the importance of locating hip hop culture within the context of deindustrialization," and pioneered this perspective among scholars of Hip Hop.

locations (see also MacWeeney 2008; Martinez-Morrison 2014; Ogbar 2007). Thus, while some Chicano rappers sustain the status quo, others challenge the system. Chicano rappers articulate oppositional politics as organic intellectuals (Delgado 1998).

Musically, Chicano rappers reflect an array of subgenres, both in terms of subgenres produced by Chicanos as well as subgenres that influence Chicano rappers (McFarland 2008). McFarland notes, for example, the influence of lowrider culture in Chicano rappers' aesthetic and flow, from cars, to clothing, to tattoos. Likewise, Los Angeles–based G-funk is influential. The Chicano penchant for funk music spans several generations, linked to West Coast locales like Oakland and Los Angeles, and influenced by Los Angeles–area artists such as Dr. Dre and N.W.A. (McFarland 2008). Indigenist streams also appear in Chicano Hip Hop, sometimes blended subtly with Chicano gang culture and elsewhere represented prominently in the names and aesthetics of artists (McFarland 2018). The interplay of these aesthetics reflect Chicano rappers' diverse stylings.

The concept of mestizaje figures prominently in LAtino Hip Hop scholarship. Mestizaje has historically provided an ideological frame in Mexico and other Latin American nations celebrating racial mixing. Though the ideology extolls the supposed superiority of racial mixing, it tends toward erasure of Black and Indigenous communities. Nevertheless, numerous scholars employ this language for speaking of cultural exchange. Los Angeles based group Ozomatli, for example, is highlighted in the work of both Kun and Medina as an example of cultural mestizaje characteristic of Los Angeles. Kun (2005) envisions an ongoing dialogue between early Chicano rock movements, the predominantly African American Uncle Jam's Army, which spurred the eventual development of gangsta rap, and the sonic bricolage exhibited by Ozomatli. Medina (2014:14) adds, "Ozomatli continues to perform music that generates resistant rhetorical productions from cultural mestizaje." In similar fashion, Wang (2010) takes readers on a musical journey highlighting the sonic life of "Viva Tirado," a song that was sampled for Frost's hit single, "La Raza"; this scholarship argues for the ongoing influence of Chicanos on Black American artists and vice versa, in Los Angeles. Similarly, McFarland notes cultural blending from Mexican, White American, and Black American influences within Chicano rap. For McFarland, this includes the influence of indigenous and Afro-Mexican peoples on Chicanos. McFarland's spotlighting of Afro-Mexicans is especially rich, noting the many contributions that peoples of African descent have made to Mexican and Chicano cultures (2013; 2006). These Afro-Mexican influences undergird Chicanos' draw to Hip Hop and fuel resistance against colonial vestiges, according to McFarland.

Crossings

A number of Los Angeles–based studies focus on the histories of Black American and brown American exchange that laid the groundwork for LAtino Hip Hop. Macías (2014), for example, notes the ongoing cultural exchange between Black Americans and Chicanos, especially the influence of Chicano aesthetics on Black American gangs and the Chicano penchant for Black American "oldies-but-goodies" music. Various scholars document an ebb and flow of conflict and collaboration between Chicanos and Black Americans. As G. Johnson notes (2013), spaces of music performance have periodically offered common grounds amid economic dynamics pitting working-class Black and Chicano communities against each other. The zoot suit era was a time when Black Americans and Chicanos came together (Loza 1993), alongside Filipino Americans and Japanese Americans. Swap meets were critical in providing spaces of exchange for cultural brokers in the burgeoning gangsta rap field (Johnson 2013). While the face of the genre consisted mostly of Black artists, Johnson notes brown creatives' involvement in shaping the scene since the 1980s. Finally, Viesca (2004) notes how the Peace and Justice Center facilitated cross-racial creativity, spurring interracial groups such as the Black Eyed Peas and Ozomotli.

Some studies spotlight Hip Hop's capacity as a site of cross-racial solidarities, ethnoracial identity coconstruction, and cross-racial social movements. Osuna (2019), for example, argues that Hip Hop offers space for envisioning new realities in postindustrial spaces for Black and brown creatives and other people of color. Magaña examines instances of mutual recognition by which Black and brown creatives influence each other's notions of ethnoracial identities. Through these processes, Black and brown creatives forge solidarities around social issues that affect their peer communities. Such solidarities may be expressed through activism, and accompanied by creative performance and artistic production. Countering notions of essentialized Black and brown competition, Hondagneu-Sotelo and Pastor (2021) echo Magaña's conception of coconstruction, documenting how Black and brown youths grow up alongside each other in South Central Los Angeles. While cross-racial conflict periodically occurs, Hondagneu-Sotelo and Pastor's volume, particularly Hondagneu-Sotelo and Thompson-Hernandez's chapter, indicates that many young, brown residents experience rich Black/brown friendships and mentoring relationships in majority Black spaces. Finally, Castillo Planas (2020) spotlights the plight of Mexican creatives in New York City, noting their ties to LAtino Hip Hop; she locates their struggles in the context of the Black Atlantic, situating Gloria Anzaldúa in conversation with Paul Gilroy. Hip Hop becomes a common vernacular for many young people in this shared space, and young residents express a sense of pride in their communities.

There are several key takeaways related to the context, content, and crossings of LAtino Hip Hop. In terms of context, LAtino Hip Hop had an early emergence in Los Angeles and gained notoriety soon after the West Coast became commercially successful. LAtino Hip Hop was boosted by various older Chicano resonances such as the pachuco movement and the lowrider scene. Hubs of Chicano creativity provided resources for the emergence of LAtino Hip Hop, especially the East Los Angeles music scene and the East Side mobile DJ scene. In terms of content, LAtino Hip Hop functions as a medium of resistance against systems of surveillance, economic exploitation, spatial segregation, and racism. Artists are said to enact a type of mestizaje as they draw from indigenous, Afro-Latinx, and Black American cultural influences. In terms of crossings, brown creatives have historically participated in the creation of multiracial musical spaces. These instances of ethnoracial coconstruction continue into the modern era among creatives who participate in Hip Hop.

Interventions and Challenges to LAtino Hip Hop

Existing scholarship on LAtino Hip Hop provides some clues as to how Hip Hop took root in Brown Los Angeles, and yet many questions remain. Certainly, the role of Chicanos in Los Angeles is indispensable, yet, approaches that exclusively center Chicanos run the risk of ignoring, erasing, or misrepresenting the contributions of non-Chicanos in LAtino Hip Hop. There are underexplored migratory patterns that contributed to Hip Hop's resonance in Brown Los Angeles. These migratory flows include Puerto Ricans moving West from New York City, and Central Americans migrating beyond the Northern Triangle. Rivera (2003) references the presence of Puerto Ricans in Los Angeles Hip Hop, but no scholars, to my knowledge, discuss in depth the participation of Central Americans in the scene. Second, framing LAtino Hip Hop as a Chicano scene flattens the histories of non-Chicanos. Artists such as Tony G and Mellow Man Ace have made significant impacts in the Chicano community; to downplay their Cuban identities ignores a major part of their musical resonances, as well as Mellow's racialized Afro-Cuban identity. Finally, Chicanos themselves are a diverse and mobile population, including those affected by generational patterns of spatial segregation. Many Chicanos have traveled to different parts of the United States and of the world; the military (Mausfeld 2019) and the arts have been two channels for this. Many are also connected to familial networks dispersed across wide geographies. These extended connections provide Chicanos with broad cultural repertoires (see Villegas 2021),[11] in addition to what was present in the local scene.

Much Hip Hop scholarship suffers from a Hollywood effect, emphasizing commercially successful artists and/or their outputs. A focus on stardom misses the formative work happening in underground spaces among grassroots artists, which is where the heart of Hip Hop creativity often resides. Many of the artists that became famous were active in the underground as well, and their formative experiences there matter. In the same vein, some scenes were of less economic viability, such as the Christian Hip Hop scene, but this scene had crossover synergy with other underground scenes.[12] In similar fashion, LAtino Hip Hop scholarship tends to focus primarily on the city of Los Angeles proper, or East Los Angeles, and less so on surrounding cities and/or counties in the greater metro region. Yet, important developments were taking place in the Harbor Area, in the Inland Empire, and in Orange County, among other places. Exploration of the greater Los Angeles area allows for a richer account of the movement's flourishing.

The concept of mestizaje merits a cautionary note; it has historically operated as a homogenizing ideology, and limits analysis of ongoing distinct resonances in the scene. Nation-building advocates of mestizaje typically sidestep questions of power and portray distinctly racialized peoples as blended together idealistically. The fine print, however, signals a racial hierarchy wherein lower status racial categories are to be washed out with whiteness (Hooker 2014; Román 2009). The reality is that the very mixing lauded within mestizaje ideologies occurred through violence. In the current era, mestizaje becomes a cultural black box into which different elements go and a unified product emerges. Furthermore, "mestizaje" is at times deployed in essentializing narratives. For example, it is problematic to assert that brown creatives with Black ancestry are naturally drawn to Hip Hop.

I argue "resonance" is a better lens for understanding the exchange taking place within the early Hip Hop scene. Resonance does not deny social distinctions, but rather acknowledges that exchange happens across social boundaries. Resonance, in fact, presupposes difference across resonant entities (Rosa 2019). Furthermore, resonance is made possible by active channels of exchange, not through essentialized identities. Some brown creatives experienced resonance with Hip Hop because they had already been exposed extensively to forms of Black American music. Likewise, some experienced resonance because of their

---

[11] Villegas's work on Filipino American contributions to Hip Hop highlights the function of circuits, social networks that facilitate epistemological loops, the sharing of cultural resources, and the sustaining of ethnoracial identities. His work provides a helpful parallel case.

[12] See DuVernay, *This Is the Life: Los Angeles: Forward Movement* (2008), for acknowledgment of a Christian emcee within the Los Angeles underground scene.

relational ties to Black Americans. Some did experience resonance in concert with their African ancestries, but through awareness of these connections and/or through familial cultural repertoires that facilitated connections with Black American culture. Finally, the mobile experiences of some Latines allowed them to serve as cultural conduits. Rather than accepting mestizaje as a matter of fact, or even as an active cultural process, I propose resonance as an active process encompassing the crossing of borders—racial, geographic, and national—to generate new creative expressions.

Methods, Parameters, and Definitions

In addition to theoretical considerations, I aim to expand LAtino Hip Hop scholarship methodologically. This book is a hiphopography, "a paradigm in Hip Hop Studies that integrates the varied approaches of ethnography, biography, and social, cultural, and oral history" (Alim 2009:104; see also Alim and Hi-Tek 2006; Durham 2014; Spady et al. 2006). I entered the project as I would enter a Hip Hop cypher, looking to be in conversation and bounce ideas off of other collaborators. Those who chose to engage with me became cypher collaborators. The project draws from four primary sources of data: (1) Oral history interviews of participants in the early West Coast scene; (2) autoethnographic observations of the Hip Hop scene in the greater Los Angeles area; (3) print, material, and sonic culture produced during that era; and (4) public user-generated information found on social media platforms related to materials and memories of the Los Angeles underground scene (i.e., podcasts, videos, posts, comments, etc.). The oral history accounts of artists and creatives, the primary data for this project, primarily come from two sources: (1) firsthand interviews conducted via face-to-face interactions, phone conversations, or online video chat platforms, and (2) secondary interviews in the public domain accessed through social media platforms. I conducted forty-five original in-depth oral history interviews with creatives as well as brief ethnographic interviews with over a dozen additional creatives. In addition, I listened to over 250 hours of secondary interview recordings, mostly from podcasts. Interviews were transcribed and coded for themes related to Hip Hop identity formation and ethnoracial dynamics. In my conversations with creatives in the scene, I worked to tap into their experiences of resonance, and their engagement within these sites of resonance. I was especially mindful of the modes of mutuality that they experienced within these spaces. Additional details and considerations are provided in the methods appendix.

There are various definitions critical to this project. First, I identify Hip Hop not merely as a genre of music, but as an art movement rooted in scenes and communities of resonant creativity. This aligns with the art worlds perspective of Becker (1984), which recognizes that art movements and art scenes are contingent on the labor of a network of participants. While acclaimed artists often receive the credit or function as the face of a movement, there are teams and networks of people that provide critical resources for the creation of art and for the flourishing of a movement. Along similar lines, speaking in particular about music communities, Jennifer Lena (2012:3) notes, "If you've ever been a member of a music community—as a fan or performer—you know that it takes tens, scores, or even thousands of people to make that community work, for better or worse. Music is a participatory, community-based activity. At different stages of development, music communities are organized to lend themselves to different forms of participation." Thus, this book analyzes the scene through insights shared by creatives undertaking an array of roles—some frontstage, some backstage, some with regional and national profiles, and others primarily known locally. This book is not an exhaustive catalog of famous LAtino Hip Hop artists, but an exploration of the sociocultural factors that shaped the emergence of underground Hip Hop scenes in Brown Los Angeles, through the eyes of participant-creatives.

Along these lines, I move beyond research that focuses on rappers and content analysis. Content analysis is a legitimate form of cultural analysis, and rappers are surely producers of valuable artforms, thus I include both forms here in this volume. However, when considering the Hip Hop field in Los Angeles, there is much that is overlooked from the experience of visual artists, namely graffiti writers, dancers—especially B-boys/B-girls and poplockers, DJs and music producers, who often set the ambience within which other artists developed their crafts, and creative promoters, who often helped create the spaces where creativity was sparked. These other creatives partnered with emcees to build the larger scene. The various elements represented, more so than emceeing, were often the primary entry-points into Hip Hop for many brown creatives. Furthermore, many of these early creatives specialized in multiple elements of expression. Their Hip Hop identities became rooted through taking on an all-encompassing mode of participation. Much of this is lost in emcee-centric approaches.

Second, I focus on underground spaces of the greater Los Angeles Hip Hop scene, which I generally refer to as the West Coast scene. Here I note the various shades of meaning that "underground" holds. Harrison (2009:1–2), for example, indicates that "'underground' has been claimed by many artists as an index to street authenticity" (see also Thornton 1994). I retain that aspect of the term, as I am attentive to the connections of the scene to the urban realities of Los Angeles. Harrison further notes, however, that the term has come to connote "an alternative to rap music's mainstream appeal." This particular meaning was popularized in the 1990s and points to underground Hip Hop as an approach that is more grassroots, less commercialized, and often socially conscious in its content (Vito 2019). I retain the grassroots aspect of the definition here as well, as I prioritize how creatives negotiated their roles within grassroot scenes. Morgan and Bennet (2011:180) most closely approximate the grassroots, localized dimension of the term "underground" that I strive to portray:

> Local hip-hop scenes shaped by artistic and cultural practices that are produced, defined, and sustained primarily by youth in their own neighborhoods and communities. In the United States, these scenes are generally described as underground hip-hop, both to characterize their critical challenge to conventional norms and to distinguish them from commercial hip-hop.

In the time of sky-rhyming, I propose that Hip Hop activity was largely underground, on the peripheries of mainstream music and rooted in the experiences of working-class creatives in the greater Los Angeles area. Certainly, some creatives sought the mainstream limelight, but I argue that the grassroots scene offers critical insights about Hip Hop as a movement. Afterall, as Vito (2019:3) notes, terms such as "mainstream, underground, and independent" are not dichotomous, "but rather, a spectrum or continuum," which may allow for overlapping. Fernandes (2011) posits that underground subcultures are often the dynamic edge of the movement. Likewise, these are often the spaces that preserve the multimedia, multielemental aspects of the culture, and do not solely focus on rap (Gill 2019). Finally, as Gill notes, in these spaces convergence of disparate Afrodiasporic elements and other forms takes place.

Third, I use the term "brown" to identify most, though not all, of my direct collaborators. I employ "brown" because of its regional significance, personal identification with it, and the possibilities it offers. "Brown" is a highly contextual label and not necessarily generalizable to all Latines. Contextually, it is a racialized label emerging from the civil rights struggles of Chicanos and others whose communities have often been contained through labor, educational opportunities, residential options, and policing practices; in terms of racial legibility, Los Angeles brown[13] people are often associated with meso-American ancestry. Yet, brown people are influenced by Black liberation struggles, Afrodiasporic ancestry and expressive cultures, and in Los Angeles

---

[13] While "brown" has been used to refer to a number of populations, including South Asians, Middle Eastern and North African individuals, South East Asians, and Pacific Islanders, in Los Angeles the term has a unique history of being used to identify people of Chicano and Latino origin. This is not to say that the term is unintelligible in Los Angeles in reference to other groups, but merely that there is a history of collective organizing and identification under that label among a sizable mass of Latinxs.

have community building histories with Black American, Asian American, Pacific Islander, and working-class whites. These ongoing histories lead to coconstitutions of ethnoracial identities across such groups, often in highly localized ways (Magaña 2022). A number of scholars use "brown" when describing ethnoracial configurations in the Los Angeles area (G. Johnson 2013; Martinez and Rios 2011; Kun and Pulido 2013). Some of the collaborators I interviewed also used this term in their conversations with me.

"Brown" is not without controversies (Busey and Silva 2021). Subsequent chapters suggest limitations and possibilities of brown as a social category. Brown, in my estimation, can be situational and intentionally fluid for some, but persistent and ascribed for others. In the time of sky-rhyming, I argue, brown-ness shares resonances with Blackness. Some Afro-Latines in Los Angeles offer important insights toward the boundaries of brown as they negotiated engagements to brown identities in nuanced ways, making important contributions to Brown Los Angeles, even if they themselves did not identify as brown and asserted their Blackness (see Rivera-Rideau 2016). To those who, like myself, identify as brown, I offer an invitation through this book to consider the ways that brown futures are intricately linked to Black futures.

The Flow

The first section of the book examines the *channels of resonance* that facilitated much of the reception of Hip Hop in Brown Los Angeles. Chapter 1 of the book chronicles the experiences of various creatives of Caribbean ancestry, noting how they drew from their backgrounds to make foundational contributions to the West Coast scene. Chapter 2 focuses on the borderlands Chicano experience as a channel of resonance. The life of one particular artist, Raul Garcia, serves as a road map for how the borderlands helped pave the way for Hip Hop receptivity as a channel of resonance. Chapter 3 examines how funk culture, and its Black American roots, impacted Brown Los Angeles.

The following section examines the emergence of *cyphers of resonance*, sites and instances of collaborations that shaped the early West Coast scene. Chapter 4 centers on the experiences of Markski, a Bronx-born transplant who transmitted Hip Hop culture and formed crews among his peers. Chapter 5 examines the place of the Radio Club, an experimental nexus of resonance between proto–Hip Hop creatives and emerging West Coast pioneers. Chapter 6 examines the emergence of the Radiotron Youth Center, a space where young people developed skills in graffiti writing, emceeing, DJing, and breaking, and formed a cohort that would spur the West Coast scene forward.

The final section, *charting the resonance*, examines how creatives navigated social and geographic boundaries in their endeavors to preserve a movement and a moment. Chapter 7 explores how creatives from Brown Los Angeles crossed boundaries of race and place to expand their prospects within Hip Hop and sustain creative resonances at a time when street violence drew media attention and sharpened racial boundaries within Hip Hop. Chapter 8 traces the emergence and spread of a Christian Hip Hop scene, which provided a form of refuge to creatives threatened by street violence and criminalization and had unexpected carryovers into the solidifying underground scene. Chapter 9 explores the efforts that some creatives engaged in to rebuild the scene, concluding with a Hip Hop shop as a center of activity. Finally, in the concluding chapter, I visit several initiatives to embody the preservation of a movement. I revisit the formation of the Tunnel Rats, reflect on a gathering of graffiti writers, and summarize the ways that the time of sky-rhyming enlivens continued efforts to maintain Hip Hop authenticity. As I argue, initiatives to simultaneously preserve and to innovate are alive and well in Brown Los Angeles.

PART I
CHANNELS OF RESONANCE
Foundational Movements

Chapters in this section explore key cultural movements and their structures of cultural transmission, the channels of resonance, that facilitated the reception of Hip Hop in Brown Los Angeles. Amid intergenerational migration flows and locally-forged artistic movements predating Hip Hop's West Coast arrival, Black and brown creatives influenced the expressions of Hip Hop that flourished in Los Angeles. The stories of creatives that helped lay the groundwork for Hip Hop in Brown Los Angeles in the 1970s and early 1980s are the focus of this section.

1
Caribbean Currents

Since as far back as he can remember, DJ Jose "Pebo" Rodriguez was at home in the Chicano community of Los Angeles. Born and raised in Los Angeles, and growing up in the Chicano majority neighborhood of Cypress Park, it was no wonder that most of Pebo's closest friends were Chicanos. Attending Cathedral High School, located along the busy 110 freeway in proximity to Dodger Stadium and Los Angeles's Chinatown, Pebo was a student of the city. Coming of age in the 1970s, he lived through the revival of the nearby Arroyo arts scene, where the Mechicano Arts Center and the Centro de Arte Publico in Highland Park became hubs of social justice work through public art (Lin 2019). In this era, Pebo participated in Movimiento Estudiantil Chicano de Aztlán (M.E.Ch.A.) and marched for civil rights. After graduating from Cathedral High School, Pebo went on to study at Pepperdine University, where he and other students successfully advocated for the university's establishment of Chicano Studies. Upon completing a degree in paralegal studies, Pebo went to work for the California attorney general's office. Young Pebo's resume read like a Chicano success story forged in the heart of Los Angeles. Yet, Pebo interfaced with a resonance channel linked to geographies far beyond Los Angeles. Like other creatives in this chapter, Pebo drew important cultural resources from sites of creative production in the Caribbean. This resonance channel influenced Pebo's creative trajectory and impacted Los Angeles's creative scene. As demonstrated in this chapter, creatives with Caribbean ancestries uniquely amplified Hip Hop's resonance in Brown Los Angeles.

Roots and Resonance

I caught up with Pebo via telephone at the height of pandemic lockdowns to talk about his music career. My job, then at Boston University, required my teaching to move fully online. I found in Pebo a kindred spirit, as he was teaching college students online and had developed a philosophy of teaching that drew explicitly on his decades-long experience as a club DJ. As I let him know, I had come across his name in various publications, mostly from the 1990s. Notably, he was featured in Brian Cross's volume on Hip Hop in Los Angeles, published in 1993. References to Pebo in relation to Hip Hop were scarce in recent decades, but publications from the 1990s made it clear that he was an innovator in the field, especially in relation to what would emerge as "Latino Hip Hop" and West Coast Hip Hop broadly. That is not to say that Pebo's musical career was not lauded, he had in fact received many recognitions as a top-tier club DJ, producer, musician, promoter, and record sales executive, among other things. Yet, his connection to early West Coast Hip Hop had received little attention in recent years and his life uncovered an important channel of resonance in the West Coast scene.

Pebo's connection to Los Angeles Hip Hop involved a circuitous trajectory, closely linked to his family's history. At some point, Pebo began to realize that he was not a typical Chicano, if such a thing actually exists. For starters, Pebo's father was Puerto Rican, which distinguished him from many of his peers. Pebo had visited Puerto Rico several times, for short stays, as his family periodically spent the Christmas holidays there. And he was not shy about identifying with his Puerto Rican family. "I used to refer to myself as Chicanorican," Pebo happily declared. At the same time, Pebo asserted, "I was down for la raza," as he described his local connections and his ties to his mother's side of the family. His connection to Brown Los Angeles felt natural, especially since his mother was Mexican. "Chicanorican" was a way for Pebo to honor both his parents' heritages.

Pebo began to understand himself differently one day when his mother pulled him aside to have a word with him. Pebo's mother told him that they were technically not Mexican, but rather *New Mexican*. Her family had generational roots in New Mexico, and much of the lore and history celebrated by Chicanos were distant from where she and her family came from, she told Pebo. "Have you ever noticed that we've never gone to Mexico?" Pebo's mother asked him one day. "We don't have family there. All of our family is from New Mexico," she continued. And one of her more conclusive statements, one that hit home for Pebo, was that "The Mexican food that we eat, it's from New Mexico!" Pebo loved his family's cuisine, and knew his mother was right. While Pebo was not disqualified from identifying as Chicano, he now paid attention to the intricacies of his family's lineage, and realized that perhaps he was distinct from his peers in more ways than he had initially recognized.

Nevertheless, Pebo did not relinquish his social ties to his Chicano friends. In fact, he continued to move in the circles that many of them moved in. He especially remained connected to his peers through popular music, even as he further explored his family roots. A significant number of Chicanos were into rock music, and Pebo was immersed in that scene. He explained, "You're gonna say 'this guy's loco,' but I'm a rocker. Rock has always been my number one. I've seen Led Zeppelin four times, and the original Black Sabbath back in the day. The Who. I've seen David Bowie the first time he came here to the states." And even as his friends became less invested in the music, Pebo continued attending live rock concerts.

As much as Pebo was drawn to rock, he had a penchant for diving into other musical scenes, and that tendency would shape Pebo's future influence in the music industry; his ability to move across genres, and to participate in distinct scenes, shaped his ear for music and his ability to guide artists from distinct genres. Pebo found himself drawn to salsa music, which especially connected him to his father's side of the family. "From rock, I would make the switch to being a salsero," Pebo explained. Pebo would dance the night away and was adept at representing the rhythms that filled the homes of his father's extended family. Then, as the disco scene took off in Los Angeles, that scene took hold of Pebo and his friends. The shift from salsa to disco felt natural to Pebo. His transition across these genres reflected the ways that salsa and disco resonated with one another within one of their primary hubs of innovation, New York City (McMains 2015). Moving from the mid-to-late 1970s, the disco scene became the craze for Brown Los Angeles and resonated for decades to come. Again, demonstrating his penchant for bridging scenes, genres, and contexts, Pebo described himself as a "disco rocker."

Crossing Waters

Even as Pebo led a successful and enjoyable life in Los Angeles, he desired to connect to his father's ethnic heritage more deeply. In 1978, he made a trip to Puerto Rico to get in touch with his Puerto Rican roots, the "traditions and antecedents" that would shape his trajectory (J. Flores 2000:117). "This is the seventies and everyone was doing the 'get in touch with your roots' thing," Pebo explained nonchalantly. The trip, which initially would be short-term, turned into a year-long stint, with major implications for Pebo's long-term career. While staying in San Juan, Pebo was reading through a newspaper; in the classified section a particular job ad jumped out at him. The ad was for a DJ job at a club called Leonardo's, one of the most popular clubs on the whole island. The job involved rotating in as a DJ during club nights. What stood out to Pebo was that the opening required applicants to be fluent English speakers and have a college degree. The description also indicated that the new hire could be trained to DJ. Pebo met both requirements and was willing to learn the skills the position entailed. After applying, Pebo was called in for a job interview. The supervisors took a liking to him and affirmed that they would mentor him in the role. Despite the fact that Pebo had little experience DJing, the opportunity seemed promising. Soon after, he received and accepted the job offer.

In those early weeks and months, Pebo admits, he was a terrible DJ. He did not know how to blend the music, and he would bungle the transitions between songs. Yet Pebo appreciated that there were people at the club willing to teach him. Pebo began to receive mentorship from some of the best DJs on the island, who were also some of the best DJs he had ever encountered. Some of the DJs that he met were, like him, of Puerto Rican ancestry and had arrived on the island from the contiguous United States. Some of these DJs were from New York City, and one New York DJ took Pebo under his wing and taught him how to DJ. Another DJ specifically taught Pebo how to blend records. One of the important skills he taught Pebo involved using two of the same records and alternating between turntables as the two identical records played. In that era, Pebo remembers San Juan, Puerto Rico, as a cosmopolitan city where influences from Europe, New York, and other locales left an imprint on the artistry of the island. He remembers, for example, that fashion was influenced by designers not only from the United States but also from Europe. In the club scene, Pebo recalls thinking to himself that many of the people, especially women, looked like they had just walked off the runway in Paris. The styles there were cutting-edge, as he remembers.

Given the many musical genres that Pebo had been exposed to in Los Angeles, including rock, salsa, disco, and various Chicano subgenres, Pebo nurtured his penchant for bringing together a variety of musical styles and sharing them with others. He was a cultural omnivore and a curator. In Puerto Rico he was introduced to a blend of the music from the island as well as music that was popular in New York City. He began to integrate these musical styles into his preferences. Learning techniques of mixing music was especially of interest to him, given his array of musical tastes and his desire to bring them together. As he continued to improve his mixing techniques, he gained mastery of reading the crowd and doing what it took to get people out on the dance floor. Soon, he was known for programming entire DJ sets that moved crowds through the ups and downs of a night on the dance floor.

Pebo's time in Puerto Rico proved to be transformational. There, he was introduced to a cultural scene that expanded his creative outlook. He was linked to cultural resources emanating from the Caribbean diaspora in New York City, cultural resources adapted from European cultural movements, and resources generated on the very island of Puerto Rico. Those creative resources disseminated by the Caribbean diaspora were likewise connected to the wider African diaspora, sustaining key resonances within Caribbean cultures and societies. And as a creative himself, Pebo carried resources that were more than a memory; for Pebo, these resources translated to skills of cultural creation and innovation. This Caribbean channel of resonance that Pebo had readily connected to, a frequency distilled through the club scene of Puerto Rico, provided Pebo with new powers of cultural creation that he would take with him through his own creative migrations.

Translated Skills

In 1979, Pebo moved back to Los Angeles, with a very different skillset as a DJ, albeit one that included the tastes he had cultivated in Los Angeles. The first order of service was to look for jobs there. Pebo found that the skills he gained in Puerto Rico were in demand, and he was able to transfer these skills to the job openings he found in the Los Angeles club scene. Even before going to Puerto Rico, Pebo had enjoyed watching DJs move the crowd. He had been an attentive observer of the skills that successful DJs drew from. Now, as a DJ himself, Pebo noticed that DJs in Puerto Rico were experimenting with and furthering techniques that had yet to hit the Los Angeles club scene. This meant that Pebo could now distinguish himself as a DJ in the very scene that he had previously frequented as a dancer.

Not all of Pebo's newfound knowledge landed well in Los Angeles. In Puerto Rico he had been introduced to forms of European disco that he had not listened to in Los Angeles. He attempted to introduce some of these records to the Los Angeles scene and discovered that crowds were not interested in these styles. Through trial and error, Pebo gained the trust of the crowds he DJed for. In Los Angeles, he played at clubs such as Fantasia, Tropicana, and Mr. J's. He dabbled in distinct musical genres at different clubs, even as he was primarily a disco DJ. He details, "At Fantasia, at the end of the night I could play everything. Tropicana was more freestyle, up tempo record music, and disco music. When I was at Mr J's., Mr. J's was like a funk club." And by the early 1980s, European disco, especially Italo-disco, would catch on in the clubs, and in the backyard party scene frequented by Chicanos. Some of the energy from the disco scene resonated in the soon-to-emerge Hip Hop scene.

Pebo's ability to match his music selections with the tastes of the masses paid off in other ways. By 1982, Pebo had picked up another job: He became a manager for JDC records, a record distribution company. Founded in 1977 by Jim Callen, JDC records gained much by hiring Pebo. Pebo's ever-expanding knowledge of the next big record positioned JDC as a major music distributor among record stores in the region. Pebo's bookish inclinations manifested in his extensive knowledge of music catalogs and music trends, and eventually drew him to better understand the music industry.

Pebo did not stop at sales. In his own words, "I had to massage my intellectual side. And so I was always involved in taking classes at UCLA at night in music contracts and recording, and I was just fascinated by every aspect of it. I used to do a lot of edits, tape edits, special remixes and take them to the clubs and stuff." Pebo's repertoire of skills continued to expand into the production side of music as well as the business side. By gaining industry skills, continuing his work as a DJ, working for a record distribution company, and periodically working at record stores, his spheres of influence allowed Pebo to build critical connections in the music industry.

Guiding a New Wave

Pebo began to notice an important trend on the West Coast—the arrival of Hip Hop music. Some Hip Hop songs started to make their way into radio station rotations, but Pebo had more of an insider perspective. He had a view of the records that were being produced and distributed. He was also tracking record sales and record pools among DJs and could see what types of records were breaking into the club and party scenes of Los Angeles. Pebo by this time had gained more experience on the production side of music and was starting to understand what it took to make Hip Hop records. While in the early 1980s Hip Hop had made modest gains on the radio, he sensed that it would be the next big movement.

Through his networking, Pebo met Dave Storrs, another cultural curator attentive to the musical landscape of Los Angeles. "These were cultural movements, and the artists had to be in your face to get people's attention!" Dave said of the early Hip Hop scene and its urban, mostly Black American precursors. Dave, a UCLA graduate program alumnus, was a successful musician, with a rising reputation as a producer and sound engineer. As an early pioneer of ambient style music concocted with electronic instrumentation, he was by no means a rookie. He had likewise worked with singer and dancer Toni Basil, holding recording session credits to his name on her early releases, but also working as her musical director for some of her live performances. Despite the fact that many of Dave's business colleagues questioned his draw to early Hip Hop, Dave kept his ear to the streets. He describes the suspicion he encountered from acquaintants: "The music wasn't what they were used to in mainstream music, with harmonies and melodies, and they asked me what I was doing here. But I knew that this was the next big movement." Dave and Pebo decided to launch a long-term project.

Pebo and Dave were attuned to the emerging electro genre on the West Coast. Electro was a genre of bass-heavy undercurrents and electronic drums, the primary style that captured West Coast Hip Hop creatives in that era. The sound carried a strong resonance from "Planet Rock," the 1982 hit by Afrika Bambaataa. The resonance also remained strong in what became known as freestyle music, a romantic, emotive, vocally driven offshoot of the electro sound, with the first song in the genre arguably being Shannon's hit single, "Let the Music Play." Freestyle music had appeal in the clubs because it was perceived as danceable, and Pebo as a DJ was well aware of this appeal. With a new crop of producers leaning into this electro sound, Pebo recognized that electro Hip Hop was poised to shake up the West.

Pebo dabbled creatively behind the scenes in the emerging Hip Hop scene, and sensed that there was something more that he could do to contribute from his own creativity. Collaborating with Dave offered additional opportunities. Still connected to Los Angeles's Chicano community, Pebo envisioned that a Chicano rapper could have strong appeal in the scene. He put the word out among his contacts that he was looking for a Chicano rapper. He had not received any referrals until his friend Richard told him he had just the right guy for Pebo. Richard referred Pebo to a young emcee named Arturo Molina. In the streets and party scene he was dubbed Kid Frost, a name he acquired from none other than rapper Ice-T. Pebo arranged to meet with Molina at a club where Pebo DJed, Mr. J's. There, he had a chance to meet Molina and get to know him. Pebo's friend Richard had hyped up Molina's reputation, saying that he had a tremendous talent for composing impromptu rhymes based on whatever he saw in his surroundings.

After the two conversed, and Pebo got a sense that Molina was someone that he could partner with, he invited Molina to share his talent on the mic at Mr. J's. Molina immediately requested that the club DJ play a particular record: "Hashim's Al Naafiysh (The Soul)." The song was one of the early hits produced in the electro style. Pebo took over the turntables. As the needle touched the vinyl, the teenaged Arturo Molina transformed to Kid Frost, a veteran emcee. He began to freestyle rhyme relentlessly, generating rhymes galore. Pebo was impressed. "I go, 'yeah, this dude is bad!,'" Pebo remembered. Pebo and Dave quickly formed their new record label, ElectroBeat Records and Molina signed a contract with ElectroBeat Records. The team had their first artist.

The ElectroBeat team jumped into the production process. Their first goal was the production of the 12" record "Rough Cut," by Kid Frost. The synth-heavy track, guided by robotic drum rhythms fit right into the era. The song included DJ scratching from DJ Yella, member of the World Class Wreckin' Cru, and later a member of N.W.A. Pebo and Dave produced the record. Their next record, "Terminator," also by Kid Frost, was named after the blockbuster film of the same name. Pebo recalls that the song's title was inspired by Ice-T, who told Frost that *Terminator* was the best film he had ever seen. In terms of the musical stylings of the song, Pebo pitched the idea to Frost, saying "Man, we got to do a Latin hip hop style record." At the time, Latin Hip Hop was the name given to freestyle music, noting its connection to Hip Hop, but also its distinct audience (Rivera 2003). Dave Storrs produced the music, and Pebo mixed the track, creating a record that closely aligned with the freestyle wave, but laced with Frost's hard-hitting delivery.

ElectroBeat Records' early hits included Chris the Glove Taylor's song, "Itchiban Scratch," released in 1984. The Glove had been the resident DJ at the Radio Club, an underground nightclub that became one of the earliest hubs of West Coast Hip Hop performance. "Itchiban Scratch," an instrumental track that sampled vocals and sounds from an array of sources, was produced by Dave Storrs, with assistance from Karlos Mongalo and Victor Flores. Mongalo and Flores were both DJs with successful careers in the club scene, signaling how creatives from the early club and disco scene, which drew heavily from Brown Los Angeles, contributed to the nascent electro Hip Hop scene. The Glove proved to be one of the most talented DJs in early Los Angeles Hip Hop, spearheading a classic track in "Itchiban Scratch," a record that Pebo considers the "first LA underground hit record."

Through Kid Frost, Pebo and Dave met Ice-T, and produced and released one of his early records on ElectroBeat. An important site of underground creativity emerged when Dave Storrs hosted Sunday afternoon recording sessions with emerging Hip Hop artists. Ice-T participated in these sessions. Dave typically worked out of a studio located in the garage at his parents' home in the Los Feliz neighborhood of Los Angeles, but also had access to a more elaborate professional recording studio in the area; he could request studio time based on equipment and expertise he had lent to the owners. Dave and Pebo worked with many artists who frequented the Radio Club, a filming location for *Breakin' 'N' Enterin'*, and *Breakin*. The tie to film proved fortuitous for ElectroBeat. Chris the Glove Taylor was invited to score *Breakin'* with electro funk tracks, and asked Dave Storrs for help. Dave and The Glove produced about a third of the film's soundtrack. Yet, the film directors wanted more. The film, which purported to capture the early West Coast Hip Hop scene, lacked an original rap track. The Glove had one day to come up with an original rap track before the entire score was mastered the next morning. He recruited Dave Storrs and Ice-T to pull off an all-nighter production and recording session. The end result was Ice-T's hit record, "Reckless," accompanied by a B-side track, "Tibetan Jam."

ElectroBeat Records had a run of roughly two years, and left an indelible mark on the nascent Hip Hop scene in that time. Along the way, Pebo realized that he could not fully dedicate himself to the critical role of managing artists, as his own musical career was ever expanding. Pebo toured with a Hi-NRG band called Stop, and he helped propel the career of the band. Hi-NRG, a musical genre often relying on high-hat-driven beats and synthesizer instrumentation, originating in the 1970s and sometimes associated with disco, was gaining fans in Brown Los Angeles. Stop's single, "Wake Up," was a hit in 1985, and Pebo helped break the record in Los Angeles clubs. Pebo and Dave continued to collaborate in a variety of ways for years to come.

The creative resonances that Pebo amplified helped pave the way for a more expansive Hip Hop scene. His connection to his Puerto Rican roots, and perhaps more so the journey of connecting, shaped his creative trajectory. Likewise, his ability to navigate the familiar Chicano context, and to access resources there, enabled him to deploy his cultural resources in creative ways. Pebo would later become involved with other primarily Chicano contexts, such as Thump Records, but it is critical to not erase his Puerto Rican ancestry (Rivera 2003), in order to understand his full impact on the early West Coast scene.

Living Legacies

Ana "Lollipop" Sanchez is known for her innovation on the dance floor, and for the living legacy she sustains through her pedagogical work among dancers of all levels. Ana grew up in Orange County, California, the daughter of parents who migrated from Puerto Rico, to New York, and finally to the West Coast. Born and raised in Southern California, Ana moved across various dance scenes from an early age. She excelled in the street dance scene in the 1970s, prior to Hip Hop's arrival, and was integral to the West Coast scene that emerged in the 1980s. She became an iconic figure in the dance world at a critical point of stylistic innovation.

When Ana spoke to me about how her parents inspired her love of dance, it quickly became clear that the inspiration was more than symbolic. When she was a toddler, as she describes, her parents "set her feet on their feet, and guided her through salsa and cha cha steps." Her parents were street dancers in their time, known for their skilled renditions of the cha cha and mambo. Without formal training, her parents competed in dance contests as a couple, and the transfer of their salsa skills to Ana laid a foundation for her lifetime of dance. By the time she could stand on her own, Ana was already moving to salsa, cha cha, and the mambo, the sounds that filled her home life.

Her extended family added to this resonant experience, as she recalls: "I grew up with all that music playing, my uncle playing flamenco guitar, my dad playing congas, and everybody's singing and dancing." Her mother added to her musicality through singing, as Ana recalls her beautiful lilting voice floating through the family home. Unexpectedly, her father's love for language learning also influenced Ana's dance knowledge. Having served in the military, her father learned multiple languages and taught Ana to pay attention to differences in dialects. He likewise taught her about the Italian heritage he carried from several generations back. His lessons to her about linguistic rhythms and cadences shaped her sensibilities toward the nuances communicated through dance. "Dances are different dialects. They mean different things," Ana explained to me.

Ana's siblings provided an important link in the chain of creative resonance that she drew from, connecting her Caribbean dance rhythms to some of the popular styles filling the radio airwaves. The Sanchez siblings, Ana's older brother and sister, took their parents' favorite pastime and plugged it into the musical genres prevalent among US teens in the 1960s. Ana's sister, Ada, moved like a trained jazz dancer, though she was primarily a club dancer. She also expressed her musicality through singing gospel music. Her brother, Angelo, gained a public profile through dance as he was a regular on the televised dance show, *American Bandstand*, with Dick Clark, in the late 1960s. He eventually became a live theater performer, appearing in productions of *Grease* and *Oklahoma*. Her brother, ten years her senior, would practice his dance moves with Ana. The practices were exhilarating to Ana, as, "He was throwing me over his head over his back between his legs practicing steps for the swing in the two step and the east coast, west coast, and then would compete in the competitions on American Bandstand." By the time she was seven years old, these moves were embedded within her kinesthetic memory.

Ana has long been a student of movement. As a child, she was fascinated by films starring Bruce Lee and his particular style; she was drawn to the physicality of it, including the precision of movement, the punctuated explosiveness, and the fluidity of sequences. Her father, noticing her attentiveness to martial arts, looked for a martial arts studio for Ana and enrolled her in Kenpo Karate for three years; at the time, her father had no idea that the instructor he found had worked with Bruce Lee. Though she describes herself as "small framed," Ana considered herself a "tomboy" who loved physical challenges. The movement styles that she learned in karate would eventually translate onto the dance floor, as she pushed herself to new levels in street dance.

Locking

Ana and her friend Stevie regularly drew inspiration from *Soul Train*. They especially noted the style of dance called locking, sometimes paired with funk music, where the most dramatic moves were expressed, but also incorporated into other genres of music. Now in their early teens, Ana and Stevie began to pick up on this dance style. They especially fixated on the Lockers, a group which Ana says "changed my life," when she first saw them on television in 1973. Ana was fascinated by how each group member distinguished themselves in their styles. She describes how, "You knew who they were. They all had their own personality, and yet were unified."

The Lockers created the locking dance style, which involved alternating between fast movements of the limbs, big steps and leaps with calculated landings, and then posing in ostentatious ways. Group member Don Campbell is known as the originator of the style. Ana and Stevie had opportunities to hone their locking skills at one of only a few venues accessible to young dancers. Specifically, she and a friend danced at an all ages club at the amusement park, Knott's Berry Farm, in Buena Park, California, not far from where they lived. This is where Ana caught the eye of other more experienced dancers. At Knott's Berry Farm, at the age of fourteen, Ana and Stevie met a group of dancers known as the Funky Bunch. The group had heard about Ana's dance skills through the scene. The Funky Bunch specialized in the locking dance style, and they maintained a style inspired by that of the original Lockers. Immediately, Ana saw the opportunity to expand her skills by working with the Funky Bunch, who recruited her to join them.

The Funky Bunch noticed Ana's excellent work ethic in dance, and began inviting her to various clubs so that she could expand her skill repertoire. Ana's sister provided her with a key resource related to dance: her ID. With her sister's ID, Ana visited new clubs and was exposed to an ever-expanding repertoire of style variations. Given her eye for movement, she began picking up on an array of details. Ana surpassed the Funky Bunch's expectations when it came to learning from what she observed at the clubs. At the same time, Ana noticed that in committing to one group, the Funky Bunch, she was limited in terms of what she could learn.

At the age of fifteen, with her sister's ID card, Ana was able to get into the Grand Hotel, a club that featured some of the best funk dancers in the Los Angeles area. The Funky Bunch took her to this club. Once inside, Ana could not believe her eyes: Most members of the Lockers were dancing at the Grand Hotel! Though she did not know all their names, she recognized Don Campbell immediately. Her dance imagination ran wild as she saw up close the very dancers she idolized. She had the opportunity to share the dance floor with Greg Cambellock Jr., Don Campbell, Fred Berry, Shabbadoo, and Fluky Luke, all legendary members of the Lockers.[1] While she could see the similarities between the Funky Bunch and the Lockers, in person she could also see the differences in the originators of the style. She realized there was another level of skills she could acquire. Ana asserts, "They had something that nobody had. There was an essence about them then. It was their dance. It was their dance, especially Don [Campbell]" (Harris 2012). During that time, Ana transitioned out of the Funky Bunch. She now had a greater opportunity to learn from the Lockers, who had altered her understanding of dance.

Ana received an open door to dance, unexpectedly, once again in connection to her sister. "Greg Cambellock Jr. [a member of the Lockers], liked my sister,"

---

[1] She met Lockers member Toni Basil at a later date.

Ana confessed. The Lockers began inviting Ana to different dance clubs such as Mavericks Flat and Blueberry Hill, often encouraging her to bring her sister along. These clubs primarily served Black Los Angeles. She witnessed some of the best dancing she had ever seen at these clubs, with moves and styles that were distinct from what she saw on television. Campbellock Jr. became the first Locker that Ana got to know. He introduced her to the others in the group. She especially learned from Campbellock Jr, who had a knack for teaching others, and made learning enjoyable. He taught her moves, and the nuances of dance tricks, positioning, and more. Soon, she felt ready to show others her look, taking a risk by performing the dance in heels. Under the tutelage of the Lockers, Ana learned to lock in her own style.

Punking and Whacking

Soon, in late 1974, Ana was taken aback by another style of dance that she first witnessed at a club called Destiny II. One fateful night at Destiny II, Ana observed a cluster of immaculately dressed men, wearing suits reminiscent of the 1940s and '50s. The men were there to compete in a dance contest held at the club that night. As each one took to the stage, Ana got goosebumps and could not take her eyes off of them. The men performed in a style that alternated between fast flailing arms, and posing bodies, holding in tension the frenetic and the intentional, and maintaining a controlled confidence. While Destiny II was a "straight club," Ana soon discovered that these men were gay. The men were risking negative reactions from other club goers by being there (Guzman-Sanchez 2012).

Two of the men took the first and second spots in the competition that night, beating out other recognized dancers. Many congratulated the men, but Ana remembers being the only person to approach the men to speak with them for an extended period of time. Just as she learned about locking, Ana felt a powerful draw to learn about this style. When she spoke to the men, and asked them what style they had performed, they described their moves: "Whack, whack, pose, punk, punking[2] and whacking." They developed the style themselves, Ana learned, in gay clubs they frequented. These men, Andrew Frank, Arthur Goff, Tinker Toy, and Billy Starr Estrada, were pioneers of this style. The men continued to compete weekly at this club, and in the process, took a liking to Ana. Her interest in the men's dance skills blossomed into friendship. She especially developed a friendship with Arthur, who would invite her over to his home; he had his own place, and the others lived with family, so his home was often the

---

[2] The designation of "punking" as a dance style, attributed to DJ and dancer Michael Angelo Harris, converted a derogatory term into a positive expression of dance innovation.

gathering place. The friends had gotten used to people wanting to copy their style, so they were cautious about letting people into their circle.[3] As Arthur got to know Ana, he saw that she was genuine, and that she cared about the friends' well-being. Soon, Arthur intentionally invited the friends over to his home so they could get to know Ana better.

Ana's interest in their dance styles never waned, but she did not merely want to imitate their style. Rather, Ana wanted to know more about these men, and where they drew inspiration from. She got to know their dreams, their aspirations, their struggles. They shared various points of inspiration with her: watching Bugs Bunny cartoons, perusing magazine images, and even taking her to underground clubs. The men recognized that she was someone they could trust, and took her in as a close friend. Throughout the 1970s, as the dance style that these men developed was growing and advancing, Ana was there not only to witness it but also to participate. Part of developing reciprocity with the friends was Ana's ability to understand the stylistic nuances of specific dancers. Her observations and perspectives on each of their dance styles proved invaluable. The dancers knew they could trust her feedback.

Ana had been accepted into the circle of innovators and recognized that she was privileged as a straight woman to have been given access into their spaces. Some of these dancers began to teach her about how to integrate more of herself into her dance performances. From her body language, to her wardrobe, to the particular moves she chose, Ana made adjustments based on what she learned. Ana expresses a tremendous sense of gratitude toward her friends. In her own words, "The creators took a chance at a straight club to share what they were creating. They took a chance with this little Puerto Rican girl." Today, Ana traces her dance lineage in punking and whacking to the very creators of the dance. Sadly, some of the friends have since passed away, making Ana's direct connection to them all the more special.

Public Performances

Moving into the 1980s, Ana was among a network of street dancers that collaborated after the Lockers disbanded. The films *Breakin 'N' Enterin*, and *Breakin 1* and *2* capture a significant portion of this dance scene. Members of this scene who shared the stage periodically included Ana, Boogaloo Shrimp, Pop N Taco, Lil Coco (Johnson 2016), Suga Pop, Hugo Mr Smooth Huizar, Popin Pete, and Shabbadoo, among others. Bruno "Pop N Taco" Falcon, became one

---

[3] Guzman-Sanchez (2012) describes how mixed gay and straight clubs were often sites where straight dancers would learn about dance styles popular among gay dancers.

of her dearest friends, and one of the most recognized dancers in the scene. The two would learn from each other as they exchanged moves from their respective styles. This circle, which garnered attention in the entertainment world via film and live performance, made an impression on a wide array of dancers, and had a unique appeal among dancers in Brown Los Angeles, as various collaborators pointed out to me.

Though Ana's background as a Latina shaped her experience in the dance world, according to her, the challenges she faced in dance were largely due to gender, more than to race or ethnicity. Ana encountered various barriers in the dance world related to the expectations that others had of her as a woman. She found that many women had internalized the expectations placed on them of what was possible to women on the dance floor. Many of the dance moves the Lockers performed were considered masculine, or for men only, by many creatives in the dance scene. Yet, Ana was determined to incorporate the full gamut of funk dance styles into her own repertoire. She recalls a particular occasion where she watched Campbellock Jr. dive off of a stage during a performance. She asked him, "What do you do when you dive off a stage?" Initially, he laughingly asserted that she would never do it, but after receiving tips from him, she ultimately dove off of the stage during a performance. She eventually perfected the maneuver, despite the fact that it was not seen as a woman's type of move. As she says to some of the students that she instructs today, "I let women know you could do all that and still be feminine. You can be strong, you can be assertive, but you still have that edge with which to beat the guys. Now you can smile and look cute while you're doing it."

As a street dancer of Puerto Rican ancestry, Ana broke new ground and became one of the most respected dancers in the scene. As is the case with some present during the arrival of the West Coast scene, she herself does not identify as "Hip Hop." Both in conversation with me and in past interviews she clarifies, "I'm a street dancer. I'm not a break dancer. I'm not a hip hopper" (Harris 2012). Nevertheless, she was a pivotal figure in what would emerge as the early West Coast scene. The resonances she drew from shaped her own trajectory, and she ultimately established her own dance styles and her own aesthetic that resonated with others. When eyes turned to the West Coast and examined whether Hip Hop had a home in Los Angeles, Ana was one of the dancers who solidified Los Angeles's place in the movement.

By 1980, Ana performed in her first music video for the Talking Heads, demonstrating her locking and whacking skills, one of the first times these styles appear in a music video. Her iconic status in West Coast Hip Hop was sealed in the films *Breakin' 'N' Enterin'*, and *Breakin' 1* and *2* (Image 1.1). She performed on a slew of other popular platforms, both as a featured dancer and as a choreographer. Her dance resume includes choreographing for the likes of Tina Turner,

Image 1.1 Bruno Falcon, Ana Sanchez, Michael Chambers, Adolfo Quiñones, during the filming of *Breakin'*. (Reproduced courtesy of Alamy)

Linda Ronstadt, David Bowie, The Beach Boys, Bette Midler, and Toni Basil. She has also performed as an opening act for Tina Turner, Dean Martin, Don Rickles, and Dinah Shore. Likewise, her performances in television and film include work for CBS, ABC, Disney, and continued work with Cannon Films. Her reputation as a speciality choreographer permeated the scene, and she was one of the few women choreographing street dance. Her boundless style sent a message to dance aficionados everywhere that women could be on the cusp of innovation within the street dance world.

Masters of the Spin

"I hated LA, at first." As I spoke to Henry "Hen Gee" Garcia, a West Coast Hip Hop pioneer, his disdain for Los Angeles was a distant memory. The Garcia family had made the drastic move from Brooklyn, New York, to the Los Angeles area. They landed in Cudahy, a largely brown neighborhood in southwest Los Angeles county. Having contributed to the rise of Los Angeles Hip Hop in the 1980s, Hen became a fixture of the Los Angeles music scene, a catalytic figure embedded in the networks of movers and shakers. Arriving in Los Angeles in the early 1980s, he had to adjust to his new settings. Hen and his brother, Evil E, attended Bell High School. There, athletics provided an important social and creative outlet for the brothers, and they excelled at multiple sports. Yet, there was another arena that would give them the most shine: Hip Hop. The siblings dipped into deep wells of familial resonance to make a creative impact in the scene.

The Garcia brothers' ability to adapt Hip Hop to their new context was rooted in their diasporic family history. The move West was not the first move the household had made. Hen was born in Brooklyn, but his family had migrated from Tegucigalpa, Honduras. His father, Justo Wilfredo Garcia, garnered fame in New York City by playing for the prestigious HOTA soccer club. The family settled in the Crown Heights neighborhood of Brooklyn, in the Weeksville Gardens Housing Development, where Hen grew up. The family held important ties to the Caribbean coast of Honduras because of their Garifuna roots. When the family had initially arrived, they were bilingual, speaking Spanish and Garifuna. In Brooklyn, they added English to their linguistic repertoire. The Garcia brothers grew up trilingual. As they explored the cultural landscape, Hip Hop was at their fingertips. The brothers began to apply their skills, particularly the knowledge of percussion that they had gained from their family, on a different set of instruments—turntables.

Alongside their father's legacy of sport, the Garcia siblings were also linked to a legacy of artistic performance. Their mother, Marciana Garcia Laboriel, had various relatives who made broad, lasting impacts in the entertainment industry, internationally. Growing up, the Laboriel name was familiar to me, as my father mentioned his youthful affinity for the music of Johnny Laboriel, a rock and roll star in Mexico. His sister, Ella Laboriel, was also known for her musical talent, especially as a jazz and blues vocalist. The two gained additional accolades through television and film. A third sibling, Abraham Laboriel, migrated to the United States from Mexico and became an acclaimed bassist, playing with some of the world's most recognized pop stars, and rising to stardom in his own right. The siblings of this branch of the Laboriel family were born in Mexico. Marciana Laboriel's branch remained in Honduras. Distinct branches of the Laboriel family reunited after migrating to the United States. Hen Gee was well connected to this extended, hemispheric (Oro 2020) Laboriel network, whose emerging generations continue to impact the world of the arts. As Hen pointed out, a number of his family members graduated from Berklee College of Music. The legacy continues (Small 2008).

Hen and Evil E arrived onto a Hip Hop landscape in the early 1980s that was a far cry from what they knew in their native Brooklyn. The talk about white t-shirts and Jheri curls that showed up in the lyrics of early West Coast rappers they heard on the streets was distinct from the life they knew in the boroughs of New York City. During those first years, the Garcia brothers were primarily becoming acquainted with the majority–Mexican American scene in the area where they lived. As they began to expand their social circle within their school, friends invited them to the house parties in the area. The Garcia brothers soon started to circulate through the house party circuit of Brown Los Angeles, especially in southeastern Los Angeles county.

As they knew to do, they began to employ their skills to rock this party circuit. Within their expanding network of friends, word got out that the Garcia brothers knew how to move a crowd, both as emcees and as DJs. Hen explains that he and his brother understood the party scene and how to interact with the crowd because of their involvement with the scene in New York. "We saw it all get started in the Bronx and spread to the other boroughs. We were right there for it," Hen recounts. Having been engaged in hyping up crowds of party guests as an emcee in New York City, Hen transposed his skills onto the party scene of Brown Los Angeles. The translation of skills went over well. He recalls those early occasions when he would be given the microphone before a crowd: "When I'd say 'Hey!,' they'd say 'Hey!'" At the time, the party scene in his area was primarily playing disco music, according to Hen. Young party goers began to see the Garcia brothers as "the Hip Hop guys," because they would introduce revelers to live rhymes and would spin Hip Hop tracks on the turntables.

As they moved through this party circuit, the Garcia brothers began to discover they were not the only Hip Hop performers in Brown Los Angeles. There were others who also identified with Hip Hop and were invested in developing a West Coast expression of the movement. Some of these young creatives would be the architects of "Latino Hip Hop." Hailing from the nearby city of Southgate, Hen and Evil E soon connected with the Reyes brothers, known as Mellow Man Ace and Sen Dog, as well as their friends that would eventually form Cypress Hill, B-Real, and later DJ Muggs. Hen remembers when brothers Sen Dog and Mellow Man would come around his block to visit two young women that lived down the street from the Garcia family. "They were hanging out with these girls, but I think they were actually trying to connect to us, because they knew what we were doing with music," Hen recounts with a chuckle. At this stage, the Garcia brothers were making names for themselves "on the block." They came to be known in the neighborhood as the Spin Masters. Their reputation was highly local, rooted in the teen networks that they were operating within. Unlike performers that would come through Los Angeles on tour, and unlike widely recognized local DJ crews who would pack arenas, like Uncle Jamm's Army, at this stage, circa 1983, the Spin Masters were "in the community." That would soon change.

"I remember seeing Frost selling cassettes," Hen explains. Kid Frost, whose name was gaining notoriety in the scene, also making his way through the party circuit of Brown Los Angeles, represented a Chicano brand of Hip Hop that was closely linked to Los Angeles. The intersection of these emerging acts—the Garcia brothers and Arturo Molina—proved to be fateful. Frost had initiated conversations with Pebo Rodriguez and Dave Storrs about recording on their label when he met the Garcia brothers. Hen remembers that "Around 83–84, Frost connected us to ElectroBeat records, with Dave Storrs and Pebo." By 1985, the two siblings released a single with ElectroBeat called "Brothers," as the Spin Masters.

Along with their musical accomplishments, the Spin Masters played an important role in generating resonance across distinct ethnoracial groups through Hip Hop. According to Hen, "We basically put the Brown and Black together." Hen attributes their ability to do that because they were "Spanish and Black." Hen also reveals that he believes his Honduran Garifuna roots played a major role in the Spin Masters' success, and in their bridge-building appeal. He explains that he grew up listening to all kinds of music, both at home and in his Brooklyn surroundings. Being Garifuna provided Hen with a particular type of cultural wealth, according to his accounts of family life. At home, "we had congas in the back," Hen explains, "and we used to get busy." He further explains, "We grew up listening to Garifuna music, with African drums." These musical sensibilities, by Hen's estimation, transferred into the brothers' ability to curate and perform music before audiences. Plus, the ability to code switch across different types of audiences was second nature to Hen, having grown up in a trilingual home where English, Spanish, and Garifuna were spoken.

The ability to integrate various musical styles paid off for the Spin Masters. According to Hen, they were adept at blending together genres of music that DJs in Los Angeles had typically not thought to bring together. As the funk era on the West Coast was one of the primary drivers of West Coast Hip Hop, Hen believes that DJs tended to stick to a more funk-based sound. The Spin Masters, however, were willing to mix together R&B and other musical genres, that shifted the ambience of the crowd during live performances. He'd mix the likes of Michael Jackson and Madonna with Hip Hop. Furthermore, their styles on the turntables differentiated them from West Coast DJs. "We introduced the backspin," Hen explains. "We had that finesse," he adds.

Hen Gee went on to amass a variety of accolades as a Hip Hop artist and power player. He linked with key crews, such as Ice-T's Rhyme Syndicate, rocked stages in key scenes, such as Uncle Jamm's Army events, and helped spur important developments, such as working as a mixmaster for KDAY's groundbreaking Hip Hop–based radio shows. He and Evil E continued to release music of their own, and continually found ways to give back to the communities they came from, even after achieving fame. Notably, Hen has continued to intentionally include Brown Los Angeles as a target within the initiatives that he designs and supports. He has helped further the career of Chicano and Honduran American rappers, among others, and has invested in documenting "The art of rap Latino."

While Hen and Evil E are recognized among West Coast Hip Hop aficionados as innovators in the field, they deserve more credit for their impact on Brown Los Angeles. Garifuna scholar Joseph Paul Lopez Oro's critique of mestizaje ideologies within Latinidad offers important insights. Regarding the racialized realities faced by Garifuna peoples, Oro (2020:2) argues that, "mestizaje discursively emerges as an ideological project of nation-building, violently negating Blackness and the existence and contributions of peoples of African descent in its construction of a racially mixed harmonious mestizo subject." Moreover, while it is impossible to negate the contributions of the Garcia brothers, often they are sidelined or their backgrounds are sidelined (Perry 2015) within discussions of "Latino Hip Hop," given the ideological tendency toward erasure of Blackness within Latinidad. Rivera-Rideau (2016:64) especially notes this tendency within "scholarship about Latinos in California." The Garcia brothers, nevertheless, sustain an indelible resonance on the West Coast scene, and within Brown Los Angeles, signaling the ways that brownness is connected to Blackness.

For various Caribbean-origin creatives, AfroLatinidad was a salient dimension of their experience in the scene. The accounts of various Black Latine artists suggest that these artists understood their own Afro-Latinidad as blurring the boundaries between ethnoracial configurations in Los Angeles. This Caribbean- and Atlantic-facing Latinidad illustrates Su'ad Abdul Khabeer's (2016:7) theorizing of Hip Hop's "grounding in a Diasporic and polycultural Blackness (in which Latinidad is always an interlocutor, if not a participant) forged by involuntary and subsequent migrations." These artists' Afro-Latinidad uniquely positioned them to broker cultural resources geographically and across social boundaries, drawing from expansive diasporic resonances. The late Adolfo "Shabbadoo" Quinones, for example, discussed having a Black American mother and Puerto Rican father, and drawing on the cultural resources of both of his parents' communities (Smith 2021). A former Latin King member in Chicago, Shabbadoo gained fame alongside his sister Fawn through their regular appearances on the dance show *Soul Train*, following the show from Chicago to Los Angeles. Shabbadoo mentored various Latine dancers (Goldstein 1984) in dance styles primarily associated with Black American communities. He emerged as one of the most influential figures in the West Coast street dance scene.

Often, Afro-Latine creatives navigated the scene distinctly from their non–Black Latine peers in relation to how they accessed Black American spaces. Many of these creatives found deep resonances with Black American traditions, and also mediated these traditions within Brown Los Angeles. Afro-Latinidad itself is tied to a wealth of cultural and technological resources, and Caribbean-origin creatives especially demonstrated consciousness of their ties to Afro-Latinidad. Nevertheless, while ties to Afro-Latinidad were prevalent among Caribbean-origin creatives broadly, Afro-Latine creatives especially maintained resonances with Black Americans in this foundational Hip Hop era (Ogbar 2007). Such connections became all the more salient when Afro-Latines and other Caribbean-origin creatives migrated to the West Coast by way of New York City, having additional access to direct cultural resources from Hip Hop's cultural center. Puerto Ricans, including Afro-Boricuas, were especially key in establishing resonance channels with Black Americans, having historically maintained a distinct resonance with Black Americans within sites of settlement (Rivera 2001; 2003).

Afro-Latine creatives also described challenges in navigating racial boundaries in Los Angeles. For example, Afro Cuban artist Mellow Man Ace discussed with Chicano DJ Tony A (Alvarez 2020) about connecting to both Brown Los Angeles and Black Los Angeles: "I have that versatility where I can go in the black community and get love. I can go into the Latino community and get love." Mellow adds, "It's not that I'm with you or them, I'm both of you, and that's the hardest part of being Mellow Man Ace." The difficulty that Mellow alludes to signals that at times Afro-Latinidad was misread in the Los Angeles context. As Mellow describes on *The Real Gully TV* podcast (Lindsey 2018), "We did get static, you know, we had to box a lot, you know, but predominantly with the Mexican cats and some of the brothers too. Because the Mexicans didn't understand how we could be Black and speak perfect Spanish and the brothers hated the fact we spoke Spanish but was Black. So, we didn't know English at that time." These interactions were particularly pronounced when Mellow and his family first migrated to California, uncovering the illegibility of and hostility toward Afro-Latinidad in some Los Angeles contexts, from both Latines and Black Americans. With time, Mellow built a niche for himself and gained a following through his music, inspiring others along the way.

Caribbean Connections

There is a plethora of examples of how creatives of Caribbean descent inspired others within Brown Los Angeles to express themselves through Hip Hop. Mellow Man Ace, for example, describes the catalytic experience of listening to "Disco Dream" by the Mean Machine (J Flores 2000). The Mean Machine was arguably the first Hip Hop group to record a song that featured an emcee rapping in Spanish.[4] The emcee in question, Danny Rivera, known by the stage name

---

[4] Another group, Spanish Fly and the Terrible Two, also released a bilingual rap record in 1981.

Mr. Schick, performed lyrics in the Spanish language, and also highlighted terms and inflection familiar in New York City's Puerto Rican community. Mellow Man indicates, for example, that the line "Wepa, wepa, alli na'mas!" caught his attention (Sullivan 2019a; see also Del Barco 1996). As an emcee of Cuban background, Mellow Man did not find the Caribbean inflection unfamiliar. Indeed, Mr. Schick attests to having had early influence from Cuban artists in the Bronx, while he was growing up. The lyric ending the same song, "Agua que va a caer," is a phrase reminiscent of the great Cuban *conguero*, Patato Valdez, whom Mr. Schick met when he was a child. As the grandson of a Cuban composer (Thompson-Hernandez 2017), Mellow Man Ace found the connection uncanny.

Even as Mellow Man was inspired by Mr. Schick, his own music inspired others. Tony Alvarez, known as DJ Tony A Da Wizard, who was already involved in the burgeoning Hip Hop industry, received a revelation of sorts when he heard Mellow Man Ace's song, "Mas Pingon." For Tony A, who was well versed in the emerging movement, being introduced to this song energized his creative imagination. He went on to be a successful DJ, mixtape producer, and song producer. For creatives from Brown Los Angeles then, hearing someone that they could identify with was an important factor in spurring them to identify with Hip Hop. It is important to note that these creatives did not solely identify with artists matching their ethnic or national-origin group. They identified with other artists based on panethnic groupings, drawing on a Hip Hop Latinidad (Castillo Planas 2020) and at times recognizing similar struggles (Fernandes 2018). Chicanos affirmed Cuban artists, and a Cuban artist affirmed a Puerto Rican artist, in the cases above. So, while Rivera offers an important critique of the way the music industry has used a homogenizing view of Latinidad to market Hip Hop among Latines, prior to this mass marketing, various Latine creatives experienced resonances across panethnic subgroups.

Sick Jacken from the group Psycho Realm also points to a record from a Miami-based rapper as serving a pivotal role in his motivation to become an artist. A record from Chulito stood out to Sick Jacken when presented to him by one of his best friends, whose brothers were DJs and had access to music not in rotation on Los Angeles radio stations. The cover of Chulito's 1989 record, *Sacudete*, includes the following statement: "Ya llego la hora de disfrutar la música que nos gusta en nuestro propio idioma." [The hour has come to enjoy the music that we like in our own language]. Moreover, this message suggests that the artists, producers, and/or executives behind this record began to recognize the marketability and demand for a Spanish-language rap song. Chulito was based in the Miami area, another hotbed of Latine Hip Hop, after New York City, and alongside Los Angeles. In terms of Latine musical production, these three cities were arguably the primary hubs of Latino Hip Hop in the 1980s.

Conclusion

Caribbean-origin creatives composed an important channel of resonance for Hip Hop in Brown Los Angeles. Puerto Ricans were among the most influential in this group, but the presence of other Caribbean origin groups, such as Cuban Americans, was also critical. These creatives crossed boundaries of race, gender, geography, and genre in influencing the West Coast scene before and during Hip Hop's arrival. As cultural brokers, many Caribbean-origin creatives made resources accessible across distinct communities and helped forge adaptive expressions in the scene. The experiences of these Caribbean-origin creatives of being caught between communities were at times difficult, and shaped their own sense of cultural adaptation. Likewise, these forms of consciousness that emerged often shaped the types of artistic outputs these artists contributed. So, while the intersections of the West Coast scene and Brown Los Angeles are often conceived of as a Chicano space, Caribbean-origin creatives provided significant cultural resources through their presence, activities, and relationalities. Ultimately, the West Coast scene is indebted to the lifework of many Caribbean-origin creatives for the resonance channel they established.

2
Borderland Blends

I came to GCS,[1] a Hip Hop shop in Santa Ana, California, to catch a live set from Zane, an emcee featured in this volume's introduction. As expected, Zane ripped the mic, losing no time to a technical glitch that delayed her instrumental from playing over the speakers. With authority, she rocked a cappella. And when DJ Soluz scratched the music in through the sound system, Zane seamlessly maneuvered her lyrics over the track, literally not missing a beat. My partner, Puanani, and I came for the rhymes, but stayed for the event, Homegurl Swap, a mutual-aid-driven gathering of mostly women who provided attendees the opportunity to swap clothing, books, plants, crystals, and artwork, among other things. Graffiti writers, poets, photographers, and other creatives came together in a resonant, uplifting manner. As I examined the art pieces represented, I couldn't help but notice the blending of Hip Hop aesthetics with older Chicano motifs, sometimes within individual pieces, and sometimes in the juxtaposition of distinct pieces. Photographer Catalina Nuñez, known as Bbygirlsolita, for example, offers an extensive catalog of images from Brown Los Angeles, featuring La Virgen de Guadalupe, classic lowrider cars, and pachuca and pachuco aesthetics. Zane's visual artwork, on the other hand, incorporates Hip Hop icons, often imposed on nature-based and indigenous print patterns. Likewise, in the aesthetics that participants wore, from wing-tip eyeliners, to "Charlie Brown"–type polo shirts, to particular tattoos, Chicano aesthetics permeated this underground Hip Hop venue. As I argue in this chapter, this stylistic blending pervaded beyond this event. In navigating Hip Hop spots in Brown Los Angeles, Borderlands juxtapositions and adaptations ubiquitously characterized a Borderlands resonance channel.

Channel of Exchange

The blending of Chicano aesthetics and Hip Hop motifs is a byproduct of Borderlands life. Yet, beyond affirming LAtino Hip Hop's emergence from the Borderlands, I argue that the Borderlands were foundational to Hip Hop's resonance in Los Angeles. Hip Hop did not first become adapted to Los Angeles and

[1] Giant Casting Shadows.

then blend with Chicano aesthetics. Rather, Hip Hop's rooting in Los Angeles, in part, happened as it resonated with Chicano culture. Brown Los Angeles is a Borderlands space, a liminal reality where resonances of past colonial histories collide with ongoing inequalities to forge adaptive cultural expressions (Anzaldúa 1999; Castillo Planas 2020). Life in Brown Los Angeles is tied to a larger Borderlands region, the expansive geographies that encompass and radiate from the US-Mexico border. It is no surprise, then, that one of the key resonance channels that shaped Hip Hop in Brown Los Angeles runs through the Borderlands. Though Los Angeles is not directly on the US-Mexico border, Borderlands extend into the experiences of people caught between the political and cultural lifeworlds of nation-states, even if they live far beyond border regions (Kun 2005 Mendoza-Denton 2015; Castillo Planas 2020; Saldívar 1997).[2] This does not mean geography is irrelevant—quite the contrary. Los Angeles is geographically linked to a broad cluster of cities extending all the way into Baja California, Mexico, crossing national boundaries. Urban theorist Mike Davis (2006) conceives of this urban cluster as a megalopolis unto itself, and one of the most influential ones at that, outsizing entire nations in cultural and material production. Thus, like the notion of Brown Los Angeles, the Borderlands are both geography and experience. In this chapter, I explore particular elements of Borderlands life that resonated with Hip Hop early on.

One key resonance of Borderlands cultural production that has had lasting impacts in Brown Los Angeles and in LAtino Hip Hop is pachuco culture. Pachuco culture, or pachuquismo, emerged from the circuits of cultural exchange most trafficked by migrants, laborers, and the rural and urban poor in the Borderlands. Despite being popular among the working class, pachuquismo was characterized by gaudy zoot suits, drape suits characterized by coats with broad shoulder pads, and high-waisted trousers that flowed widely on the legs and finished tightly on the cuffs. In Los Angeles, versions of the suit were worn by both men and women. Some pachucas, women associated with pachuquismo, also sported high pompadours, v-neck sweaters, pleated skirts, and fishnet stockings or bobby socks (Ramírez 2009). The movement traces key influences to Black American culture in 1930s Harlem, and was blended and remixed along the Borderlands. Stylistic blending and resourcefulness may be noted in how some pachucas wore huarache sandals with their outfits (Ramírez 2009). Communities most affected by the outgrowths of war, left in the lurch of industrialization, transitioning between rural and urban life, and rendered liminal through legal-juridical surveillance mechanisms, have historically accessed

---

[2] While Rodriguez (2009) offers a valid critique of exclusionary forms of Chicano nationalism that have emerged in the Borderlands, I am most interested in forms that blur boundaries in the Borderlands.

strategies of survival and adaptation in pachuquismo. Pockets of pachuquismo have existed for nearly a century across the US Southwest, with Los Angeles emerging as a hub of pachuquismo. Pachuco culture's influence on the West Coast scene is best understood as part of a larger Borderlands resonance channel.

Borderland Visuals

As was evident at the Homegurl Swap event, founded by Sally, a graffiti artist, urban Chicano visual aesthetics that evolved from Borderlands pachuquismo resonated significantly with Hip Hop; graffiti writing was one of the key arenas where this resonance emerged. According to John "Zender" Estrada, who rose to prominence as a graffiti writer, urban Chicano culture informed the aesthetic milieu of the city's urban neighborhoods. Zender's work often reflects the coming together of Hip Hop and pachuco culture. One of his recent murals, for example, features a man and a woman that reflect pachuco aesthetics, alongside of Hip Hop graffiti lettering. Zender explained how this Borderlands milieu shaped his artistic creations:

> Because I grew up in East LA, right in the heart of LA, so I was part of Chicano culture from the get go man, from like five [years old]. So to me Chicano culture was my first, you can say, my upbringing. My dad wasn't a good father. He didn't say, "I got some advice for you," you know? Yeah, it was more like the homies said, "Ay little man, orale! Caile [drop in] homie! What's up? How old are you, ese?" "I'm five." "Orale!" Yep. I was educated by the street, because I was my own dad.

In being welcomed into the street scene in his childhood, Zender became familiar with a style of writing that was common among Chicano gangs: Old English lettering. He also reproduced on paper a writing style he saw on the walls, referred to in the neighborhood as "placas." Implicating the dearth of attention he received from his father, Zender indicates that local gang members provided him with the affirmation he sought. As word of his lettering skills spread, the local gang recognized how they could benefit from Zender's talents. Zender explains:

> Writing on the wall, you know, that came into my life in 1976. Okay, when my older people kind of caught on that I had a flair for lettering, and Old English writing, and placas, as a little kid, they were like, "homie, do a roll call for us." And you kind of begin to play. That's your intro to a spray can. It's in the block letters, and that's graffiti art. That's LA's version of graffiti. And Chaz, Chaz

is the guy who was notorious for explaining that process because that's what happened to him. He mastered the groove of the calligraphy of gang letters to the next level till he did it in a Japanese profession, almost like a tao, you know?

Zender was immersed in the writing forms and practices of the neighborhood "older heads," which presented a key phase in Zender's artistic development. The roll calls were especially engaging processes of creation in which he would list the names of different people from the neighborhood. While there were particular conventions that were associated with these types of art practices, for Zender they opened doors to more expansive repertoires of expression. Zender especially credited his inspiration to Chaz Bojorquez, a key innovator in the field of Los Angeles graffiti. Bojorquez harnessed the styles and aesthetics from the streets and developed expansive hybrid styles of lettering and imagery that earned him entry to art shows in highly respected international museums. As Latorre (2008:121) argues, Charles "Chaz" Bojorquez "galvanized and legitimized the graffiti influence on Chicana/o art." Speaking of how Bojorquez transitioned from a youngster writing on city walls to being featured in highbrow art institutions, Latorre notes, "He is often regarded as a figure who reconciled 'counterculture' aesthetics with the visual discourses of European and North American modernism." Even as an outlier, Bojorquez drew from the art of the Chicano communities he emerged from and made the art accessible to wider audiences. Zender's awareness of Bojorquez's work served as a source of legitimation for Zender's work.

Before New York City–style graffiti had gained notice in Los Angeles,[3] Zender was experimenting with the motifs he spotted in the gang graffiti, prison art, and tattoo imagery that were in his vicinity. As Zender recalled:

People are coming in and out of prison with their little prison art package, and that kind of imagery began to filter through the communities of the underground scene. A lot of homeboys would try to figure out how to project that on the walls. So you would have the guys from 38th Street gang begin to include the Diablito [little devil] character that you see a lot of in the tattoo industry. That was their trademark. And when I would see that little drawing on the wall with the three and the diablito in the middle of the eight, that would fascinate me, "holy smokes they incorporated a cartoon!" Next there was something like a Playboy Bunny. And then I thought about my nickname, which was Night Owl. So I said, "Man, I'm gonna put a little tecolotito [small owl] in between

---

[3] Creatives note the early work of graffiti writer "Soon," in bringing New York City–style graffiti to Los Angeles. Alski was another Bronx-born transplant to Los Angeles who was a prolific graffiti writer in the early 1980s.

my letters." And I did that, I was putting it down for Clanton, the gang, cuz I was from Clanton at one time. They had a trademark character, a little character with a huge Mexican sombrero and mustache as big as himself. But with a shotgun coming out of the side. That was Clanton's character.

Nobody unless you were in that culture would know what I'm doing. Little by little, these gangs would adopt imagery as part of their propaganda. And I remember there was this one gang doing this amazing thing like what Andy Warhol was doing in New York. This gang was doing it in LA in South Central. The gang was called Barrio Loco, BL, and they used an image of Emiliano Zapata in a stencil. So, in 1978 Barrio Loco would stencil Emiliano Zapata everywhere and sometimes in different colors because they didn't always have the same color. I didn't know who Andy Warhol was at the time. But I know now as an art historian that whole idea of multiple propaganda, like Shepard Fairey, was already being done with the gang genre.

Hip Hop–associated graffiti would become a powerful mode of expression among creatives in Los Angeles in part because Chicanos had already been blending elements of visual culture within their own repertoires, sometimes conveying revolutionary images. These skills later adapted to New York City styles. The ability to use spray paints for writing on walls was not a new skill to people like Zender. Likewise, the vision for creating characters on walls was not a new discovery that came with Hip Hop. Recognizing names on walls was also a common practice among neighborhood gangs, and something that Zender was engaged in.

Chicanos were exposed to visual art beyond Chicano street aesthetics. For Hector "Hex" Rios, a key contributor to the visual backdrop of the West Coast scene, the various forms of visual arts represented in the city spoke to his racialized experiences. Speaking at the Los Angeles Festival of Books, Hex drew in the audience by weaving together a historical account of how he and his peers found a creative outlet in graffiti. Despite mounting racial divisions, according to Hex, and perhaps because of them, Hip Hop took root in Los Angeles. It was in response to disempowerment and resistance that Hex saw street art emerging. The image that Hex described was one of people crying out for recognition:

> People started screaming out "I am someone, and I have an identity." All of a sudden and once you start seeing portraits going up and African-American muralists putting up pictures of African Americans on walls. In downtown LA you see the phantom shadow of Joey Krebs, putting up big shadows and saying "We mean something, we represent something." East LA, Estrada Courts, we are a minority. All of a sudden you start seeing the people screaming out saying, "We are important, we mean something." And that is where the Long

Beach Pike, all of the bikers, a lot of the guys that came—white guys and Hispanics—and they started going down to Long Beach and getting tattoos and riding their bikes. And that's where I first saw the first colors that were vivid on people's skins.

The murals and the colorful tattoos held prominent places in Hex's imagination. Hex connected these visual representations to a desire to be known, to be valued and understood, as young people growing up in the city. The internalization of these visual representations was eventually infused by Hex into his own art. Creatives in Brown Los Angeles were demonstrating agency in how they integrated the visual cultures surrounding them. In the process, many of them became active producers of visual culture, adapting the resonances that they were exposed to.

For Hex, the opportunity to blend West Coast aesthetics with East Coast visuals came early, via a Borderlands reality. Hex, who has family roots in the Borderlands region around Mexicali Mexico, had family members who migrated throughout the United States. These labor-migrant relatives made their way to disparate locales around the United States. In visiting Hex, these relatives shared photographs of sites they visited in places like New York and Chicago. In these photographs, Hex caught glimpses of graffiti. Some of these photographs portrayed graffiti images before Hip Hop graffiti had reached Los Angeles. Hex caught a vision of what could be and began to fuse the images in the photographs with the visual culture that he took in from his surroundings (Image 2.1). The Borderlands reality of migration unexpectedly amplified Hex's creative imagination and his penchant for visual fusion.

The influence of Chicano visual culture through these borderland frequencies also influenced non-Chicano creatives. Kyu Min Lee, known as OG Chino, for example, migrated with his family from South Korea to Colombia while he was a young child. According to Grace Jahng Lee (2015), "Chino's family was among the first Koreans in Colombia. In the mid-1960s, his father, a diplomat, went to Colombia to help establish the Korean embassy there. A few years later, he brought his family to Bogotá, where Chino lived from age one to ten." At the age of ten, Chino and his older brother were sent to live in the United States. They first landed in Carson, California, but soon after moved to Koreatown in Los Angeles.

Because of his familiarity with Latin American culture, Chino was able to integrate readily among diverse peer groups. In his early teens he associated with a Chicano gang, though he was not an official member. Having already expressed a penchant for writing on walls as a child, he soon learned to perfect Chicano calligraphy. Similar to Zender's experience, His homies would ask him to write their names on walls. When New York City–style graffiti gained popularity in

Image 2.1 Graffiti mural produced by Hex, 2012, demonstrating blending of Hip Hop and Borderlands aesthetics. (Reproduced courtesy of Hector Rios)

Los Angeles, Chino already had skills to build on, which he had developed in Colombia and attuned to a Chicano aesthetic in Los Angeles. Chino would become a successful Hip Hop entrepreneur, cultural influencer, and artist at an international level, playing key creative roles in Los Angeles, Dallas, and New York, as well as in Colombia. He opened what was arguably Los Angeles's first Hip Hop record store, Bboy Records, on Slauson Avenue in South Central Los Angeles. The Chicano aesthetic was part of the repertoire he drew from, as someone who had readily integrated into the community and had gained acceptance there.

Transborder Cultural Formations

At some point I realized my father was well versed in Caló, Chicano street slang. He still answers the phone with "Que-húbole," calls pants *tramos*, and refers to a head of hair as *greñas*. My father grew up in Ciudad Juarez, Chihuahua, Mexico, bordering El Paso, Texas, a city known as "El Pachuco."[4] Caló was the argot he

---

[4] This nickname for El Paso was often shortened to El Chuco, which became more popular than the full name, El Pachuco.

and his peers from the region communicated in. The twin city border region of his youth, it turns out, was the cradle of pachuco culture, the transnational subculture forged by Mexican and Mexican American youth for which Caló was an important signifier. Caló emerged as a blend of Spanish, US phraseology, and covert gypsy terms harkening back to the old crime world of Spain (Macías 2008). As Garcia notes (2009:25), "Pachucos appear to have spoken in the same creative, neologistic style as did the Spanish gypsies." This transnational subculture for generations influenced the cultural toolkit that many ethnic Mexicans drew on as they moved through the Borderlands. Inadvertently, it would influence West Coast Hip Hop (Kelly 2004).

The channels of exchange within Borderland cities, and across the border, were part of a larger web of cultural trade, interlinking the underground culture of the expansive southwest corridor that produced pachucos (Cummings 2003). With the expansion of railway systems in a previous era, young pachucos from this border region hopped trains and made their way to Los Angeles (Barker 1958). My father and his family were later participants of this migratory path as they migrated in cars to Los Angeles. While they came of age after the height of pachuco popularity, my father and his peers were undoubtedly inheritors of its legacy, and were among the many Mexican and Mexican American youths that carried forth resonances of this aesthetic into later cultural expressions.

After several back-and-forth moves, my father and his siblings eventually settled in Fullerton, California, in the 1970s. There they encountered older Mexican Americans who had come of age in the wake of the pachuco era. Fullerton became home to El Pachuco Zoot Suits, a clothing store founded in 1978 specializing in zoot suit fashion (Miranda 2023). In the period surrounding World War II, Los Angeles became the epicenter of Mexican American pachuco youth culture, echoing back to the Juarez/El Paso Borderlands an adapted version of the original pachuco wave. The zoot suit, uniform of the pachuco, was evermore emblematic of social oppression, and a response to this marginalization, among not only Mexican Americans but also Black American, Filipino American, and Japanese American youths (L. Alvarez 2007). The so-called Zoot Suit Riots brought this subculture to the fore, and placed Mexican American young men and women in the spotlight, as US military servicemen roamed the streets of Los Angeles and assaulted Mexican American pachucos. For Mexican American youths, the pachuco remained an expression of adaptation, and survival. As R. Rodríguez (2016:114) notes, the pachuco embodied elements of "resistance and empowerment." Duran (2002:42) aptly characterizes pachucos in the following manner:

> As a "border crossing" subject ("sujeto transfronterizo"), the pachuco is constantly translating cultural, linguistic, and economic realities on both sides of

the border. Appropriating a constructed border language-slang (calo)—that is already a reflection of the multiple realities they inhabit, pachucos translate culture and politics into a theatrical performance that is usually on the margins of the law (or officially sanctioned behavior) so as to produce and represent the unstable, marginalized, and marginal conditions of existence on these multiple borders, both in reality and as cultural metaphor.

This experience of the pachuco, its cultural antecedents, and its progenitors, laid the groundwork for the arrival of Hip Hop in Brown Los Angeles, especially among ethnic Mexicans (L. Alvarez 2007; R. Rodríguez 2016). Urban Mexican American culture had been informed by the transcultural pachuco reality for multiple generations. Much of this ongoing stream of adaptation, in response to marginalization, was evident both in the creative output of artists and in their personal accounts of life experiences.

Bridging Eras through Music

In journeying through the Borderlands of Brown Los Angeles, I found an unexpected conversation partner in Raul Garcia, an artist known for his ties to pachuco culture. While he passed away in 1992, Garcia's creative body represents an important road map of sonic cartographies in the Borderlands. The work of Raul Garcia, popularly known by various names —most recently Jonny Chingas— maintains creative touch points along the Borderlands. Garcia was a Mexican American musician, singer-songwriter, producer, and eventually rapper. Garcia's life is a window into the creative contributions of Borderlands culture informed by pachuquismo, and highlights various ways that West Coast aesthetics draw from Borderlands culture. While Garcia is no longer corporeally in this world of the living, through his living legacy, he remained a collaborator in my creative cypher.

Through his musical career spanning over three decades, Garcia curated a Borderlands resonance channel. As an artist who was part of an existing cultural scene, he lent resources to the incoming Hip Hop subculture and facilitated the emergence of a modified, indigenized version of the subculture in the new context. Specifically, Garcia's artistic work demonstrates the transcultural adaptation characteristic of pachucos and how this particular cultural toolkit interfaced with the arrival of Hip Hop. I was immediately drawn to Garcia's story when I discovered that he, like my father, was from Chihuahua. When I began to examine the extensive catalog of music that Garcia produced, it made sense that the transculturality of the Borderlands was part of his family history. In Garcia, pachuco culture did not merely interface with Hip Hop theoretically; rather, Garcia reached a point in his career where he performed Hip Hop as a pachuco.

Garcia faced many challenges as an artist in the Los Angeles music industry and often responded with an entrepreneurial spirit. After hustling in the industry for several decades, he was rewarded with a music contract from Columbia records (Snowden 1984). Some of his music received international airtime, gaining acclaim from London (G. Wilson 2003) to Ibiza (Brewster and Broughton 2011). Through the span of his career, Garcia performed a wide array of genres, from Rock and Roll, Chicano Soul, disco, and funk to corridos, samba, and cumbia. Late in his career, Garcia released several rap records. He transitioned from the Chicano Rock and Roll era to Hip Hop, and excelled at everything in between. A humorous thought experiment, to put Garcia's career in perspective, would be to envision the late rocker Ritchie Valens as a rapper. Garcia was two years older than Valens. One of Valens's early bandmates played music with Garcia. Garcia's incursions into Hip Hop would be similar to Ritchie Valens, or another of their Rock and Roll contemporaries, becoming a rapper.

Still, it is difficult to find a substantial amount of published information on Garcia. Only a few scholars of Chicano culture have acknowledged him in print. Raegan Kelly makes a passing reference to Garcia related to his contributions to Chicano music in the 1970s. Kelly (2004) indicates that Garcia and his band from the 1970s, The East LA Congregation, were a hit with the Chicano lowrider crowd. Tatum (2011), in writing about Chicano lowrider aficionados, also points to Garcia's popularity with that crowd as indicated by his being featured on the cover of *Lowrider* magazine.[5] Tatum (2011:46) notes that Garcia was "dressed in a long white zoot suit coat standing proudly next to his 1949 Ford lowrider." Garcia featured vehicles for album art, a nod to his lowrider-driving audience and to his own penchant for cruising boulevards. DJ Gary "Ganas" Garay, who also embarked on a quest to uncover more of Garcia's story, remarks in a recent *LA Times* article that searching for Garcia is like "trying to find Batman" (Garay 2022). Columnist Gustavo Arellano (2013), too, provided an overview of Garcia's career in response to a reader's question, "Whatever happened to Jonny Chingas?"

Newspaper archives as well as social media posts contained some references to Garcia, and of particular assistance were accounts from people who knew him personally. Still, Garcia's career was anomalous to me in that fans raved about him on various social media platforms, and he had an extensive library of musical

---

[5] The centrality of car culture within Chicano communities and the place of Chicano car culture as a channel of resonance for early West Coast Hip Hop speak to the "ethnographic locomotion" that Zanfagna (2017:14) describes in relation to exploring Los Angeles Hip Hop as a culture intertwined with automobile transit and movement. Chicano car culture contributed to this aspect of Los Angeles Hip Hop.

Image 2.2 L to R, Carlos Hernandez, founder of the party promotion company the Orange County Music Commission, Jonny Chingas, and Anselmo Rascón, DJ from Santa Ana, California. (Reproduced courtesy of Manuel Villaseñor)

works, along with a larger-than-life persona, but few accessible publications celebrated his contributions. Scholars and cultural analysts had either forgotten him, did not know of him, or intentionally overlooked him. I began to understand that a convergence of factors led to the dearth of information on Garcia (Image 2.2). Some of these factors were related to the type of art he produced, while others were related to larger challenges that mired the broader Chicano artistic experience.

The Transcultural Beginnings of Rulie Garcia

Raul Medina Garcia was born in the Mexican state of Chihuahua on April 12, 1939. A record of "Alien Arrivals" from the state of Texas indicates that Garcia, presumably with his family, migrated through El Paso, Texas, at the age of four (NARA 1952). The document indicates that Garcia had been born in Camargo, Chihuahua. Though Camargo was not a border town, it was directly connected to the El Paso/Juarez border cities through railway. The Garcia family, then, would have had access to the border region with relative convenience, for that time period. The steady flow of goods, people, and culture would have been part of the Garcia family's extended Borderlands experience as they resided in Camargo. It is also within reason that they resettled closer to the border for a season before eventually migrating to the United States. The records do not specify, but such was the case with my father's family, and such continued to be the case with many Mexican migrants, settling in the border region before resettling in the United States. An additional detail that is specified in the record is that Garcia's destination in the United States would be Glendale, California (NARA 1952). After moving to the United States as a child, Garcia would call Los Angeles home for the rest of his life. An *LA Times* obituary provides the following details regarding Garcia's life and career:

> Garcia came to the United States when he was a child and began playing music in junior high school. He played a variety of instruments, including saxophone, piano, bass and vibraphone. After graduation from Glendale's Hoover High School in 1956, Garcia formed Rudy [sic] Garcia & the Imperials, which recorded many Latin and rock "n" roll singles on Garcia's own label, Katinga Records. (LA Times 1992)

As Garcia was a contemporary of the late Ritchie Valens, he shared in some of the musical scenes that Valens participated within. Jimmy Carlos and Pete Antoniano, two brothers who released records as the "Shadows" and as the Carlos "Brothers," played with both Ritchie Valens and Garcia, known then as Rulie Garcia. In fact, the Carlos brothers at one point sang with Garcia's group, Rulie and the Imperials (Aversa 2011). The sibling duo, who grew up in the Cabrillo projects of Long Beach, was influenced by the doo wop and R&B vocalizations familiar to their Black American neighbors (Aversa 2011). Gilbert Rocha, bandmate and close friend to Ritchie Valens, also played for several years with Rulie and the Imperials in the early 1960s, after Ritchie Valens passed away. Rocha informed me that he watched Garcia play bass guitar alongside renowned Black American saxophonist Joe Houston in 1959 at the Calypso Inn.

Gilbert Rocha provides a hint as to why early in his professional career, Garcia was not receiving the credit he deserved (Guerrero 2020). According to Rocha, the band Rulie Garcia and the Imperials was having a great run appealing to local crowds. Racism was a limiting factor, however:

> We played for five years in Los Angeles at different places. And then as soon we were trying to go make the demo tapes and send them to all the different studios, selling the band, but when they saw "Rulie Garcia," they immediately

did, this is the truth, back in the era it happened, they figured anybody who would do that wouldn't get past the California border because he was Mexican.

Bearing an ostensibly Spanish name, at the time read as being Mexican, was a hindrance to Rulie Garcia and the Imperials. The appeal of the music was not enough to draw an investment from record labels, despite the fact that Garcia was practically a one-man band when it came to musical composition. As Rocha points out in an interview with Chicano musician Mark Guerrero (2020), Garcia had the talent to do much of the work on his own: "He recorded most of that stuff. He did his own backgrounds. He played the bass, he played the piano, on some of them he played the drums! He did all the background by himself!" The lack of support from the music industry would haunt Garcia for a good portion of his career. Ethnic identities, and how they were represented, mattered for artists of that era. Garcia's contemporaries, the Shadows, for example, changed their name to the Carlos Brothers. Local music historian Guy Aversa (2011) posits a reason for the name change: "They recorded 'Under Stars of Love' and 'Jungle Fever' under the name the Shadows. It was released in September of 1958 but the record went nowhere possibly because using the name the Shadows, they were thought to be black." Similarly, Ritchie Valens bore one of the most famous name changes among Chicano artists, having changed his last name from Valenzuela to Valens.

Garcia had a productive decade in the 1970s, with a style that primarily reflected local tastes. In this era, Garcia's music would have been classified as Latin Rock and Roll and Latin Soul. He built a name for himself weaving together sounds that harnessed the East Los Angeles penchant for rock, soul, and Afro-Caribbean percussion. According to Sal Medina (1992), "in the early seventies he recorded a series of singles for U. A. Records such as 'The East L.A. Congregation' and 'Sabrosito.' Unfortunately the gabacho record companies didn't do right by him. They wouldn't spend the time or money to promote him. This didn't deter Jonny." In alignment with Medina's observation, many Chicano artists of this era struggled to find the backing needed to reach a larger audience.

Garcia himself expressed his frustration in an *LA Times* interview with Don Snowden (1985):

Vocalist Jonny Chingas sank $8,600 of his own money into the first of a series of self-promoted and distributed albums in 1980 that ultimately paid off in a Columbia deal. He says that the usual route of submitting demo tapes is "like hoping to jump on the moon or something. I knew the label people wouldn't understand the music or the market I was going after with my first albums."

As already noted, Garcia had launched his own label, Katinga Records, but he also started various other labels (S. Medina 1992). His obituary adds that, "Later, Garcia renamed his label Billionaire Records and wrote and produced his own material" (LA Times 1992). Gil Rocha remembers that one day, as Garcia visited the Rocha family, he asked Rocha's mother for a hundred dollars to start his own record label. She obliged, and helped Garcia launch his label. "Garcia went on to record about a dozen albums and toured the Southwest, Central and South America and Europe" (LA Times 1992).

Making Music in an Era of Chicano Struggle

Garcia was rarely one to shy away from controversy, and having his own record label allowed him to speak his mind openly, especially on issues affecting the Chicano community. In 1971 he released "The Ballad of Daniel Ellsberg," a song memorializing Daniel Ellsberg, a military analyst who during the Vietnam War released to the press classified documents from the Pentagon, known as the Pentagon Papers. Ellsberg hoped that leaking the documents would precipitate the end of the war (Ellsberg 2003), as he understood the war to be unjust. Some who held views similar to Ellsberg's not only saw the violence meted on the Vietnamese people as unjust but also identified injustice in how military recruiters targeted communities of color. Indeed, the Vietnam War was taking a toll on the Chicano communities of Los Angeles as a disproportionate amount of Chicanos were dying in combat. Garcia's creative intervention into this issue indicated his commitments to peace and justice and to his own community. Memorializing Ellsberg in song was an act of protest, and Garcia had positioned himself within the chorus of Chicano dissenters against the war.

The issues that Garcia was addressing resonated in the lives of several of my collaborators. Graffiti artist Hector "Hex" Rios, at a public presentation, reflected on the legacy of the Vietnam War for Black and brown communities in general, and for his own family in particular (Rios 2018). His account, highlighting the experiences of his family, illustrates what Garcia would have been experiencing and witnessing during this era: "They were sending Blacks, and they were sending Hispanics. My father was here working the labor unions in the garment district of Los Angeles. Sure enough they sent him. they were sending mainly the minorities of all of the major cities of the United States to go fight a war. And the rich, the son of the rich, were the last to go." The mid-1960s and early-1970s proved to be a critical era for communities of color in Los Angeles, by Hex's estimation. He continued, "In that chaos, the Watts Riots, the Brown Berets, the Hispanics were fighting in East LA, they [the police] were arresting—police brutality. As a little kid I would see cops beat down women and children and guys my color, guys his color [pointing to a black copresenter on stage] and slammed their heads on the, on the police—the cop cars." Prominent in his account, given his father's own service in Vietnam, Hex recalls how veterans returning from Vietnam, "coming back to LA and they're mistreated even worse because they're meant to go kill people that they didn't even want to go kill in the first place, to represent a nation that's supposed to be all of us together helping each other move on to the next step." Many from the communities of color in Los Angeles were experiencing collective marginalization as an outgrowth of the war.

The Chicano Moratorium March, a protest against the Vietnam War staged in East Los Angeles, marked a defining moment in the Chicano community. Ruben Salazar, acclaimed journalist, was killed during the 1970 March; he was struck by a tear-gas projectile fired by a Los Angeles County sheriff's deputy. Salazar was referred to as "La Voz de la Raza." Recognized for his work as an *LA Times* correspondent and as a news director for Spanish-language network KMEX, channel 34, Salazar's voice was an important one among ethnic Mexicans in Los Angeles at a time when few voices represented this community in the public square. His stint with the *LA Times* lasted from 1959 to 1970. During that time he covered everything from the Vietnam War to issues in the Dominican Republic, Cuba, and Mexico, to local matters affecting the Chicano community in Los Angeles. It happens that Salazar shared a birth state with Rulie Garcia—Chihuahua, Mexico. Born in Ciudad Juarez, Chihuahua, and brought to the United States as an eleven-month-old, Salazar reflected a deep grasp of the Chicano experience in his journalism; he too was born a *fronterizo*, a person of the Borderlands.

Salazar's martyrdom contributed to the development of a localized Chicano identity, and the music of the era reflected these collective notions of belonging and resistance. Salazar's work challenged the discrimination wielded on the Mexican American community, and brought to light how identification with terms such as "Mexican" and "Chicano" were acts of resistance. Though he could easily have been mistaken for a US-born Chicano, he was technically an immigrant, whose quest for US citizenship was long and belabored. With his experiences throughout Latin America, his status as an immigrant, and his association with later generation Chicanos, Salazar embodied a panethnic reality, even as notions of Latinidad were still being cobbled together at a national level. For Salazar, a word that more appropriately captured the experience of Chicano Los Angeles was the term "Raza." A key voice from the community was silenced when Salazar was killed; musicians continued to do their part in amplifying a Chicano voice amid the deep loss for the community.

During that period, in 1971, Garcia released a record under the band name "Brown Brothers of Soul." This is among his most celebrated works, capturing an East Los Angeles, Latin Soul sound. Here, Garcia functions as a celebratory host, drawing Chicanos out onto the dance floor. "Heeey Chicano!" Garcia calls out jubilantly to his listeners. The decidedly Afro-Cuban rhythm that comes through signals the types of sonic resonances present in the East Los Angeles sound of the era. The name of this group, Brown Brothers of Soul, had racialized connotations. On the one hand, the use of the word "brown," in distinction to "white," points to the racialized positionalities that working-class Chicanos inhabited in this era. Furthermore, the use of the term "brothers," resonates closely with the Chicano concept of *carnalismo* (Garcia 1997), an aspirational brotherhood imbued with ethnic loyalty and support. Finally, the term "brothers" suggests a nod to the Black American convention of calling fellow Black men "brother." Again, Garcia's music highlights the Chicano experience in Brown Los Angeles of the era.

Within Garcia's music, the construction of Chicano identity takes place in collaboration with the construction of Black American identity, and not simply in contrast to it. The romantic oeuvres that Garcia makes to hypothetical love interests in his songs, for example, do not emphasize Eurocentric standards of beauty, but rather, often highlight melanated beauty. In the song "Rosita," for example, Garcia describes his love interest, a woman in Mexico, as having "sexy chocolate skin." In his song "Sabrocito," he shares a similar description of his romantic interest: "Big brown eyes, long black hair, and chocolate skin that just drives me wild!" In other songs, he makes references to his love interests as having dark hair, and dark eyes. Rather than seeing Chicano brownness as moving away from Blackness, Garcia's descriptions suggest proximity to it. At the very least, Garcia is not maneuvering around terms associated with and approximate to Blackness. Instead, he is finding commonality in his descriptions of beauty.

The expanding musical range evident in Garcia's creative catalog reflected the expanding musical tastes of Los Angeles's Mexican American community of that period. Young Chicanos coming of age in the period in which Garcia was active as an artist often speak of the wide array of musical influences that they were exposed to at home. This expansive range of tastes also figured into Brown Los Angeles's reception of Hip Hop. Stepping away briefly from Garcia's music and examining the accounts of Chicano creatives points to the parallels in Mexican American musical tastes and Garcia's musical outputs. Especially of interest is the way that various Chicano creatives tied their inclination toward Hip Hop to musical exposure, both in listening to and in creating music, that they gained from their parents or family members. Frank Contreras (n.d.), for example, a member of the group Spanish F.L.Y., points to the musical skills he developed as a child due to his father's musical influence. His father, Frank Sr., was respected for his artistry in the timbales and the congas in Southern California, pointing to a trend among a cohort of Chicanos to incorporate Afro-Cuban musicality into their musical repertoires. Frank Jr. credits receiving a keyboard and a set of drums from his father at five years of age as an important milestone in his creativity. Moreover, some Chicanos were committed to passing on their love for music to the next generation. Frank interprets this as a key stepping stone in his development as a DJ and producer. He developed his skills as a DJ by sneaking old records from his parents. Parents' record collections, in fact, were a resource that various creatives identified.

In similar fashion, Chicano artist Rocky Padilla discussed his musical influences in an interview with Tony Alvarez (2020). When asked about his musical influences, Padilla responds, "I'm glad you asked that. So, my mother being from Texas, my dad, Daniel Padilla, being from East LA, he's OG. He likes the good'ol boleros. Yes, so, I mean to this day he listens to cha-cha-cha. He lives in bolero, so we grew up listening to that." Padilla's love for music was sparked by playing in his father's band: "I was in his band since I was 10 years old. My dad, my 3 uncles. My uncle Fito taught me everything I know." His grandmother asked him to learn to sing in Spanish, and he followed her prompting. Learning how to play the music popular among his family members opened the door for Padilla to learn to play the music popular in his peer group, which included bands such as Cameo, Lakeside, and Confunktion. After learning to play music, and learning to sing, Padilla learned to rap. With his musical agility, and the familial creative resources at hand, he was among the first brown creatives to release Hip Hop–infused records. The accounts of these Chicano artists suggest that the musical resonances in Chicano households showed up in their Hip Hop productions. Garcia, too, would bring these influences together within his own musical career.

The propensity for musical adaptation is especially common among Borderland communities. This pattern fits right into what various Borderlands theorists describe as a type of hybridity that is enacted in the cultural exchange in the Borderlands (Saldívar 1997). Young people coming of age in Brown Los Angeles, in the 1980s, were especially well positioned to draw on a wealth of resources from their parents, in a pre–social media age. Many of them were still engaging with the tactile elements of records and musical instruments, and embodied their parents' musical influences even as they became conversant in the popular sounds of the era that may have distanced them from their parents. Nevertheless, I caution against understandings of hybridity that are essentialized, ones that assume cultural adaptation through passive absorption due to geographic residency and social proximity; creatives engaged in active processes of performative formation that gave rise to new artistic expressions.

The Legend of Jonny Chingas

By the 1980s, Garcia's musical endeavors encompassed a hodgepodge of genres under the artistic name Jonny Chingas. The pachuco image seems to have become the most prominent persona Garcia took on through his final decade of performing and into the beyond. Acclaimed Chicano artist Ruben "Funkahuatl" Guevara, though he did not meet Garcia, did have the opportunity to see him live in concert in the early 1980s at a club called Lingerie. Guevara notes that Garcia created a buzz and was developing a loyal following. As Guevara describes him, "Jonny wore a zoot suit and spoke in caló, pachuco slang. His music was a mix of swing and pachuco boogie-woogie. The audience was mostly Chicano but many curious white Hollywood scenesters showed up." Snowden's write-up on Garcia corroborates that Garcia indeed did play gigs at Club Lingerie (1985), indicating that Garcia did have a following in the area.

Music historian Vicente Mercado had the opportunity to interview Garcia in 1979, and acknowledged that Garcia was a "mystery." At that time, Garcia spoke about performing at a club in Boyle Heights called the Calypso Inn. The Club was owned by the parents of Brown Berets founder Dr. David Sanchez. Sal Medina's 1992 write-up on Garcia in *Firme* magazine corroborates Mercado's account, indicating that the Calypso Inn was indeed one of Garcia's primary performance sites. Mercado reminisced that Garcia played shows with a number of artists popular in the Chicano community, including Gilbert "Gil" Rocha, who played with Ritchie Valens, and Little Julian Herrera. Moreover, Garcia was deeply embedded in the creative networks of Los Angeles.

The content of Jonny Chingas's lyrics, more so than his musical stylings, likely distinguished him from other artists; the downside is that his lyrical content was one of the reasons his music failed to receive as much mainstream play as it could have received. Jonny Chingas's songs, in many cases, contained explicit lyrics and described lurid scenes of sexual encounters. In a 1992 issue of *Firme* magazine, a Chicano magazine, Sal Medina writes a tribute to Jonny Chingas, commemorating how in its 1979 inaugural issue, the magazine called for social action against radio stations that refused to play Jonny Chingas's records. The magazine's call for action was on the cusp of Garcia's musical release as Jonny Chingas. The launch of Garcia's career as Jonny Chingas began with his music being censored. Garcia must have suspected as much would happen, given his choice in artistic names. The word "chingas" is a curse word in Spanish likened to the term "fuck." Medina reports that bilingual radio station staff turned radio programmers against Garcia's music when they translated the meaning of Chingas.

In commemorating Garcia's career, Medina (1992) points to the ongoing struggles that Garcia faced in the music industry:

Jonny's path to success was strewn with "puro jale duro" [only difficult labor]. It was a tough climb to the radio's pop chart list. Jonny had his share of obstacles. Using themes and words that are usually reserved for the camaradas when the viejas are not around Jonny sang off beat, some might say off color lyrics that had Raza cracking up all over Aztlan.

The comedic performances that Garcia shared with the Chicano community, sometimes built on machismo braggadocio and sexually explicit content, but often reflecting popular Chicano cultural trends, began to appeal to a broader audience. Snowden (1985) sums up Garcia's rise to fame in the following way:

> His ticket to success there was "Se Me Paro," in which he played on the street slang double entendre in the backing vocal of the Moonglows' classic R&B oldie "Sincerely." The song has enjoyed a new surge of popularity since new wave station KROQ-FM began playing it recently.
> "It's about making love in a car, and that's a song the kids just eat up everywhere I go," said Chingas, whose vulgar (in Spanish) surname reflects his iconoclastic approach.
> "Se Me Paro" gave him a strong foothold in the Chicano market, but his other minor hits have included ballads ("I Want to Marry You"), Latin rock ("Funky Salsa Party") and disco ("Automatic Lover"). "Phone Home," a play on the "E.T." phenomenon, cracked the Top 50 in England and induced Columbia Records to sign him three years ago.

The song that made Jonny Chingas famous was the very song that a friend introduced me to while we were junior high students. My friend, Julio, whom I knew from church, had Guatemalan immigrant parents as committed as my parents to raising us to live as respectable adults. We were in junior high at the time when he stealthily directed me to the cassette player in his room. I understood that if Julio wanted to share something covertly, I needed to take him seriously. His mother, a woman of prayer, had a supernatural sense of what her children were up to. As Julio moved sneakily, I followed suit. To my surprise, Julio played a song in which the singer described in detail a romantic, sexual encounter he had with a woman. I was enthralled by the lascivious lyrics of the song, with its comical delivery and unique interweaving of English and Spanish rhymes. The bilingual lines were interspersed with Caló, the familiar Chicano slang jargon. It was unlike anything I had ever heard. The two of us listened with restrained chuckles. The artist, I learned, was called Jonny Chingas.

Having endured discrimination in the music industry, it appears that Garcia adopted the persona of Jonny Chingas as an affront to those that had rejected him. Gil Rocha suggests that the meaning of the name Chingas was not immediately understood by people in the industry, and appeared to be a distancing from Garcia's more recognizable Spanish name. Simultaneously, the vulgar meaning of the name was like a middle finger to the industry. "Jonny," sounds like the Spanish words "ya ni." Attached to the last name Chingas, the name sounds like "ya ni chingas," which could translate as "not even give a fuck," or "you don't fuck anymore." It seems that Jonny Chingas was ready to pull a fast one on the industry and to do it his way. Ironically, it was under the name Jonny Chingas that he achieved his biggest record deal, with Columbia Records.

Jonny Chingas as Proto-Rapper

In the early 1980s, the rise of Jonny Chingas was taking place just as Hip Hop was catching on in Southern California. As a cultural observer, Garcia took note of the styles that were hitting in Los Angeles and began to integrate them into his repertoire. In 1984, Garcia released a Hip Hop themed record, "Break, Pop, Lock," which spoke to the different dance styles that had caught on in the area. In typical Jonny Chingas fashion, the song comes across as a parody of the dance styles. Nonetheless, it is meaningful that a cultural mainstay like Garcia was spotlighting these dance styles in his songs. As Jonny Chingas speaks over the track, he peppers his delivery with Caló phrases. The musical style of the song itself is most akin to funk music, and all the while clearly integrates Chicano performativity.

Inclusion of a Hip Hop–themed song was a logical progression for a Jonny Chingas record. Several of Garcia's previously released songs were already within the funk genre, and funk was an integral component to West Coast Hip Hop. Garcia had a history of experimenting with funk and soul sounds since the 1970s. Also, moving into the decade of the 1980s, his songs started to take on a more electronic sound. His track, "I'm Looking for an Automatic Lover," features a sound that blends clap drums with a funky bassline and eerie keyboard pulsations. Another of his early funk tracks, "Hey Motherfucker," from 1984, features Garcia speaking over his track in near rap fashion. Even in some of his older tracks, his singing vocals could have sounded right at home as hooks for later West Coast Hip Hop numbers.

One of the revolutionary aspects of Jonny Chingas's tracks, however, is that they speak to the Chicano condition in clear, honest, and raw ways. His song, "Hey Motherfucker," for example, details an encounter with police in which he, the singer, is harassed and beaten by officers. In the song, the singer is brought to a court of law and made to stand before the judge. The judge declares, "I find you guilty, you Blacks and Mexicans are all alike, and I sentence you to prison for the maximum time allowed." Jonny Chingas not only draws attention to the potential for Chicanos to be brutalized at the hands of police but also suggests that "Blacks and Mexicans" are viewed as having similar status in the eyes of the law.

The theme of discrimination faced by Chicanos appears in various Jonny Chingas songs. His song, "El Corrido del Vato Loco," depicts a scene wherein police beat him in a back alley, and then declare him to be "loco," or crazy. Perhaps the most forward of his tracks on this front is the song "Yo Quiero Tirar Chingasos," which translates as "I want to throw blows," with the more direct connotation of "I want to fuck someone up" (Arellano 2013). In this song, Garcia describes that he is looked down on and discriminated against by "gabachos," or white people, and he is ready to fight back, physically. The musical mood of the song is celebratory and cheery, paradoxically so, given the confrontational message of the lyrics. Yet, Jonny Chingas emphasizes the humanity of "Latinos." As he expresses in the song, "Yo no soy marrano, yo soy un Latino, con un corazón mejor que nadie" [I'm not a pig, I am a Latino, with a heart better than anyone]. Garcia conveys a strange tenderness when he sings these lyrics. The message purports to include all Latinos, not just ethnic Mexicans. Jonny Chingas both confronts racism against Latinos and asserts the full humanity of Latinos.

Garcia also speaks of more mundane topics such as finding love, getting a job, and cruising down the famous Whittier Blvd. The funk song, "I Gotta Get a Job," describes the challenges of finding work for motivated job-seekers in the city. Implicit in this song is the idea that the singer, Jonny Chingas, is getting played by would-be bosses, possibly because of racism. That is, that roles that he could legitimately fulfill are being kept from him. These are matters that resonated with a segment of Brown Los Angeles and beyond, and they are often communicated over catchy instrumentation. Despite the fact that his songs dealing with matters of romance present a dominant, macho figure who succeeds in attracting romantic partners, or experiences rejection because of his own promiscuity, his depictions of attempts toward social mobility deal more with hardship. Romance and partying, then, often assuage the difficult conditions faced by Chicanos and Latinos. In some ways, these messages presaged themes that would be made common in the expanding world of rap, and especially in West Coast Hip Hop.

Chingas the Rapper

By 1986, a Jonny Chingas release titled "Night Stalker" was a clear rap track. In it, Jonny Chingas warns of the dangers of the Night Stalker, a true life homicidal figure that had local communities living in fear. The style and flow of rhyme in this cut was more upbeat than his previous incursions into potential rap attempts, where those presentations sounded more like talking. Garcia's vocal recording, rhyming with a bouncy cadence, positioned him to sound as a distant observer cautioning locals about a roving terror. Finally, in 1988, Garcia released a Jonny Chingas track called "Mini-Truck Lover." This song was fashioned much more as a traditional rap song, and again, made reference to a recognizable cultural symbol in the Chicano community—mini-trucks. The song was produced by J-Vibe, a Chicano producer from East Los Angeles who had been producing electro tracks for some years and had developed rapport with Garcia.

Garcia's foray into the world of rap records is best understood within the emerging field of Chicano rap. Garcia was among the first crop of Chicano rappers to release a Hip Hop–themed record, and soon after a record containing actual rap. However, by the mid-1980s, a particular Chicano rapper was already setting a standard for other Chicanos—Kid Frost. Frost would release his first track in 1984, "Rough Cut," produced by Dave Storrs and Pebo Rodriguez, at ElectroBeat Records. That same year, Frost released "Commando Rock" with C-Jam, produced by Dave Storrs alongside Allen Parada. The following year, in 1985, he released "Terminator," with ElectroBeat. Kid Frost was gaining fans in the burgeoning underground scene, at times showing up at Ice-T's gigs, and at times opening doors for Ice-T in Brown Los Angeles. Frost's street authenticity, engagement with multiple performative elements, and respect for Hip Hop's New York City roots set the tone for others.

While in terms of age cohorts Frost and Garcia occupied distinct social worlds, there were points at which their worlds intersected. Jose "J-Vibe" Jimenez, one of the producers who worked on Jonny Chingas's rap records, recalls Frost attending some of Garcia's shows. Frost, at the time, was early in his career, but was eager to perform. Jimenez explains:

> There was a videotape that Jonny Chingas showed me. It's a video of Kid Frost rapping, and he was really young. In the 80s. It was a show where Jonny Chingas was performing at. It was at a hotel, some Howard Johnson. This guy came up and said he's a rapper. It was Kid Frost. He used to do a lot of shows. A lot of car shows. Parties. He was a hustler—rapping all the time. He's a performer.

Based on Jimenez's recollections, Frost was making an impact on the underground scene. Because Kid Frost was developing a following around East Los Angeles, he would have shared some of the same audiences as Jonny Chingas, who participated in the lowrider events circuit and other gatherings. Aside from their generational differences, Frost was likely exposed to Hip Hop sooner than Garcia was, outside of Los Angeles. Frost encountered New York City Hip Hop while attending military school and while growing up on military bases with his family. The resonances Frost encountered on the bases he lived at, including in

Guam, Germany (Rodriguez 2016), Panama, and throughout the United States (Mausfeld 2019), shaped his affinities toward Hip Hop.

Both Frost and Garcia emerged from sites of transcultural exchange, but for Frost that included distant locales, while Garcia's formation was primarily in the Borderlands (Mausfeld 2019). Frost explains, in an interview with Michael Khalfani (2017b), that at a military academy in Texas he heard Private Sloan, a Black American private from Brooklyn, reciting rhymes (Mausfeld 2019). A number of his friends at the academy were from New York City and embodied a Hip Hop aesthetic. This took place as early as 1978. Kid Frost, then, was already experimenting with Hip Hop performativity, through his stints in military institutions in the 1970s. While conceived of as homegrown talent from East Los Angeles, he is simultaneously a translocal broker who had exposure to Hip Hop sooner than many of his Chicano peers. In Garcia we find an artist adapting older resonances to a new creative scene. In Frost we find a translocal broker ushering newer resonances into the old. As a rapper, Garcia was on the last leg of his career; Frost's career was just taking off and would influence the scene significantly. Still, Garcia, as Jonny Chingas, embodied a Borderlands Hip Hop resonance that few others represented.

Few have explored Raul Garcia's impact on Hip Hop in Brown Los Angeles. Jose "J-Vibe" Jimenez laments that Garcia has not received the credit he deserves for his contributions to Hip Hop. Jimenez started producing and recording with Garcia in 1987, and found in Garcia a prolific artist. He lauds Garcia for his work ethic, which he remembers to be incomparable to any other artists he worked with:

> The thing about Jonny Chingas is that when he started to work, he would work and already show up in two, three days with the records already pressed. He's the fastest thought-recording-to press, that I ever met. No one ever was faster than Jonny Chingas. He was a hustler. He would record it, I'd mix it down, and as soon as he would hear it, he'd say, "yeah sounds good," and he'd say, "I'm going to go get the plates made." He'd take off with the car, he'd drive over to the record plant, and then he'd get the plate made and then a couple days when the plates were made, he'd have the records pressed.

When Jimenez and Garcia first recorded the song "Mini-Truck Lover," it was written in both English and Spanish. Jimenez remembers that Garcia would flip back and forth, between English and Spanish, while he was writing and practicing his music. The song was about 40% Spanish, according to Jimenez. Garcia began to show the demo tape of the song around to different contacts in the recording industry to get their feedback on it. Many listeners laughed at the lecherous lyrics of the song. Some of the criticism he received, however, was that the song contained too much Spanish. Jimenez believes that the song was much more humorous in its original state but understands that Garcia hoped to achieve the widest appeal for his song, and thus altered the lyrics to be almost entirely in English. Jimenez especially laments that Jonny Chingas is not recognized in the pantheon of rappers who produced bilingual tracks.

Even during this last leg of his race, Jimenez notes that Garcia was faced with forms of discrimination because of his linguistic inclinations. "At that time, when we shopped around his demo, record companies were hesitant to sign a Latino. Some people we talked to, for example, said they wouldn't go for a rap record that didn't sound Black enough." Jimenez recalls having such an experience with a track of his own that he produced in the late 1980s: "Some executives said 'it's cool, it's cool, but it doesn't sound Black enough.'" To these white record executives, these artists did not perform in a way that signaled the Black American linguistic conventions they looked for. Jimenez suggests that this hindered Jonny Chingas's recordings from being more highly promoted. Throughout Garcia's career, distinct racialized borders continued to surface. And yet, his work surfaces in unexpected places. Recently, I encountered a sample of his within "Lil Loco Youngsta," a song from Chicano rap group Spanish F.L.Y.; I discovered that dance legend Boogaloo Shrimp recently recorded a cover of his bilingual song, "I Want to Marry You"; and I found out that a video game, *Dark Souls III*, includes his song, "Looking for an Automatic Lover," on its soundtrack.

Conclusion

Borderlands resonances permeate the West Coast scene in subtle and obvious ways. Along with the creatives spotlighted in this chapter, various other Borderland creatives made an impact in the West Coast scene. Graffiti artist Shandu was born in Ciudad Juarez, Mexico, and lived in El Paso before migrating to Los Angeles with his family. Producer Johnny J, one of Tupac's most esteemed producers, was born in Ciudad Juarez, Mexico. Carmelo Alvarez, who appears in Chapter 6 of this volume, spent part of his childhood in El Paso. The Borderlands have transferred important resources into the Hip Hop scene. The combination of marginalization and adaptation, characteristic of Borderlands life, as reflected in the pachuco experience, especially positioned Borderlands creatives to adapt Hip Hop expressions in Brown Los Angeles.

The story of Raul Garcia traces the flow of this resonance channel as it manifested in the early Hip Hop scene. In reality, the Borderlands resonance does not rest in a limited cluster of individuals, but is rather an expansive consciousness and positionality that connects to many expressive facets of West Coast culture. And while the Borderlands retain deep histories of resistance and survival, they are a site of continual innovation, thus inviting sustained interrogation. Indeed, many who have continued to traverse the Borderlands, and remain in a Borderlands reality, find a place in Hip Hop, in spaces like Brown Los Angeles.

3
The Funk Frequency

The Observatory theater in Santa Ana was packed to the brim with "foos."[1] I was at the 2021 Foos Gone Wild live show, a blend of concert and comedy. A social media account turned cultural movement, on Instagram, @FoosGoneWild boasts over 3 million followers, and has spawned spin-off and parody accounts. The account features humorous and inspiring posts depicting life in brown communities, privileging Brown Los Angeles perspectives, though increasingly spotlighting other communities that share affinities with Brown Los Angeles. The original account is itself part parody, earning critiques from cultural purists. Nevertheless, the movement captures key cultural motifs that permeate brown communities. Event attendees, overwhelmingly men, sported fashion items such as plaids, Old English lettering, and dickies pants, with many remixing and reinventing these markers of belonging. One cultural signifier came through loud and clear that night: funk culture. A DJ crew called the Funk Freaks performed extended sets, playing classic funk cuts such as "Double Dutch Bus," by Frankie Smith, and "A DJ Saved My Life," by Indeep. A poplocker took to the stage and energized the crowd with crisp tut and wave movements. He sported a traditional uniform of Brown Los Angeles: A flannel shirt, dickies pants, and Chuck Taylor shoes. I met him at Bboy Summit weeks later, and found out he was Cambodian American, Long Beach–based dancer Johnee Blaze. Funk culture, which I call the *funk frequency*, has so influenced Brown Los Angeles that phenomena like the Funk Freaks are emblematic of Brown Los Angeles. As a precursor to Hip Hop, funk culture's unique resonance in Brown Los Angeles set the stage for Hip Hop's embrace therein. With *foos* going wild over funk that night, funk's expansive resonance in the community was evident. This chapter examines how the funk frequency resonance channel attuned Brown Los Angeles to Hip Hop.

Legacies of Funk

I was astounded when Ace Rock uttered the following words: "There was no Hip Hop to us." I had only heard of Ace Rock as a West Coast Hip Hop pioneer. He

---

[1] Foo/s is a variation of "fool," used in similar fashion to the term "homie."

had been touted as such atop a variety of performance stages. Yet, over a phone conversation, Ace Rock explained that he became involved in street dance before Hip Hop's arrival in Los Angeles. In the late 1970s, before the term "Hip Hop" meant anything to West Coast crowds, and before breaking had been observed in California, Ace Rock participated in a West Coast scene that was an amalgamation of Chicano and Black performativity, which Ace Rock especially represented through "poplocking."[2] I refer to this particular resonance channel, which attracted many Chicanos, as the *funk frequency*. The funk frequency already present in Los Angeles was the assemblage of cultural aesthetics proximate and compatible with the broader funk culture that emerged from Black American communities in the 1960s. Chicano street culture aligned with this frequency, albeit in an adapted manner incorporating Chicano aesthetics.

Near his home in Claremont, California, Ace Rock became involved with an innovative dance crew called the Groovatrons, with whom he both learned and adapted funk dance forms. Just as his dance skills were hitting optimal level, Hip Hop arrived on the West Coast. Ace Rock functioned as a cultural curator in that he excelled in the artistic, urban forms present in the local scene prior to Hip Hop's arrival and welcomed the arrival of Hip Hop as a movement associated with New York City. Ace Rock began his street dance journey in the late 1970s, and dance provided him with opportunities to travel beyond the Los Angeles barrios where his family lived. The greater Los Angeles area became Ace Rock's stage, as he maneuvered the expansive urban landscape to hone his craft, taking names in the process. He was part of the cohort that embraced Hip Hop, but he specifically drew creative resources from the funk frequency. Ace Rock describes a street dance scene at the start of the 1980s where the music of Cameo, Parliament Funkadelic, and the likes provided the soundtrack to frenetic encounters between poplocking crews. Poplocking was Ace Rock's style of choice, and the dominant dance style among his peers. Even in his early teens, Ace Rock would travel up to fifty miles across the Los Angeles area, hitching rides with friends, riding public transportation, and even riding his moped or bicycle to participate in the dance scene of the early 1980s. According to Ace Rock:

> We were like gangs and we would literally find out the underground hotspots where everybody was hanging out. One of the biggest ones was the corner of Hollywood Boulevard and Highland Ave, during that time before the buildings were built there. So there was a huge lot right there and people would walk up with the ghetto blasters, like ten deep, with matching sweatshirts with names in Old English letters in the back like a barrio, like a gang, and would

---

[2] While I retain the terms used by my collaborators, factions in the local dance scene debate whether "poplocking" or "popping" is the correct term.

start getting off on each other and that was a real thing. That was around '81, '82, '83. Another hotspot was Venice Beach. Another hotspot was when they would throw dances at skating rinks: World on Wheels over at South Central, Compton had Skateland, Skate Junction in West Covina, we'd meet at malls, Puente Hills Mall. Different places like that. Anytime where there was any kind of get-together, at Legg Lake in Whittier narrows, the fairgrounds, anywhere where there was a place like that we could walk around with ghetto blasters. And getting to like around '82, Hollywood and Highland and Venice Beach were the two biggest spots that people would come to from all over. I was living on the other side of Pomona and would shuttle from there to Venice Beach just to go get off on people.

In the season prior to Hip Hop being embraced in Los Angeles, the street dance scene was alive and well. Yet, even as the sites of street dance were spread throughout the Los Angeles basin, there were particular locales where artistry and creativity were especially cultivated. Ace Rock's fascination with street dance was precipitated as his family moved from East Los Angeles to La Puente, and then farther East to Claremont, next door to Pomona, California. Pomona in the late 1970s was a hotbed of street dance talent. After moving to the area, Ace Rock met the Groovatrons dance crew, and soon became a member. He quickly excelled at the artform, and began to add his own stylistic innovations. Performing publicly with the Groovatrons fortified Ace Rock's identity in street dance prior to Hip Hop's arrival. The more he invested in this performative identity, the more he excelled at his craft, and vice versa.

The funk/poplocker identity was all the more persistent because it was bound up with other aspects of neighborhood life. From Ace Rock's vantage point, "[Poplocking] was all about, and was surrounded in gang culture. That's how it was back in the early days, from like '78 till like '85." It is no wonder that when Honduran American Hip Hop pioneer Henry "Hen Gee" Garcia initially experienced the electro funk scene in Los Angeles, after moving from New York City, he referred to the musical styles as "gangbanging music" (Viator 2020). As the Groovatrons traveled throughout the Los Angeles basin to dance, the sites that they frequented were spaces especially accessible to Black and brown youths, but they had to be aware of the neighborhood politics present within distinct sites. Often, accessibility meant finding spots that were neutral territory, so that neighborhood affiliations would not perturb dance battles. Poplockers toed a delicate balance. Many of them were closely identified by the neighborhoods where they lived, but many crew members wanted to compete with their dance skills and not lead off with confrontations over neighborhood gangs. The connection between gangs and poplocking presented an ongoing negotiation.

Funk Culture

West Coast Hip Hop creativity was especially energized through creatives' direct engagement with the Black American funk movement, largely associated with funk music and its accompanying dance styles (Pabon 2006). The West Coast funk frequency was itself a confluence of various regional Black American cultural resonances. The Bay Area of Northern California, in earlier decades, especially the 1960s and 1970s, played an important role in distilling particular music and dance funk styles that would later be integrated into Los Angeles's own funk styles. Some Bay Area funk culture elements were adapted from other regions and some were developed in the Bay, with much early innovation happening in Oakland, along with other surrounding cities, and spreading outward. Certain dance styles took root and developed in the central valley of California, specifically in Fresno, and were then brought to Southern California. "Boogaloo Sam" Solomon is credited with developing the popping style of dance, and later, his brother, Popin Pete, helped to further develop and popularize it. The Solomon brothers moved to Long Beach, where they expanded their dance squad. Forming the Electric Boogaloos, they would rise to fame on the street and through mainstream media (Guzman-Sanchez 2012).

In Los Angeles, the dance style known as locking was developed by Don "Campbellock" Campbell. While the story goes that Don Campbell developed the style by accident, after being ridiculed for his lack of dance skills, locking would gain national attention as it was featured on the television show *Soul Train*. Along with Don Campbell, Toni Basil, Fred "Mr. Penguin" Berry, known as Rerun, Leo "Fluky Luke" Williamson, Greg "Campbellock Jr." Pope, Bill "Slim The Robot" Williams, and Adolfo "Shabbadoo" Quiñones composed the famed group, the Lockers (Goldstein 1984). By the late 1970s, with locking in full effect and popping entering the scene, some Los Angeles dancers contentiously dubbed the Los Angeles dance style as "poplocking." These styles came together to form a distinct Los Angeles funk culture.

Though funk culture largely developed within Black American communities, in the 1970s, dancers of other backgrounds who lived in close proximity to Black Americans or had access to these styles learned them as well. Guzman-Sanchez (2012) exemplifies this pattern in the San Fernando Valley, and Bruno "Pop N' Taco" Falcon (Golonka 2021) exemplifies this pattern in Long Beach, both perfecting funk dance styles present in their communities. Guzman-Sanchez, a key figure in street dance himself, intricately documents much of this movement in his own writings (2012). Likewise, a number of my collaborators pointed to Adolfo "Shabbadoo" Quiñones as a key link in translating these styles to creatives from Brown Los Angeles. His spectacular dance skills and his relational deployments of his Black American and Puerto Rican ancestries positioned him as a central connector of Black and brown creatives. Ace Rock expressed that some brown creatives had ties to Black American funk dance pioneers; his group, the Groovatrons, was composed primarily of Black Americans, and included one dancer who later rose to fame as an underground emcee—Medusa. Ace Rock remembers with detail the lineage of the styles he was invested in:

> I inherited a Compton style of poplocking, really before I moved to Pomona, but then it was stamped on even further because I met a dude named No Bone Tyrone and he was from Compton. He moved to Pomona in '79. He went to Dominguez High School and brought a way different robot style of poplocking to Pomona. They were already popping their own style in Pomona and their main thing was waves and things like that. But now, suddenly, they had this guy that was doing robotics stuff and twist-o-flexes.

Ace Rock's account illustrates the power of place in influencing the performative styles of creatives. According to Ace Rock, Black Americans and Latinos "shared the same ghettos." Through these cross-group interactions through social proximity, poplocking became popular among brown creatives as well. Brown creatives who interacted with Black Americans could also share their skills and talents throughout Brown Los Angeles. Given that many Chicanos already had an affinity for funk music, many naturally gravitated toward poplocking.

Funk Roots

Dance, for Ace Rock, was about movement and mobility—corporeal and geographic—but it was also about rootedness, about being from a community. Despite his travel throughout the area, Ace Rock expressed a deep connection to the neighborhoods he grew up in, a connection that emerged in part from his personal awareness of his family history. As he explained, "I was born in East LA. My parents were born in East LA. My grandparents were born in East LA. And before that, it was probably Mexico." Ace Rock situated his family's legacy within the deep history of Mexican Los Angeles; he understood his ancestry as deeply anchored within the Mexican barrios of yesteryear and within the Chicano culture that emerged from these communities. More than simply understanding the term "Chicano" as a neutral ethnic label, for Ace Rock being Chicano was a racialized identity he wore with pride, recognizing that it sprouted from a history of civil rights struggles against injustice. The Chicano legacy that Ace Rock embodied permeated his involvement in street dance, even as he engaged in a scene that was predominantly Black American. His connection to both Chicano culture and to Los Angeles's Black American culture positioned him as a curator of a legacy within the street dance scene.

In discussing his ties to his Black American friends, Ace Rock simultaneously expressed his pride in being Chicano. In other words, for him, being committed to his Chicano identity, and being committed to his mostly Black American crew, were not mutually exclusive. Nevertheless, Ace Rock especially stressed that he believed the Chicano contribution to West Coast aesthetics was understated. He illustrated this issue by describing an exchange he had some years back when he took a trip to New York City:

> When I went to New York, I was talking to some Puerto Ricans and they started asking a question about lowriders, because there weren't really lowriders out there. They're saying, "Yeah, how did that start? Man that was started by Snoop and all that right? All the Crips and Bloods?" I said, "No." And they said, "Well, that's what we see." I said, "Wow. Now, let me give you some history. That was created by us. It goes way back to the zoot suit days."

Because of encounters like this, and because of the neighborhood aesthetics where he grew up, Ace Rock still made it a point, even in current performances, to represent himself through Chicano fashion; from the pant, to the shoes, shirts, and sunglasses. According to Ace Rock, during the rise of gangsta rap, much of the dress code that Black gang members took on was influenced by Chicano gang members. "Just look at NWA in their first days," he emphasized. His words echo Macías's (2014:64) observations about Chicano aesthetic influences on Black gangsta rap pioneers: "Central to the look of this lifestyle were the many elements that the Crips and Bloods appropriated from Chicano gangs, particularly Chuck Taylors, khakis, Dickies, Pendletons, bandanas, baseball caps with the brim flipped straight up, hand signs, Old English tattoos, black block-letter calligraphic graffiti, and low riders. Los Angeles African American gangsta rappers like Ice Cube, Dr Dre, Snoop Dogg, and Ice-T borrowed Chicanos' cool cholo street style." In light of these observations, Ace Rock was committed to maintaining these styles as a Chicano, even when he performed in Black majority spaces.

Funk as Hip Hop

For a younger cohort of creatives, funk culture provided an on-ramp to identifying with Hip Hop. Chicano DJ Ralph Medrano the Mixican, renowned for his work in the group Funkdoobiest, illustrates this phenomenon. In an interview for the National Association of Music Merchants (2020), Medrano states that his parents took him to a Halloween party and that was the, "first time I saw Hip Hop." The party took place in 1982, according to Medrano, in the city of Lynwood. He was in fifth grade at the time. Medrano continues, "I saw kids—Black and Latino kids—dancing and poplocking. That was the first time that I heard a lot of funk music, good party music." Medrano's description of his own experience is insightful in that he relates aspects of West Coast funk culture, the music and the dance styles, with Hip Hop. The funk frequency blended into many creatives' interpretations of Hip Hop as it arrived.

Some artists recognize that there was something distinct about these earlier modes of expression, but interpret popping and its precursors as "Hip Hop related," understanding its foundation for West Coast Hip Hop. Acclaimed beatboxer, Click the Supah Latin, has one such recollection of funk culture. As he recounts:

> My earliest memory that I have of anything Hip Hop related, I was in the seventh grade and I was playing in band. I loved being part of band. So one night, they had a talent show. And so the band was scheduled to play. You know so I got dressed up in my suit and played the clarinet and stuff. So I'm sitting there behind the curtains and all of a sudden a song, "I Heard It through the Grapevine," by Zapp, comes on. And then all of a sudden the room was dark, but this strobe light was on. And the music, it caught me, so I go, "Okay, let me see what's going on." So I looked through the curtains and there's this crip. His name is Mister, and he's popping to that song. But dude, I never seen that ever, and the way he moved, the way he popped, it was unique, even though I didn't know how unique it would be at the time, because it was just brand new to me. But that was like that West Coast gangsta pop and I don't care if you're from New York. I don't care where you're from. No one has that style like the West Coast, man, at gangsta popping. So that was my first introduction to THAT part of Hip Hop.

Looking back at this particular introduction, Click identifies the distinction of styles, but is forceful about connecting popping to Hip Hop. Notably, identifying popping as a West Coast contribution to Hip Hop, for Click, is a source of pride. He sees it as fitting within the umbrella of Hip Hop, but identifies with the West Coast origin aspect of popping. It is also worth noting that Click's first glimpse of popping, or anything "Hip Hop related," came through watching a Black American young man performing. For many brown creatives, being inspired by Black American peers and then learning the skill themselves was common. The personal nature of these experiences seemed to especially compel observers to become participants.

Along the same lines, one of the pivotal moments for famed B-boy Lil Cesar was when he came across a group of highly skilled poppers who were battling. Seeing advanced level poppers, after only having experienced the dance style from novices, left a memorable impression on him. More than that, it drew him in, and forced him to consider the potential of excelling within the art (Xhaferi 2020).

> I actually stopped by an arcade and outside the arcade there was a circle, there was a cipher, and I remember they were just going off this was more like in a battle tactic, you know, in popping. So I first saw the attitude of poppers going at it. You know what I'm saying, because I you know, I just saw the some of the basic stuff in popping but these guys were actually more advanced so it was outside an arcade and that's where people started to gather around to actually watch this actual battle and you hear all the oohs the aahs, like, So it was such a magnificent, You know, centrifugal force that was pulling towards the cipher, right? So I was very fascinated.

Fortuitously, Lil Cesar witnessed this spectacle on his way to visit Radiotron, a youth center where many learned the Hip Hop elements for the first time. As a world class B-boy, in retrospect, he made the connection between witnessing popping and being motivated to become the best dancer he could be.

For some, the funk frequency facilitated stylistic adaptation. Some brown creatives noted, for example, how funk's influence on the popular disco scene ultimately influenced the West Coast scene. Although scholars such as Ewoodzie (2017) point to the differentiation between disco and Hip Hop during Hip Hop's emergence in the Bronx, some Los Angeles participants early on siphoned creative resources from local disco scenes and into the new Hip Hop scene, with funk functioning as an important mediator. Indeed, West Coast rap originator Michael Khalfani was known as Disco Daddy; teaming up with Captain Rapp, the duo released the first West Coast rap record, "Gigolo Rapp," rhyming over a funky track.

Active in the local disco scene, John "Zender," Estrada described how "The disco scene prepared my mind for the Hip Hop scene." As a preteen, Zender ventured into the disco scene, an experience he describes vividly: "In 1978, I was going to clubs, disco clubs, as a little kid and I would paint my mustache with shoe polish to make myself look older. And most of the people at the door knew the people that I was coming in with. And we went to Gino's, we went to Star Wars, we went to the Copacabana, we went to all these disco clubs, just like *Saturday Night Fever*." Zender observed that the fusion of different styles in this disco scene expanded young brown creatives' performative repertoires:

I started seeing people locking, the Shabbadoo kind of locking, that was being fused in there. I mean, you've probably seen the early episodes of *Soul Train* when they do the Soul Train line. I can watch an old '70s disco thing and say, "that's this move from disco." Then you will see them introducing it with locking, you know, the splits and the locking, then you start seeing people introduce popping in there. All those forms begin to fuse. As the music changes, you're dancing, and the dancing changes. I hung out with this guy named Popping Pete, not the real Popin Pete, but another Filipino Popping Pete; and he was the one that was notorious for popping and I kept telling him, "Hey man, show me how to do that." Then we would do routines and he would show me the pops and then we would do them at the club, like as a team.

Based on Zender's account, styles were being fused in this pre–Hip Hop disco stage. Locking, for example, was associated with funk music. According to Zender, at clubs and parties, disco and funk were being fused together, both in terms of musical genres played side by side and in terms of dance styles. Zender suggests that creatives who had access to a broader array of artistic aesthetics, or who were attentive to the distinct streams of cultural movements around them, had more resources to draw from when Hip Hop arrived. This ability to recognize distinct cultural resources and integrate artistry from a vast array of sources, positioned creatives to innovate and collaborate with a broad array of people. Creatives that were already used to crossing cultural, ethnoracial, and social scene boundaries could readily step into the role of cultural curators.

Joining the Army

One dominant source of the funk frequency in Los Angeles was the mobile DJ party scene. Uncle Jamm's Army (UJA) arguably garnered the most attention within this scene. At a time when the local club scene had a dearth of venues catering to the tastes of urban Black Los Angeles, UJA represented a revolutionary grassroots movement of young Black creatives, especially DJs and promoters. Spearheaded by Rodger Clayton, UJA took flight as a backyard party DJ crew centered initially around the Harbor Area of Los Angeles, where Clayton and his associates grew up. The crew was originally named Unique Dreams Entertainment in 1978, when Clayton and his high school friend Gid Martin joined forces to launch the creative enterprise (Hess 2009; Viator 2020). As the movement grew, UJA started to host events at larger, rented venues. Eventually, the crew would fill arenas with thousands of people, mostly young, Black attendees, and provide DJ-centric dance parties.

With these events gaining notoriety, crew promoters were able to draw respected Hip Hop acts from the East Coast into their lineups. Yet, even with known rap acts such as Run DMC, Whodini, Dr. Jeckyll and Mr. Hyde, Kurtis Blow, Real Roxanne, and LL Cool J gracing UJA events (Hess 2009), the DJs commanded the stage at these gatherings. Other skilled DJs also rose to prominence and established their own crews. Thus, UJA competed with other crews in the scene to become the best, and continually distinguished themselves. Additional front-running DJ crews included the likes of the World Class Wreckin' Cru, headed by Lonzo Williams, and counting a young Dr. Dre in its ranks. Williams had built a name for himself by running a successful nightclub, Eve After Dark, which, given more relaxed regulations in its Los Angeles County location, often served as an afterparty spot for club-goers from around Los Angeles. Lonzo's club was a talent incubator for his DJ crew. The competing crews, as suggested by Hess (2009:232), held sway in territorial fashion, with UJA controlling the region "from Long Beach to the Valley" and the World Class Wreckin' Cru dominating "Compton and the Watts area."

Viator (2020) argues that UJA filled a gap that was present in the Los Angeles scene in terms of the promotion and development of local talent. In New York City, the rise of commercial Hip Hop was largely predicated on "a handful of independent labels based in New York, including Sugar Hill and Profile Records. These enterprises discovered talent and showcased their signed artists inside a thriving, industry-driven New York nightclub circuit. Here, DJs played supporting roles, spinning records to serve the needs of labels and the acts they represented. Most early New York DJs, including DJ-cum-rapper Bambaataa, were supporting actors for talent scouts, the true stars of the city's nightclub circuit" (Viator 2020:77). UJA especially, along with some of its competitors, established a scene in which DJs themselves would eventually crown some of the biggest names in the local scene. Perhaps more importantly, this was a grassroots effort that represented the tastes and creative energies of young, Black Angelenos. It was not merely an imitation of the New York City Hip Hop scene, but was rather a scene that emerged organically from the communities of Los Angeles.

Though the UJA scene catered predominantly to Black Americans, the scene influenced Brown Los Angeles as well, drawing attendees from these communities also. B-boy Mike "Iceman" Rivera, who grew up in Wilmington, close to where UJA originated, remembers UJA parties, mostly as places to go dancing in his teens. Robert "Ace Rock" Aceves has similar memories of UJA parties, particularly as events where he and his dance crew could gather and test their skills. Aceves and his crew traveled from the Pomona area to spots throughout Los Angeles to attend UJA parties, among others. Renowned street dancer Michael "Boogaloo Shrimp" Chambers recounts seeing Chicano poplocker Pop N Taco at UJA events as well. Chambers describes Taco as "the only Hispanic in a sea of chocolate," (Golonka 2021) but also emphasizes that Taco's reputation as a dancer preceded him. Indeed, Chambers claims that he "had to see a Mexican that danced better than black people" (Khalfani 2017b). While Ace Rock, Iceman, and Taco may have been exceptional as brown creatives, accounts of their engagement at UJA illustrate that UJA events provided opportunities for some brown creatives to learn and innovate.

UJA also traveled beyond their usual territories in South Los Angeles County, and covered places like "Pasadena, Pomona Fairgrounds, San Bernardino" (Chang and Nardone 1994:70), particularly as they moved from the early to mid-1980s. In these disparate excursions, the crew encountered diverse audiences. Some of these places and audiences had sizable brown constituencies. One such encounter is recorded in an interview between Hip Hop journalists Jeff Chang and Michael Nardone (1994:70–71), and UJA associates, Rodger Clayton and Egyptian Lover:

> [Rodger Clayton]: When we went to San Bernardino, it was like a whole 'nother world. We drove out there to look at the San Bernardino Convention Center, and they treated me like a king. I went in and got on the microphone, told them and they screamed. So we went and got a bus and took about forty people out there and drove up. They was lined up like it was a damn concert! That's when we used to wear muthaphukkin' spikes and belts and leather, chains.
>
> [Egyptian Lover]: Girls damn near passed out when they saw me! We was starving, we was just DJs! It was four types of crowds. One group was just dancing. Three hundred, 400 deep on the wall, just amazed, looking at the people dancing. They had the breaking and poplocking shit in the corner in the circle, and they had people just looking at me DJ.
>
> [Rodger Clayton]: That was the first time the crowd was really diversified too. There was Mexicans, some whites. All the Mexican DJs and Mexican breakdancers and white DJs. They all came and stayed there at the front. Then we taught them all how to freak.
>
> [Egyptian Lover]: We told them, "This is the dance we do in LA." We had somebody up onstage, this little groupie, and taught them how to freak! They was still doing the LaCoste and all that shit! A few people started doing the freak, then some, and then all of them was doing it!

UJA's interview presents important insights about the relationship that UJA had to brown creatives, identified as Mexicans by Clayton. First, according to Clayton, Mexicans were a sizable segment of the San Bernardino crowd. For Clayton, this also meant that "Mexicans" were likely not a notable segment of attendees at previous events. This resonates with accounts of early UJA attendees that I spoke with, such as Iceman and Ace Rock. Chambers's impression of Pop

N Taco as being in a "sea of chocolate" makes sense for earlier contexts. That had changed in San Bernardino, a city nearly sixty miles east of Los Angeles with a sizable working-class Latine population. Clayton's comments also suggest that diversified crowds were not a one-time occurrence for UJA. This was their "first," but not necessarily their last diverse crowd.

Clayton's account describes A transference of creative capital between UJA and brown creatives. As Clayton indicates, Mexican DJs, Mexican breakdancers, and white DJs stayed near the performance stage. The suggestion here is that these DJs and breakers were learning from the UJA crew as they were performing. These brown creatives, along with some of their white counterparts, were expanding their skills. Nevertheless, the fact that Clayton identified a part of the crowd as "Mexican DJs and Mexican breakdancers" indicates that these brown creatives were already active in their crafts. These creatives were there to learn from UJA precisely because, as active performers in their local scenes, they aimed to learn from the best. UJA energized the creative talents of these local scenes, and also passed on new forms of expression and performativity originating in locales more central to LAs core.

Participation in UJA events served a pedagogical aspect for many brown creatives, as onlookers were inspired and observed particular skills. As relayed by Egyptian Lover, regarding teaching this new crowd about the freak dance, "We told them, 'This is the dance we do in LA.'" Though music could spread through the radio waves, these events were important for disseminating performative expressions such as dance. Some Latine attendees at UJA events also report that they learned skills or were inspired to perform in a particular way through the events. DJ Ernie Gutierrez of the Chicano group Proper Dos, for example, in an interview with DJ Tony Alvarez (2019), specifies that he was inspired when he saw a UJA DJ scratch at one of their events. Gutierrez, who was about sixteen at the time, indicates that the event took place in his hometown of Santa Monica. Gutierrez identifies this as a pivotal moment in his formation as a DJ. He went on to become one of the innovators among LA's early Chicano Hip Hop boom in the 1990s.

Much of the creative resonance featured thus far flowed from Black American creatives to brown creatives, but there were cases of brown creatives contributing artistry to the predominantly Black American mobile DJ scene. DJ Pebo Rodriguez remembers meeting Rodger Clayton in the early 1980s, while Pebo worked as a record buyer at JDC records in San Pedro. He formed a positive working relationship with Clayton, recalling that Clayton would purchase records from him at JDC. Pebo remembers that Clayton and other DJs, "Came straight to the source because I was the buyer and I had everything imaginable. Everybody came to JDC records."

As a DJ in the disco scene, who was very much active during the advent of the West Coast scene (and still is as of this writing), Pebo's knowledge of the music industry was not incidental. He had an ear for music and had influence over records that were being distributed and played in the DJ scene. Furthermore, Pebo and Dave Storrs's ElectroBeat Records became an important source for the signature electro sound from the West Coast. The relational connections that Pebo had in the DJ scene allowed him to make important connections with UJA by brokering an opportunity for Kid Frost to perform with UJA. Pebo spoke with Rodger Clayton to set up this feature at an event where Egyptian Lover was performing. As Richard Rodriguez notes (2009:112), Frost's rap career was propelled by "joining the ranks of the hip-hop outfit Uncle Jamm's Army (UJA), and performing as the opening act for rap groups like Run-DMC who were beginning to make their mark on the scene." This amplified resonances between Black and brown communities.

Other key contributors to the electro funk scene include Lizette Rodriguez, known as Lisa Miss Rockberry Love, member of the musical act, the LA Dream Team. The LA Dream Team had two hit records that Rodriguez contributed her vocals to, namely "Rockberry Jam" (1985), and "The Dream Team Is in the House!" (1985). Rodriguez, who was Cuban American, was just starting her recording career when her life was cut short in a car accident in 1986. Her vocals are memorialized as part of the signature Los Angeles electro era. Other such participants include Ventura County–based DJ John Manzella. Also known as DJ J Scratch, Manzella recalls DJing at several UJA events (Manzella 2017). He recounts how he recognized that he had to be at his best when performing at a UJA event because of the quality of artists affiliated with the collective. Manzella is of Mexican and Italian background and grew up primarily in a Mexican American neighborhood.

Chicano DJ Scene

In similar fashion to UJA and other majority Black DJ crews, brown DJ crews established a vibrant party scene that drew from the funk frequency, along with other channels of resonance. This majority brown scene also influenced the broader Los Angeles landscape. Manny Villaseñor, a cofounder of Boogie Motion Productions, a party promotion crew based in Orange County, has extensive knowledge of the brown DJ scene. DJ Freak Daddy, as Villaseñor was known, started Boogie Motion Productions (BMP) in the 1970s, in Santa Ana, about thirty miles South of Los Angeles. He started BMP at around the same time that Rodger Clayton and Gid Martin started operating as UJA. BMP saw much success through the 1980s, hosting popular large-scale concerts in the region. Some BMP events featured UJA members. "We especially worked with Egyptian Lover," Villaseñor recalls. "We didn't do promotion work with them," Villaseñor adds, "but hired some of them as individual artists." Because of regional geographies, these scenes developed in parallel to each other and did not necessarily compete for the same residential audiences. Racial demographics factored into the distinct audiences as well. BMP was only one of a plethora of brown DJ Crews scattered throughout the Los Angeles area, but it was one whose events were at a scale that approximated UJAs, at first. Many other DJ crews hosted events at smaller scales, but were still active in the region.

Villaseñor's collection of flyers, photographs, and VHS cassettes, which he shared with me, capture snapshots of the group's extensive history. The earliest flyers, from the late seventies, appear as hand-drawn designs, reflecting the calligraphy and writing styles familiar in Chicano neighborhoods. One of the flyers states that the party being advertised is sponsored by "The Spanish Club," without further detail. I asked Manny about it, and he explained that it referred to the Spanish Club at one of the local high schools. In the first couple of years of the 1980s, the flyers began to advertise events at places like hotels, and small rented halls.

BMP activities started scaling up when Villaseñor began collaborating with a friend named Carlos Hernandez. Carlos had his own party promotion company, The Music Commission, but had a slightly different target audience. While Manny was having success with younger crowds around Santa Ana, Carlos drew from a broader radius in Orange County, from a slightly older young adult Chicano crowd. Carlos was successful in drawing the lowrider crowd, for example, and had contacts in the Chicano music scene, including many live bands. The name "The Music Commission," proved effective in promotion, because people often assumed it was a city-sponsored civic organization. The Commission operated using a hotline offering the latest information on parties happening in the area. Manny recalls that he and Carlos sometimes taped dimes on the back of their business cards so that potential party goers had the needed funds to make a call on a payphone and would be encouraged to call the hotline. Their events were booming.

At first, Carlos's events featured Manny and Boogie Motion Productions as part of the DJ lineup. By 1982, Manny was sharing leadership with Carlos on large-scale events. Coincidentally, one of the venues that Manny and Carlos hosted events at was Old World Village in Huntington Beach, a site that shared owners with Alpine Village in Torrance, one of UJA's first venues of operation. The flyers and printed items reveal not only a change in scale of events but also a change in musical genres being featured at the events. One of Manny's business cards from the '70s indicates the following musical genres that he specialized

Image 3.1 Business card for Manuel Villaseñor's Boogie Motion Productions, c. 1979. (Reproduced courtesy of Manuel Villaseñor)

in: Punk, Latin, Nu Wave, Funk, and Disco (Image 3.1). In 1982, one of his flyers advertised that there would be a "Pop-Break" contest, highlighting cross-coastal dance hybridization. By 1983, BMP included a plethora of artists and DJ crews, including UJA artists and several mainstream Hip Hop artists. By 1985, numerous Hip Hop artists were featured.

Partnerships with party promotion crews like Boogie Motion Productions helped to amplify the profile and sounds of some UJA members and their contemporaries. While he does not have photos with specific UJA members, Villaseñor shared photos showing him and his promotional crew together with a fresh-faced Dr. Dre, DJ Yella, and Ice Cube, circa 1987, prior to a show they hosted (Image 3.2). These young artists, then members of N.W.A., had been contracted by Boogie Motion Productions for a show in Anaheim, California. Villaseñor had known some of these members from their work with the World Class Wreckin' Cru. Villaseñor was able to put on a sizable event at the Anaheim convention center with N.W.A. because of connections he established with these mostly Black American DJ crews in years past. Moreover, in the brown communities of Orange County, brown promoters helped break Black American artists.

Some scholars suggest that the relationship between the UJA scene and the brown DJ scene was more complex than the contracting of artists from one scene to the other. Moreover, some scholars propose that an earlier wave of mostly Chicano large-scale concerts influenced UJA's promotional model. Cultural historian Joshua Kun, for example, speaks of this cross-pollination. Kun (2005:222) describes how the band Ozomatli makes reference to UJA in one of their songs, and suggests broader resonances across ethnoracial groups: "The UJA parties were modeled after the Chicano 'Woodstocks' that Ruben Guevara used to throw, back before he saw rock's reconquista charging over the hill." Kun's proposition is that an older history of Chicano rock platformed through large-scale concerts resonated with the model that some Black DJ crews established.

Image 3.2 Manuel Villaseñor, front center, and Ricky Sosa, left center, members of Boogie Motion Productions (BMP), pose with Eazy-E, top left, and Dr. Dre, bottom left, along with members of Home Boys Only, after a BMP sponsored event, 1987. (Reproduced courtesy of Manuel Villaseñor)

Guevara, whom Kun references, had been staging large-scale events mostly on Los Angeles's East Side, catering to Chicano audiences, but more accessible to diverse crowds in comparison to white events at the time. These events were mobile, too. In his seminal work on Hip Hop in Los Angeles, Brian Cross (1993) makes a similar association between these so-called Chicano Woodstocks, and the model developed by UJA. He attributes the flexibility of the UJA events to the Chicano events of an earlier era. Jimenez (2011), citing Cross (1993) and Kelly (1993), follows this same line of reasoning when talking about UJA. In this case, Jimenez documents the emergence of "electro hop" music, noting that Latino DJ crews helped to popularize it as well.

Adding another observation along the same lines Gregory "G-Bone" Everett, a 1980s- and 1990s-era DJ, also associated the approach of brown DJ crews and UJA's approach. G-Bone observed the following: "We pushed the name of the organization and the DJ's, that is the way the Hispanics were doing it, and that's the way Uncle Jam's Army did it" (Cross 1993:164). According to G-Bone, the promotional style of his events was modeled after the way "Hispanics were doing it," alongside the way UJA had done it. That is, models emphasizing DJ's and the organization gained notoriety among fans, more than musicians and headliners.

88　IN THE TIME OF SKY-RHYMING

Image 3.3 Boogie Motion Productions event flier, 1989. (Reproduced courtesy of Manuel Villaseñor)

The DJ-centric approach, according to G-Bone's observation, reflected a resonance between Black and brown DJ Crews (Image 3.3).

Disco Scenes and Backyard Parties

As important as clubs and large-scale mobile DJ parties were to integrating the funk frequency in Brown Los Angeles, the backyard party scene provided a unique space of resonance. Scholar and DJ Gerard Meraz (2008) points to how the backyard scene of the 1980s developed in part out of the discrimination experienced in the disco scene. The club disco scene was inaccessible to some brown creatives, who turned around and channeled their creative energies to the neighborhood. During an interview, Meraz, who is Mexican American from East Los Angeles, and helped shape the homegrown East Side backyard party scene of the 1980s, explained an important generational transition that contributed to the growth and entrepreneurial spirit of this scene:

> A lot of older brothers and sisters would go to discos, you know from the late '70s and early '80s. Those older brothers and sisters eventually would get pissed off by the treatment they received at these discos because they were usually in the white areas. We had some in our hoods too, but you want to go check it out and you get dissed, and maybe the ones in your neighborhood are too ghetto. There were some class, economic, and social differences. Then those older siblings said, "We can buy this equipment and throw our own parties." And

they got the younger siblings to learn the music and DJ. So the older brothers would buy the equipment and know the electronics cuz some of them would take an electronics class at a community college or what not. And they would know how to set shit up, and the light boards, and run power. And they'd have the little brother who is in school taking music classes be the DJ. I've heard that story a lot. It was the older brothers that came from the disco scene, saw the lights, and the speakers and said, "You know what? We can buy this shit and make our own."

Discrimination and lack of opportunity, along with familiarity with the technical side of sound and lighting rigs, helped spur the entrepreneurship of the East Side backyard party scene. Younger siblings would help set the ambience for their older siblings, according to Meraz, yet these younger siblings would grow in their skill and creativity as well. While the backyard scene was not, generally, a Hip Hop scene, it did allow for experimentation with Hip Hop.

One brown creative who capitalized on the backyard scene as a space for Hip Hop performance was Arturo Molina, known as Kid Frost. As Hochman (1990a), a journalist for the *LA Times*, revealed about Frost's rise to fame, "Frost hooked up with the group DJ Tropical, performing in East L.A. and the San Gabriel Valley. 'They let me do a show, and soon I started doing three or four house parties a night,' [Frost] said." Markski, featured in Chapter 4, remembers crossing paths with Frost in the house party scene of the East Side and rocking the mic with him at these events.

Frost facilitated the performances of some Black artists in the backyard party scene. Cross (1993:24), in his account of the early West Coast scene, for example, describes how Ice-T's early performance sites included, "the east side circuit with Tony (G) Gonzalez and a young Kid Frost, an electropop house jam scene with a primarily Chicano constituency." So while Frost is generally recognized as Ice-T's protégé (Rodriguez 2009), even being dubbed "Kid Frost" by Ice-T, Frost helped open the door for Ice-T on the East Side. Frost also acknowledges bringing rapper Coolio into the East Side circuit. In an interview with Michael Khalfani (2017b), Frost, who first went by the name Gemini during the period in question, explained that a treacherous mishap marred their first Hip Hop performance at a backyard party in the East Side: "Two East LA gangs decide that they're going to have a shootout," Frost explained. Coolio, who was present during this incident, according to Frost, told Frost, "I didn't come out to East LA to be involved in something like this!" (Khalfani 2017b). Frost dated this event to 1982. Thus, while some distance existed between some predominantly brown and Black American scenes, points of convergence did exist.

Beat Geeks

Some brown creatives drawn to more technological aspects of music found fertile soil for experimentation in electro funk. Jose "J-Vibe" Jimenez remembers that the technological aspects of the electro sound is what piqued his interest. J-Vibe and his brother Santiago, growing up in East Los Angeles, had dabbled in electronics. The futuristic aspects of the electro sound resonated with them in how it spoke to their technological interests. In gaining awareness of his musical preferences, J-Vibe naturally sought opportunities to gain further exposure to his preferred music. He and his brother would frequent two arcades that were across the street from each other on Broadway Street in downtown Los Angeles. One of the arcades would often play electro music, and J-Vibe would ask the arcade manager about the different songs that he would hear. His knowledge of the music was expanding, and he was also associating the music with his excursions into downtown and with playing video games. As J-Vibe describes it, there came a point early on where he moved from being a consumer to a creator:

> What got me into the music was, I can isolate down to saying it was a synthesizer. My brother is five years older than me in school, and it was junior high school. He had electronic classes and he built a strobe light and was building stuff. So, I got really excited about that and started digging into it and I learned some electronics. He taught me things. And I just took it from there and hung out at Radio Shack and started doing stuff, eventually building my synthesizer.
>
> So, when I started doing a lot of the music, the music that was using synthesizers is really what drew me to Electro. When that started, I was hearing Kraftwerk. Then I was listening to Jean Michel Jarre, which I discovered from two older cousins in Mexico. They were playing this total ambient space music that I totally fell in love with. And they showed me the album of Jean Michel Jarre, and I was like, wow, and then from there I discovered Tangerine Dream and these other groups. And in the process of doing the synthesizers and hearing the music, I heard Arthur Baker, Jon Robie, and what they were doing with Afrika Bambaataa, Planet Patrol and all that.
>
> When I first heard that song ["Planet Rock"] I was at Zodie's in Montebello. There was a Zodie's right off the 60 freeway. And I was at the boom boxes and all of a sudden, I hear "Planet Rock" playing. Man, I was like, What the heck is this? It was like Kraftwerk, but different. It had the big heavy beat on it, the 808 and all that. And I was stuck to the radio, and I was waiting for them to say what it was and didn't get to hear it. They didn't say anything. I was so frustrated, man. Eventually I heard it again later somewhere else and eventually got the name of the song.

J-Vibe's affinity for the technical and technological aspects of electronic-based music guided him toward Hip Hop. Even as his draw to "Planet Rock" was described as a sudden experience, his sensibilities toward electronic music had been cultivated over time through various sources, including through the music that he was introduced to by his cousins in Mexico and his brother. As "Planet Rock" reverberated through the airwaves, and Hip Hop swept through the streets of Los Angeles, J-Vibe was immersing himself into the technology of beat-making. To fund this endeavor, he remembers, "I got a job at a bakery in East LA so I could buy my own synthesizer. My whole goal was to make beats. I'm going to make some music! We're going to go downtown and we're going to break dance and I want to crank it and blast it so that we can show it all over downtown echoing the way we're breaking to the other music. I wanted to do that too, only to my music." Eventually J-Vibe would reach his goals, and produce an electro track, "VSF," that would get radio play on KDAY. J-Vibe's account of technological interest is important because it demonstrates that Hip Hop was not merely about street reputations but also about technological skills and practice. This is reminiscent of Egyptian Lover's description of how he was drawn to the Roland TR-808 and excelled at his craft in part because of his dexterity with that device. Without technologically minded creatives, Hip Hop production would not be possible.

Conclusion

Even as Black creatives were the primary drivers of the emerging Hip Hop scene, Black and brown resonances emerged through the funk frequency. Parallel movements catering to young Black and brown people through DJ-centric acts provided platforms for local artists to perform and develop their skills. Through the movement of artists, these DJ scenes contributed to cross-racial resonance. The overlap in part took place as artists were contracted from one scene to another. The partnerships of artists fostered opportunities for cross-pollination and for resonance amplification. Nevertheless, the contracting of artists seems to have been mostly of Black American artists being hired into brown community events, with some notable exceptions. Still, some brown creatives supported the predominantly Black DJ scene in front stage and backstage ways, and likewise boosted the resonance of many Black American artists within their own localized scenes. These funk frequency resonances opened the door for Brown Los Angeles to identify with Hip Hop.

PART II
CYPHERS OF RESONANCE
Sites of Proliferation

Chapters in this section illustrate how sites of creativity shaped Hip Hop's adaptation and dissemination in Brown Los Angeles once the sights and sounds of Hip Hop became accessible on the West Coast. Early underground sites of Hip Hop innovation were especially important toward developing early cohorts of Los Angeles creatives who identified deeply with Hip Hop in the early-to-mid 1980s. From neighborhoods, to a club, to a youth center, creatives from Brown Los Angeles were among some of the early innovators that interacted with East Coast transplants to translate Hip Hop into a West Coast phenomenon.

4
Translating Elementary Knowledge

Mark "Freeze Rockin Markski" Santiago was a rare type of "new kid," at North Park Junior High School in Pico Rivera, one whose heart and mind seemed to be located elsewhere. Having been uprooted from his home in the Bronx, New York, the prior year, Markski's family sought new opportunities in a mostly Mexican American suburb, less than two miles from East Los Angeles. Speaking to Markski during an interview, he recalls how he was received: "In LA, people were like, 'That guy's a freak, that guy's from another planet.' In New York City, I had been that kid with the knack." Leaving New York City in 1981, Markski's family, en route to California, had a brief stay in Puerto Rico. As a Nuyorican, Markski found others like him in Puerto Rico—sojourners who lived between the island and The City—occupying a border-island space. While finishing seventh grade on the island, Markski was heartened by his encounters with these like-minded peers. He was especially drawn to other Nuyoricans who transacted in the Hip Hop elements he had excelled at in the Bronx. After staying on the island only a few months, his next, and final destination, California, would prove less familiar. Still, in the moves from the Bronx, to Puerto Rico, to Pico Rivera, Markski discovered that some of the cultural resources he held onto were especially valuable for acclimating to his new social surroundings. Among the tools that would animate him through his settlement process, Markski's identification with Hip Hop proved especially meaningful (Recinos 2010). Markski may not have known it then, but his efforts to preserve his own sense of wholeness positioned him as a teacher to others.

In reflecting on his journey from the Bronx to Los Angeles, Markski enthusiastically mused, "I was the personification of Hip Hop." As he presented his personal Hip Hop history during our interview, I became increasingly convinced by his assertion. The classic creation myth, the Bronx-origin development of Hip Hop, came through loud and clear in Markski's account. Mass media provided an important channel of transmission from the geographic source of Hip Hop culture, connecting creatives from around the globe to Hip Hop's epicenter. Markski's story, however, uncovered another layer of creative absorption in the culture's dissemination. Personal, translocal connections helped to propel Hip Hop into the social imaginary of Brown Los Angeles. These connections provided new audiences means by which not only to observe Hip Hop but also to internalize it. The translocal associations that were forged by creatives and the practices and conventions (Ewoodzie 2017) they developed through these connections came to define Los Angeles Hip Hop. Markski's story spotlights the pedagogical aspects of Hip Hop's resonance, the ways that creatives with connections to New York City had a major impact on Brown Los Angeles.

Given his connections across distinct geographies, Markski functioned as a translocal broker in the West Coast scene. Translocal brokers are cultural *translators*, in the fullest sense of the word "translator." They translate by making comprehensible a new cultural vernacular from one context to another and by transporting the materials of a culture from one locus to another. Through translation, translocal brokers boost the resonance of particular movements across geographies (Morgan and Bennet 2011). The knowledge Markski translated was *elementary*—related to the Hip Hop *elements*. A living, breathing conduit of the movement, Markski maintained ties across multiple geographies. For eventual West Coast participants of Hip Hop, Markski became an embodied, authentic expression of Hip Hop. Perhaps more importantly, Markski was accessible to young aficionados wanting to learn and grow in their skill. There was only so much that West Coast creatives could gauge from media examples. And certainly, many tried to learn, but there was no substitute for having contact with a translocal broker like Markski, who knew the ins and outs of the elements. For many Hip Hop neophytes, Markski became a critical link in a chain of resonance, starting in Pico Rivera, California.

Planet Rock, Puerto Rico, and Pico Rivera

Markski's role as a teacher began with his efforts to preserve his own sense of self. Hip Hop provided a sense of continuity for Markski as he moved through cityscapes, and across coasts, tying him to his home neighborhood in the Bronx. For Markski, Hip Hop had been in the air he breathed. Since his childhood in the Bronx, Markski recalls, he was drawn to the Hip Hop elements. As he describes it, "I used to go to elementary school and sometimes I'd take the train by myself, you know, nine years old, 10 years old, 12 years old and so sometimes I'd start venturing out like, 'Okay, well what if I miss my first class, but I go to Manhattan for a little while and look at the subways?' Right? So, I was already venturing into the [graffiti] writing scene. I knew crews, I knew their styles, and so not only did I feel mature in life being exposed to bad stuff, dangerous stuff, but also firsthand watching Hip Hop and writing develop." Hip Hop colored the way that Markski saw the city. It oriented how he related to the geographies of his social world. His daily routines were increasingly paced to the rhythm of Hip Hop.

At the start of the 1980s, Hip Hop culture was still largely a New York City phenomenon, popular among mostly Black American, West Indian, and Puerto

Rican young people. Markski arrived in Los Angeles, a young teen, in 1982, just as mass media gained interest in Hip Hop and Los Angeles became a receptacle for Hip Hop sights and sounds. Some artistic expressions that Markski knew as commonplace, started to become commodities in Los Angeles. However, on his initial arrival, Hip Hop for Markski was more a source of personal stability, and a marker of difference. He explains that, "I missed my hometown. I knew my craft and I really deeply continued all of my avenues, my rhyming, my graffiti art, my dancing. And so, I'm a guy that's been connected to the street life." Markski was essentially a practitioner of all the Hip Hop elements; this was typical of many early participants in the movement and a source of pride among practitioners in underground scenes today. In Los Angeles he continued to practice these modes of expression, albeit at times in a reserved, solitary manner. Markski found solace in the familiar images of graffiti lettering that he produced, in the B-boy poses that he positioned himself into, and in the rhyme schemes that he jotted down.

The predominantly Chicano context of Pico Rivera required continual adjustment and adaptation from Markski. He reminisces about being "Right in Chicano culture," experiencing "the East Coast, West Coast culture shock and the Nuyorican versus Chicano Angeleno. You know that there's a lot of differences—there's similarities—but there's differences." At first, blending in was not an option for Mark. He describes how even his physical appearance drew attention from peers: "I was like 'blam!' right in your face, customized gear head to toe, vain, color-coded, color coordinated, layered with you know stuff that I found that my mother was gonna throw away. Because we're poor kids we would create, you know, from nothing, and so, you know, I was rocking stuff like from another planet, and then I got treated that way too!" Markski quickly became aware that his wardrobe, typical in the Bronx, made him stick out in Pico Rivera.

It was difficult for Markski to ignore the differences he had with his peers, because these manifested not only as diverging tastes and opinions held internally, or as distinct cultural styles, but rather as outward confrontations, which at times entailed the threat of violence. In school, and in his neighborhood, he developed a persona that vacillated between facing-off directly with people that questioned him, and quietly retreating into his private modes of artistic expression. He gained a reputation for spouting off grandiose explanations of who he was when he grew agitated by the barrage of questions he received. Conversely, he was also known for being quiet and for isolating himself, sometimes focusing on his Hip Hop craft away from others. In his early days in Pico Rivera, in eighth grade and later in his first year at El Rancho High School, these highs and lows were especially pronounced.

As much as he enjoyed retreating into his art, retreat was not always an option for Mark. For a season, he was repeatedly confronted by a group of "Chicano cholos" at school. In such situations, he had to quickly decide how to respond to aggressors. He notes:

> Some of the neighborhood little guys were the little brothers of cholos, so they were all with their kind of cholo stuff on—and they surround me! They heard about me, how big I talked and they wanted to come check me out and so, you know, in between classes, people would surround me. They would ask things like, "Who are you? Who do you think you are?" So, I had to, in my own brain, I had to counter what I perceived was happening. People would tell me, "be careful with those guys, they're from a gang." In my brain, I would think gang life, like what I experienced in New York. The police are scared and the police won't hardly come around and basically the mafia is the graduated gang. So, they come through and they basically protect the neighborhood, and so I thought, but man, I'm in a totally different place.
>
> I was thinking those vatos were the younger brothers of the mafia, okay, so basically they surround me and I was like, "well, you know what? We moved out here because we're from the mafia!" And you know, so I start coming at them like "Yeah, you don't know who you're messing with here! We're from the mafia and we will chop you up and put you in the ground and no one will find you!" And so, I was talking to like twelve cholos that were around me and I was talking like that, right, because I thought, man, New Yorkers are talkers for sure, we know how to talk. And so, to get out of potentially being beat up or something that I thought could happen, I started talking my way out. I'm gonna make these guys afraid you know, like they're not gonna want to mess with me.

The ruse that Markski concocted seemed to work, as the local gang members eventually left him alone. What he did not expect, is that some of his teachers were catching wind of the stories he was sharing—and were believing them! This brought an unexpected benefit. Markski explains, "My teachers would also listen in on that, and they were giving me A grades, without me having to work. They were like, 'You get an A, I don't want any part of you!' They were scared of the big stuff they heard me saying." Markski was getting through with his verbosity, and continued to practice his art.

Adapting to the West Coast

As much as Markski was committed to preserving his ties to Hip Hop, he did so not solely through a rigid reproduction of past practices but rather by sustaining a Hip Hop habitus—an embodied mode of Hip Hop expression that could flow and adapt to his new environment. The notion of habitus, as proposed by Pierre

Bourdieu (1990), speaks to the feel for the game that Markski describes in relation to Hip Hop. His embodiment of Bronx Hip Hop culture through his habitus enabled him to adopt and adapt forms of urban expression that he encountered in the Los Angeles scene. Aspects of urban West Coast culture resonated with Markski. The resulting adaptation was consistent with Marski's embodiment of Hip Hop authenticity in that it allowed him to stay true to his culture but also to innovate. That is, Marksi was finding points of resonance in West Coast culture and integrating these into his habitus; this assisted in the adaptation process of the movement.

His propensity to engage urban modes of expression quickly drew Markski to the poplocking scene in the Los Angeles area, because, as he observed, "they were popping on the streets in LA." To become a teacher, Markski also became a student. He began to learn from the dance styles that he witnessed in his area, explaining, "I picked that up like real quick. I was real interested. So, I was doing my B-boy stuff which they never saw, and then I started popping LA style." He recognized the creativity of the local artform, asserting, "to me, that's one of the things that I give props to LA for, that very fine-tuned popping style compared to New York. I didn't learn popping in New York. You know, so when I learned it in LA, man, that was like another branch added to what I did." Popping, then, was authentic to Los Angeles. Markski was blending what he knew from New York City with what he encountered in Los Angeles.

One of the conventions that Markski was socialized into in the Bronx Hip Hop scene was that "biting," replicating what others were doing, was taboo. This was a major marker of authenticity for Markski. Originality was of highest importance in the scene that Markski grew up in, and as such, he took care to develop his own version of the popping moves he was observing. He would practice them on his own, knowing that soon enough he would be called on to battle others. Battling, in fact, was another tradition that Markski was all too familiar with. As a B-boy, breaking was part of Markski's repertoire. By practicing his own version of particular popping moves, he was adding additional skills to his dance repertoire, which in turn allowed him to live out his commitment to originality.

This striving for originality, as a way to demonstrate authenticity, was put on display at a high school event. Markski recounts:

> So, I was popping at a school dance. All of a sudden these cholos and the neighborhood guys surrounded me and they start battling me. Well, after like various rounds of that, I ran out of the moves that I had made up. I had these different popping moves like you know, I go, I cut your head off. Well, once I exhausted that against these bunch of dudes, then I took it to the floor [doing B-boy moves]. And then, they didn't know what that was. They didn't know what to do, but I knew I was rocking those guys, right? So I'm on the floor. I'm doing my

footwork shuffling, very elementary, basic stuff. But nevertheless, I have some top rocking moves, I have some bottom rocking moves, and they didn't know how to respond. So they started laughing going, "oh that's that disco dancing—oh!" You know, they were mocking me!

Though the group of neighborhood boys attempted to ridicule Markski, he eventually felt vindicated. With the increasing exposure to New York City Hip Hop that people in Los Angeles received, what Markski knew how to do became coveted knowledge. As he observed, "The next year at the same Fall school dance, guess who was on the floor doing the exact, identical moves that I rocked on them? Those same guys were doing my moves! They were a year behind you know, doing my moves. So I had one up on them." A shift had taken place, and New York City Hip Hop was becoming not only familiar and acceptable but also popular in Los Angeles. By then, for example, the 1983 film *Wild Style* was gaining popularity throughout the country. So, while Angelenos had increasing access to representations of Hip Hop, Markski's embodiment of Hip Hop made him a model to emulate, essentially a teacher.

Rather than being excited about Hip Hop gaining acceptance in Los Angeles, Markski was upset that his skills were being replicated. This was contrary to what he understood as authentic to the culture. As he described, "I resented it because to me, part of the Hip Hop code was you don't bite. That's like you can get punched in the mouth for biting." He recalls that this value in Hip Hop applied to all the elements. For example, in graffiti writing,

> If you bit somebody's letter E, or somebody's arrow, you can get punched in the mouth. Biting is against the code but creativity is really required. When I saw people in LA biting off of me, that was another part of the culture shock. They were starting to see *Wild Style*. I saw *Wild Style* too, and it reminded me of what I knew, but then I would go to the dances, or to breaking events and I would see carbon copies—people that dressed like they thought they were the guy from *Wild Style*. And they were doing, you know, the graffiti style that they saw. Back then that burned me inside. Number one, you're violating the code. Number two, you're not from the place where this originated. That was my attitude back then.

"Skip hoppers," Markski explained, was the term that he coined to describe this form of Hip Hop mimicry. At the time, Markski felt that some Angelenos were inserting themselves into a history, a culture, that they had no role in creating: "I saw my life experience as what we developed there in New York. Okay, I saw the life experience as being part of the process of how Hip Hop was developed. And so I saw it as if you haven't gone through this process, then you're jumping ahead and you're just biting." Whether it was through observing him, or by consuming what was displayed via mass media platforms, Markski wanted to do his part to minimize mass production of the New York City culture he was familiar with. He was engaged in a form of authenticity policing, albeit, typically at a personal level. For a period of time, Markski became increasingly secretive with his craft: "I basically hid a lot of what I did from others. And then, what would happen is I would just break out my work all of a sudden—like I landed from Mars—I would just break out and rock something, like dump it on someone, like blast them and dump this expression, and then break out." In becoming strategic about when he was sharing his craft with others, Markski felt more at ease about continuing his artistic development.

Markski remained connected to New York City in more ways than one. He spent most of his summers back in New York City, visiting family, during his teenage years. This allowed him to remain fresh in his skills, and not merely continue to base his innovation on memories. He continued to be part of a living culture, even as he spent most of the year away from its epicenter. Furthermore, his heart was largely still in New York and his desire to remain authentic was largely a commitment to self. In fact, he recalls that, "For all of the years that I stayed in Pico, I used my original suitcase like a dresser drawer for my normal clothes. I had an NYC poster that stretched across my main wall." Wanting desperately to return to the City, Markski found a way to live with family friends in Long Island for his eleventh grade year. He would trek into the city from Long Island to participate in the graffiti writing scene during that year. Nevertheless, he eventually returned to his family in Pico Rivera, and completed his senior year at El Rancho High School. After graduating from high school, he orchestrated a trip to New York City with some of his friends from Pico Rivera, introducing these Chicano friends to the sights and sounds that shaped him.

On a Detour, Catching Glimpses

During the season that Markski's peers were meeting him with ridicule and then intrigue, creatives from around the LA basin were having distinct experiences in which Hip Hop grabbed their attention; many creatives were seeking ways to be taught in the elements. Especially for those in the working-class suburbs of greater Los Angeles, some created communities of learning, extended cyphers, essentially, in which they taught each other from the bits and pieces of the culture that they were able to procure. As Dino Mayorga, a dancer and visual artist articulated it, "It was such a new thing that if you were diehard about it, you were willing to do whatever it took to go to where it was." In other words, if something Hip Hop related was happening somewhere, interested creatives would make the effort to go. The primary urban corridors of Los Angeles became material avenues of resonance for Hip Hop, but for those farther out in the suburbs, it was difficult to gain access to expressions of the elements. Initially, many of these creatives latched onto whatever representation of the elements they could access.

Some creatives recall watching video segments that spotlighted B-boys and B-girls before seeing them in feature-length films. B-boy Don Sevilla, a Filipino American B-boy who often collaborated with Latino B-boys, indicates that a segment of the television show, *That's Incredible*, which aired on the ABC network in 1982, was pivotal in his identification with Hip Hop. B-boy Don goes on to describe the way that he would learn from video segments on television, using techniques that some of his contemporaries also engaged in. Learning dance skills from mass media required extensive effort in the early days, and B-boy Don was willing to put in the work:

> I would watch almost every music video channel that was available to us on TV and I'd have to find videos that had popping or breaking in it. So that was my, I guess you could say that was my YouTube tutorials back then, catching music videos that had any kind of dancing. because I didn't have a VCR, I had to catch dance moves. You know, for however long and good for a few seconds I had to take a *picture in* my mind, and then go in front of a mirror, which was my backyard sliding glass door during the day to see the reflection on it and then practice what I saw for hours. Music videos like "Buffalo Gals." You remember "Buffalo Gals" by Malcolm McLaren? I would catch that video and try to emulate what I saw. Real quick. There's a video by Gladys Knight and the Pips Called "Save the Overtime" and there was some footage of the New York City breakers doing their moves. I would catch that and I'd try to emulate what I saw.

Still an active B-boy at the time of our interview, who is involved in both street dance performances and in teaching university classes, it is impressive that B-boy Don learned his skills largely through memorization of what he saw briefly on television. This was an important avenue that some neophytes had at their disposal in the early days. Exposure to these videos and images involved chance, as well as time and patience.

Koolski, a Chicano B-boy from Fullerton, California, vividly remembers the moment at which he became transfixed by Hip Hop. "I was just mesmerized and I was like, 'Yo! I want to do that!'" Having gone to a drive-in theater, he glanced away from the film he and his party were watching and spotted an adjacent screen showing a different movie. A child of eight years old, he could not peel his eyes away from the sights being projected onto the other screen. He would later learn the film was called *Beat Street*. He recalls, "So I can't hear the audio, but I can see what they're doing. I see people dancing. It's that part where the battle at the Roxy comes up." Later that night, upon describing to his older brother David what he saw, his brother interjected, "Oh yeah, that's called breaking. My friends do it."

Koolski wanted to learn. He recalled, "One day my brother and his friends came over to our house after a school dance. They started dancing in front of my house, and I said, 'Yeah! That's it!'" To Koolski's dismay, David did not want him around. David convinced his friends to head over to another home, about three blocks away, in part to get away from Koolski. It was nearly nine o'clock at night, and Koolski trailed his brother and his friends. When they reached the house, he inconspicuously attempted to follow the group into the house.

Get away from here! Get the hell out of here! Go home!" his brother admonished him. So Koolski walked away and walked around the block, cutting through an alley behind the home. As he recalls: "This was a bad part of town, I was on Valencia, in the alley between Valencia and Truslow on Highland and Richmond. That was a bad time in the early '80s, the mid-'80s. And I'm seeing people doing drugs and they're drinking, they're partying and they're looking at me like, "Why's this little kid walking down the street?"

Eventually, Koolski found the right house, and peered over the fence to see the friends dance. Someone from the group spotted Koolski and alerted his brother David, who proceeded to yell at him, "¡Ay, que te vayas!" [Hey, go away!]. One of David's friends, a young man named Chucho, reasoned with David: "Let him hang out with us. It's okay, no big deal!" Begrudgingly, David gave in and accepted that Koolski could stay. Chucho invited Koolski in and said, "Do you want to learn?" Koolski was elated. From this point on began Koolski's journey into becoming a student and eventually a master of B-boying. Years later, Koolski would go on to fulfill his dream of joining the West Coast contingent of the Rock Steady Crew, one of the very crews whose dexterity had captivated him on film at the drive-in theater.

Famed West Coast beatboxer, Click the Supah Latin, whose parents migrated from Peru to the United States, remembers his first experience with Hip Hop music catching his attention:

I heard the Fat Boys, and when I heard the Fat Boys, it blew me away because I never heard beatboxing before. And that's the one thing that stuck because I believe before that I may have already been trying to rhyme or what not, but it just, it wouldn't, you know, I wasn't great at it yet but, beat box, once I heard that, man that that just took me in and then that that's what I focused on after that. But I want to say, man, shoot at maybe '81, or '82.

Click had already heard Hip Hop music, and had dabbled in emceeing at that time. Nevertheless, hearing the Fat Boys moved him in a different way. In this music from the Fat Boys, Click recognized something particular that he sensed he could be good at—beatboxing. Soon enough, he excelled at this artform. Click went on to become an emcee, beatboxer, and producer. In 1987, he met Markski at a community Hip Hop showcase sponsored by KDAY. It was Markski who encouraged me to reach out to Click.

Alvin Trivette, known as ALT, points to the experience of watching Ice-T and Frost battle each other through rhyme as something that was formative to him. The rap battles he witnessed early on inspired him to become the no-nonsense emcee he would be known as. In later years, having worked with Frost, he was surprised to learn something about the battles that he witnessed, which he shared in an interview with Arnold Sullivan of Dusty Vision Radio (2019b): "What broke my heart is when I got to know Kid Frost and Ice and found out that all that shit was staged! They were homies." ALT described himself as one of the "little kids right there looking over the turntables. We could barely stand over the turntables watching them battle." Though those particular rap battles were scripted, the performances served to inspire him. These rappers were no strangers to real battles, and their skills were on display, written rhymes or not. ALT's story indicates that exposure to the Hip Hop performances of West Coast pioneers sparked his imagination before he himself would emerge as a pioneer to subsequent generations. These performances motivated him to engage as a rapper committed to lyricism. He would later go on to work with Frost and Markski as part of the collective called the Latin Alliance and released his own music beyond that.

Dino Mayorga entered the dance cypher at a precocious age, learning from a talented teacher who moved to Dino's city. In 1983 the apartment community where he and his family lived in Buena Park, California, became a local hub of dance activity. According to Dino, a lot of creative energy flowing through his community came from transplants that were showing up to the neighborhood. Dino remembered, "One of my influences was this dude named Teddy Medina, who went to Buena Park High School. He was in high school when I was still in elementary school. He was originally from Flatbush Brooklyn, New York, and he and his family moved to Southern California. He was Puerto Rican." Teddy was part of a crew with a fitting name, Generation One. In California, they were part of the first generation of B-boys and B-girls. Many of the dancers also incorporated funk dance styles developed in the West Coast. Dino continued, "Teddy visited his girlfriend who lived at the same apartment complex as us, right across the street from the high school. The first time, for example, I ever heard "White Lines," that classic Hip Hop song, was out of Teddy's radio. As a kid, he was the coolest because of how he danced. His crew would meet at the high school across the street from us and battle other crews." At one of those battles, with Generation One, Dino got into the cypher for the first time. He has never stopped dancing, amassing a wide array of dance styles to his dance repertoire.

These accounts highlight moments of inspiration and translation that West Coast creatives experienced in disparate locales around the region. Firsthand exposure to performance of the elements, especially in communal settings, was helpful to the learning process of these creatives and facilitated opportunities for greater innovation. As media carried increasing amounts of Hip Hop, it also mattered that creatives found expressions of Hip Hop that inspired them and that they identified with. The emergence of West Coast creatives who furthered the culture was contingent on their learning to develop the skills for themselves and for them to develop an identity within the movement. Finding a balance between skill and inspiration was important for these early West Coast creatives. Teachers of the craft were difficult to come by, especially for the young cohort coming of age during the movement's beginnings. Yet, the cohort that formed the vanguard of the Hip Hop generation on the West Coast were willing to make sacrifices to find teachers. For those that had proximity to Markski, perhaps many did not initially appreciate the resources that were accessible to them through him, but that would soon change.

Resonance through Crew Building

In his later teenage years, before graduating, Markski became more intentional about sharing his cultural capital with his friends translocally (Morgan and Bennet 2011). He became more aware of and strategic about the agency he had in deploying this knowledge. Whereas some opportunists sought to profit from the cultural knowledge that Markski had, he recognized that among his peers some were genuinely interested in who he was, including his expressions of Hip Hop and his personal story. According to Markski, "There were some kids that really liked me and really were interested, and they related to me. So, I made some friends like that and I always kept them as really close friends." Marski was attentive to those peers that had an authentic, nonexploitative interest in him and his cultural knowledge, and some of these peers would eventually join him in his artistic endeavors.

Having a crew in Los Angeles enabled Markski to venture out in more generative ways and engage in his creative expressions in a more public manner. He was even able to expand his Hip Hop skills in Los Angeles: "I did break in public a lot—breaking and popping—in public a lot. I learned to windmill in LA." The peers that Markski linked up with developed a sense of mutuality with each other, and learned to facilitate and improve the expression of the Hip Hop elements as a crew. This group of friends would eventually be known as United We Stand, or UWS. UWS was primarily based in Pico Rivera, but it also drew members from surrounding cities. It even included as an affiliate one of Markski's associates from Long Island, New York. These young men, and a couple of young women, had access to key resources from Markski. He would sometimes share mixtapes, for example, that he acquired through his contacts in New York City. Eventually, members of the crew developed their own affinities toward particular Hip Hop elements, and learned to express them in original ways.

The UWS crew grew in local popularity in the mid- to late-1980s, and opportunities to perform expanded. The crew began to catch the eye of local organizers and promoters, and the group gained an increasingly public profile in the neighborhoods of the San Gabriel Valley, and beyond. Markski and one of his rhyme partners, for example, performed at an event in 1987 sponsored by KDAY, the Los Angeles radio station known for pioneering Hip Hop radio play in the region. At this event, he met Click the Supah Latin, who was also performing. Events sponsored by local schools also provided stages for these talented teens. In some cases, the teens asserted their way onto the platform, but by this time their performances were lauded and well received by crowds. Most often, UWS was performing at house parties, which were common in the area, with the long-standing mobile DJ scene popular in the Chicano community energizing the party circuit (Image 4.1).

At a high school in the nearby city of Rosemead, Markski recalled, he and his UWS crew attended a school dance specifically to participate in a popping contest that was being hosted there. After the popping contest, Markski casually inspected the DJ's set up. He noticed that periodically, the DJ would make announcements on a unique microphone, a classic looking one that reminded Markski of vintage, 1940s equipment. Stealthily, Markski made his way to the DJ and asked him if he could rap. In the process, as Markski picked up the microphone, the DJ stared at him quizzically and interjected, "you're gonna what?" Markski responded, "I'm gonna rap! Throw on this instrumental," all the while pointing to a particular record that he could rhyme over. "Check this out!" Markski coaxed him: "One two, one two!" Markski proceeded to wow the crowd with his rhyme skills. Markski recalls receiving a positive response from those in attendance. Years later, he was approached by some Chicano recording artists who confessed that they were students at that Rosemead high school and that his performance had inspired them to rap.

Image 4.1 Members of United We Stand, clockwise starting at top left, Gremz, Freeze Rockin' Markski, DJ Faze 3, and Lyrical Engineer Genius G, 1987. (Reproduced courtesy of Mark Santiago)

Amplifying the Scene's Resonance

Among the creatives that Markski collaborated with in the 1980s were two Chicana sisters, Delilah and Denise Gonzales, known as Lilah and Neecee respectively; their stories present important insights into the processes of knowledge transmission in the West Coast scene and how creatives in Brown Los Angeles sought opportunities to grow in their crafts. This included avoiding opportunities that would draw them away from their crafts. In a setting like Los Angeles, finding the right opportunities sometimes required moving around across the broad landscape (Zanfagna 2017). At other times, opportunities appeared close by, and creatives needed only to recognize them. For example, the Gonzales sisters attended the same schools as Markski in Pico Rivera, and knew Markski through his older brother, Kato. They began to cross paths with Markski in the house party scene.

Lilah and Neecee had an abundant love for dancing that manifested publicly in the early 1980s. At the time, as Michael Jackson was charting on the radio, gaining the status of the king of pop, Lilah and Neecee were engaging in a pop of their own, to Michael's music. "Everyone was dressing like Michael Jackson with the red jacket and pants and, you know, the belts and the spikes." The music of Michael and his contemporaries was the natural backdrop to the popping scene that Lilah and Neecee engaged with. Popping was a dance style that caught on the West Coast. A commitment to dancing provided an important outlet for sisters in the early 1980s. As Lilah explained, "My intention was to be a homegirl, but I have more love, instead of going in that direction, toward the music and dancing direction because I knew I could do it."

Dancing gave Lilah an alternative. Upon elaboration, Lilah made it clear that being a "homegirl," in her case, referred to being involved in gangs. For many of their peers, given the era when Lilah and Neecee were coming of age, and the location where they were growing up, gangs were a visible option for them. Not only was dancing an alternative, though, but what made it that much better was that, in her words, "I had the perfect partner, and that was my sister. So, we started being really drawn toward that early '80s, '81, '82, '83." Lilah, the older of the two sisters, formed a dance crew with her sister and friends, including their next-door neighbor, all from Pico Rivero. The crew began to gain notoriety in the San Gabriel Valley area of Los Angeles County.

The young women knew where to showcase their talents against other dancers, as the scene became competitive. One of the closest spots to them where dancers would gather to battle was on Whittier Blvd. The crew would make its way there by whatever means necessary. Lilah recalled, "we walked Whittier Blvd we battled with the Poppers, Tiny, Tic Tac, Boogaloo Shrimp.

I mean if we weren't in Long Beach, we were in Elysian Park. We'd do three different places a night." Sometimes their quest to hone their skills took them to places where they would have traditionally been barred from, namely nightclubs: "We were going out to all these places, when we were only sixteen and we shouldn't have been in the Florentine Gardens, we probably shouldn't have been in the Casa Camino Real, you know different things like the Vault in Long Beach." Yet the sisters knew their way around the scene and knew how to access these locations. In this way, Lilah and Neecee reminisced about some of the recognized dancers of the era, as well as the distinct spots that drew the best of the best. This was a West Coast scene, fueled by a dance style that developed in the West—popping.

While Lilah and Neecee were deep in the Los Angeles popping scene, they saw how Hip Hop's arrival began to influence their scene. For them, much of this started to show up in their fashion and in the dance styles they started to incorporate. As early adopters of Hip Hop fashion, Lilah recalls how she and her crew were distinguished from other crews: "We had gear that nobody was wearing with the Puma suit and no laces, or fat laces, my name plate, belt buckles, you know, my big earrings." In that early phase, Lilah and Neecee saw this as giving them a competitive edge when they faced off against other crews. As Lilah remembers, "all my girls had a different style to them so we were in it like by ourselves first. We really got on that hard. We brought something different." Neecee added, "We were up rocking, we were top rocking," indicating that they started to incorporate B-girl moves into their dance repertoires early on, making them more competitive.

While some of these styles were brought in from watching and learning about Hip Hop through mass media, Lilah and Neecee also credit Markski for presenting them with up-close access to the Hip Hop elements. As already mentioned, Markski was one of the first in the area to demonstrate B-boying to others, live. Graffiti writing was another element that Markski brought to the sisters in person. They were drawn to the aesthetics of graffiti, and even learned to write themselves. The introduction of freestyle rapping was another form of expression that Markski modeled to his community, and Lilah in particular gravitated toward that form of expression. She described the type of scene that would sometimes unfold at house parties: "I would also freestyle a little bit, any chance that I could, you know, maybe pick up the mic and do something. Right before we'd start dancing just blew the party away. They're like 'dang, she's just, even if a guy's right there, she's not afraid to battle!' But that was a natural thing for me." Creating this ambience was part of Markski's contribution to the scene, but it also involved creatives like Lilah and Neecee who were willing to step out and work on their skills.

Chicano Translocal Brokers

Teaching others about Hip Hop later in high school had brought more joy to Markski than when he first arrived, but gaining reinforcements would come to make a difference for him. On a fateful day in 1986, classmates started to approach Markski telling him he had to meet a new student that was so unique. Soon he was informed that it was not one, but two new students that he should meet. Markski remembers catching sight of these supposed extraterrestrial new students: "All of a sudden there were two of them and they looked like twins. They had Kangols on, and Cazals, and golden nameplates, you know, the epitome of B-boys! Fila socks, Fila this, Fila that, everything!" Students became invested in making the encounter happen. At lunch time, schoolmates attempted to draw together Markski and the two new students, with several peers eventually bringing the new pair over to Markski.

Markski got the impression that, "the school kids were putting us together to watch us interact. Like they wanted to hear us speak the same language or something, you know?" Markski agreed to connect with the new students, and contact was made. As the encounter unfolded, Markski remembers, "everybody in the school quad is looking at us because to them, this is a big entertaining thing." Perhaps the orchestrators had stumbled onto something. Markski instantly felt a sense of connection to Steve and Pat, the Roybal brothers, who had moved back to Los Angeles from Denver, Colorado. Pat, the younger of the two brothers, was known as Lil Blitz. Steve, the oldest of the two brothers, went by the name Zulu Gremlin, a name that points to his ties to the Universal Zulu Nation and the Rock Steady Crew.

Markski and the Roybals found opportunities to partner together through the Hip Hop arts. Already, from the inception of their association, they started to test each other's skills. On that first day, they walked over to the gym and Markski called on them to show their abilities. The Roybal brothers were impressive. In Mark's words, "they were sharp and so we clicked immediately." They verbally exchanged Hip Hop resumes, and mutually concluded that they were in the presence of authenticity. Soon after, Markski and Steve, also known as Gremz, began writing their first songs together. Markski took from rhymes that he had already written, and combined them with lyrics that Gremz wrote.

The Roybals were translocal brokers themselves. Born in Los Angeles, and growing up in Denver, the brothers were used to traveling across disparate locales. Even while growing up in Denver, they annually traveled back to Los Angeles to visit family. One characteristic that positioned the Roybals as translocal brokers was that they had high levels of exposure and access to performing arts resources. Steve Roybal Sr., the young men's father, was a musician and choreographer who had toured across the United States with different bands, especially as a drummer. The young men had already traveled to various regions across the United States because of their father's work, before arriving in Southern California in their midteens. Besides their draw to New York Hip Hop culture, they had especially learned from some of the funk and soul culture in Northern California's Bay Area. Gremz recalled seeing dancers in San Francisco's Fisherman's Wharf engaging in robotin and struttin, for example, some of the dance styles originating in Northern California. With a keen gift for kinesthetic learning, Gremz was soon testing out what he observed, and adding his own twist to the movements he witnessed from distinct locales.

In Denver, the Roybal brothers had participated extensively in local performing arts movements. There, the boys had opportunities to perform publicly on major city stages. In fact, their involvement in the arts had given them access to some of the New York–based innovators of Hip Hop culture, particularly B-boys. As New York City B-boys started to tour throughout the United States in the early 1980s, the Roybals had the opportunity to meet and interact with some of them in Denver, including members of the famed Rock Steady Crew and the New York City Breakers. The Roybals even won a competition where they were selected to showcase their own B-boy skills in Denver during the national live performance tour of the TV show *Fame*. That performance was televised, allowing the Roybal boys to grow accustomed to being in the spotlight.

Yet a significant amount of the Roybal's work was also performed behind the scenes, and that was no less important. Gremz, in particular, took his knowledge of the arts a step further than performance. By the age of fourteen, he was already teaching dance classes to college students at the University of Southern Colorado. Furthermore, he began to flex his skills in both production and entrepreneurship. He helped plan large-scale events in Denver, such as the Beat Street Tour, and assisted in other concerts. As an entrepreneur, Gremz would eventually start his own music production company as well as clothing businesses. He would become the founder and planner of some of the largest B-boy/B-girl centered competitions in the nation, if not the world. Most of that would come later, but on a smaller scale, the core of these skills was evident in his and his brother's innovative approach to fashion, their networking abilities, and their inclination toward adapting creative elements. The meeting of these creative translocal brokers, Markski and the Roybals, was catalytic.

The Roybals' creative trajectory challenges notions of Chicanos as a sedimented population that could only receive creative inspiration from others who had traveled the land. The Roybals themselves were inheritors of a creative legacy from their father, and learned important skills from him. Likewise, they were exposed to a variety of creative expressions through following in their father's footsteps. The brothers should also be credited with developing an awareness of the creative expressions in the distinct locales that they visited. They were able to observe the unique expressions within distinct places. Through these forms of exposure, the Roybal brothers developed their own creative repertoires. Gremz, in particular, became a catalytic figure in the dance world, gaining notoriety around the world. In the United States, he came to bridge the dance scenes of locales as distinct as New York City, Miami, and California's Bay Area. As a teen who encountered Markski, though, the creative resonance that these teens experienced through their collaborations spilled out into Pico Rivera's scene and beyond.

The Roybals boosted the signal of UWS and became integral members of the crew. As UWS's profile grew, Markski was also able to build ties with other key artists in the area, including none other than Arturo Molina, known then as Kid Frost, and now simply as Frost. At the time, Frost resided not far from where Markski and his family lived in Pico Rivera. Frost was already a pioneer of Los Angeles Hip Hop, one whose star was quickly rising. According to Markski, Frost was a talent scout of sorts, seeking to network with other young artists. Frost was a few years older than Markski, and "was very business-minded." Markski and his crew were getting opportunities to perform at local events even as Frost had already released his first records in 1984. In the burgeoning scene, "we would pass the mic to each other at house parties a lot, so Kid Frost knew me. In fact, my brother used to rap together with Kid Frost." Mark's older brother, Kato, was closer in age to Frost and maintained communication with him, which helped to keep Markski on Frost's radar.

Markski and his crew continued to hone their craft, and their stock rose to the top. Along the way, Markski and some of the UWS members became affiliates of Frost. Markski would eventually pen the lyrics to "Straight to the Bank," one of Frost's songs on his landmark album, *Hispanic Causing Panic*, featuring the acclaimed single, "La Raza." Frost's momentum would come to provide additional opportunities for the UWS crew. The performance schedule for the group grew increasingly busy. As Markski outlines, he and his friends were, "doing lowrider shows, LA sports arena lowrider events, we're doing, you know, Juanito's birthday party. I mean, we were doing whatever! Because that's just how we were rolling with it, you know, and we had a lot of fun and interesting times." Essentially, the UWS crew became a source of entertainment throughout the San Gabriel Valley area of Los Angeles, with most of the opportunities to perform being presented within the Chicano community. These connections that were built with key figures in the emerging Hip Hop scene, and throughout the expansive LA region, allowed Markski and the UWS crew to function as Hip Hop evangelists of sorts, preaching and modeling to an audience of mostly Latines a particular Hip Hop aesthetic.

From the Ground Up

I bumped into Markski at an event called B-Boy Summit, in the summer of 2021, hosted at the Graff Lab in Los Angeles. As its name suggests, the event was a rendezvous of B-girls and B-boys, mostly from around the greater Los Angeles area but also including various out-of-state and international dancers. Attendees were treated to battles from dancers of different age levels, including children. Even among the youngest of contenders, the skill level did not disappoint. The event also featured representatives of the other elements, including emcees, DJs, and graffiti writers, some of whom performed live, and others who were primarily there to "build" (Alim 2008). Gremz was there as one of the organizers of the event. He had been one of the key figures in preserving B-girl/B-boy culture in Los Angeles through the 1990s, so it made sense to find him still curating the culture. That day, he rotated from area to area, overseeing the battles, directing participants, and hyping up the crowd. Gremz worked to put on the event with Asia One, a B-girl, educator, and organizer with roots in Denver Colorado who founded B-Boy Summit in 1994 and was also a key cultural curator in the scene. I observed as older generations of B-boys and B-girls convened in clusters with those from younger generations, sometimes solemnly dropping knowledge, sometimes sharing in laughs.

I found Markski getting busy at a section of the Graff Lab complex designated for live graffiti painting. It was nearly forty years after he arrived in Los Angeles, and his graffiti skills had continued to expand. He was in deep concentration as he painted, but he happily stepped away from his work to greet my daughter Kalea and me. The piece he painted consisted of his name, "MARK," in expansive twisting letters of red and blue, with interlocking shadows and outlines in green and black. These were done in "wildstyle" format. In red letters, below the primary name, in a much smaller script, he wrote "ski," completing his name as Markski. Hidden within and around the focal letters were various initials denoting crews that Markski had associated with: UTI, UWS, MSK, KDM, BLT (Image 4.2). These initials, as cryptic as they might appear to the uninitiated, revealed Markski's history of working with others. The name of the piece was "Bronx Transplant Revenge, Number 36." Ironically, the notion of revenge seemed far removed from this act in which Markski was sharing his gift with others.

I learned that Markski was taking his pedagogical energies in a different direction: He was working on a book about graffiti writing. Unlike many graffiti books focused on documenting the art through photographs, this book, which Markski had largely completed and was now revising, would be a weighty tome on the definition and philosophy of graffiti writing.[1] Markski was eager to publish the

---

[1] I later learned that the title of the book would be *Graffthetics* (Santiago 2023).

Image 4.2 Original piece by Markski, 2021. (Reproduced courtesy of Mark Santiago)

book and get it into the hands of others. He also still wrote rhymes and on occasion recorded songs. He was still creating art. Through his art, he was building with others. He had found many like-minded comrades on the West Coast, and had a respect for the movement in California that differed from his earlier takes when he first landed in the Golden State. I especially noticed his availability in sharing his knowledge with others. The movement which he once considered to be a local Bronx phenomenon had now gone worldwide, and quietly, Markski had been on the cusp of that move. The once-reluctant teacher had now been teaching and collaborating with others for decades. It was through these cyphers of creativity, these cultural building blocks (Alim 2008), that knowledge was transmitted, and the movement was ingrafted onto Brown Los Angeles.

5
Game Recognize Game

Starting my freshman year of college, I wondered how I would fare at an institution where many students were from conservative upper-middle-class suburban households. I grew up in a working-class home minutes from the college, Biola University, but my high school alma mater seemed worlds away. Buena Park High, in 1990, went from a white majority school to being minority-majority.[1] The year after the Los Angeles uprisings, my freshman year, 1992–1993, demographic shifts accelerated. Many Black, brown, and Asian American families relocating away from Los Angeles landed in my high school zone just outside the Los Angeles County line. I loved my high school experience, enjoying wonderful teachers and friendships that expanded my understandings of the world. Yet, amid the social dislocations of the day, some students began seeking recognition by claiming sets and neighborhoods from throughout the region and across racial groups. During my junior year, racial tensions escalated. On various occasions I was caught between cross-racial clashes. My senior year football squad made the news after a game in which a "10-minute brawl" between fans and players of both teams broke out (Jones 1995). That year I chose to attend Biola University, a Christian college, planning to study psychology and Christian theology and hoping to speak to the social realities I experienced. Moving into this new world, I held tightly to two things: A faith grounded in my lived experience, and Hip Hop. Would I encounter other like-minded souls? Would my experiences be legible to my peers? I wondered.

The day I moved into my dorm, I discovered that I was already familiar with my new next-door neighbors. These floormates, Akida and Ray, were emcees. Two years prior, I had purchased a compilation album that happened to contain a song of theirs—a song that I had played out on my cassette deck. We soon conversed about emceeing and beat-making, a welcomed surprise. Game recognize game. I quickly learned that I would succeed at college as I learned to recognize and be recognized. Mutual recognition was an experience of finding peers to build with, in essence, "collaborating, challenging, and theorizing," as described by Samy Alim (2008:vii). That semester we performed our original Hip Hop music at a university coffee shop. Hip Hop heads came out of the

---

[1] The percentage of white students at the high school was 4.4% in 2022: https://www.schooldigger.com/go/CA/schools/1476001809/school.aspx.

In the Time of Sky-Rhyming. Jonathan E. Calvillo, Oxford University Press. © Oxford University Press 2024.
DOI: 10.1093/oso/9780197762479.003.0006

woodworks, both as spectators and performers. By my junior year, a group of us established an annual Hip Hop concert that became a staple of university life. With the help of a friend, Liza Gesuden, and some creative input from another friend, Carlos Aguilar, the event was called "Sola Soul," and was institutionalized into the university calendar. Maintaining a decidedly underground vibe, local acts like Propaganda, the Procussions, Click the Supah Latin, 4th Avenue Jones, I.D.O.L. King, and LA Symphony graced our stage. The annual event persisted for two decades.

The mutual recognition continued. Through these events I met Gio Stewart, a Los Angeles emcee who grew up in the shadow of underground sacred spaces—The Good Life Cafe and Project Blowed. A graduate of Fairfax High on famed Melrose Ave, across from where Hex's Hip Hop Shop was located, Gio knew his way around a good slice of the Los Angeles underground scene. We recognized we could build and collaborate on music together. Performing at a college Hip Hop night, Gio and I were introduced to Jason Mytar, a DJ from the San Fernando Valley. Again, we recognized the potential to build. Together, the three of us formed the first iteration of a crew called Homestyle, consisting of a Black American emcee, a brown Mexican American emcee, and a white DJ. For a couple of years, I marauded through Los Angeles generating resonance with this expanding crew.

In the campus scene that my peers and I helped form, mutual recognition meant finding our people. An experience of conscious creative resonance, in mutual recognition two or more individuals recognize each other as potential collaborators within a shared creative field. This recognition often involves shared or comparable social locations, investment in shared struggles, and desire to build a new world together. Experiences of extended mutual recognition led to the formation of cyphers of resonance, where participants saw themselves as belonging to a movement or subculture through creative participation. Historically, this led to the formation of many of the earliest Hip Hop crews, which Tricia Rose (1994:34) characterizes as "alternative families." Recognition provided grounds for "mutual engagement" through "shared repertoires" in the nascent scene (Harrison 2015b:156). Moreover, such interactions allowed for the development of microscenes (Harkness 2013), where members engaged in a set of creative activities with established conventions (Ewoodzie 2017). As Harkness (2013:157) notes, "local music scenes can produce specific sites, populated by certain scene members, where collective ideologies, attitudes, preferences, practices, customs, and memories took place." As I found, instances of mutual recognition were important toward harnessing creative resources and strengthening norms of creativity in the early scene.

At a time when the boundaries of Hip Hop were still blurry, and more spectators were passing through the scene, creatives were recognizing who their collaborators were. In this chapter I examine the rise of Club Radio. Club Radio was a site that drew a variety of participants from distinct subcultures, but helped define what West Coast Hip Hop would be; it was a site of mutual recognition. Various crews emerged from this gathering point, and many norms and conventions were established for subsequent West Coast cohorts. For many creatives, mutual recognition often meant crossing boundaries of difference, such as racial boundaries; yet it was this act of crossing boundaries that often led to key developments in the scene. In this chapter, I draw on the accounts of Radio Club participants, especially a graffiti writer known as Crase, to examine how creatives' experiences of resonance and recognition fueled the scene's emergence.

Recognizing the Context

For about two years, Byron "Crase" Marquez dedicated himself to perfecting his craft of graffiti writing. Born in Guatemala to Guatemalan and Honduran parents, Crase was a child when he and his family migrated to New York City. He reached his teenage years in the Bronx just as Hip Hop was moving onto the world stage. Crase's parents were concerned that their teenage son's dedication to graffiti would burden his future prospects with a criminal record—or worse— make him a casualty of street violence. The solution they arrived at was to ship Crase away to Los Angeles, where some close family friends were willing to take him in. In 1983, graffiti was largely thought of as a New York City phenomenon; sending Crase clear across to the opposite coast would shield him from the deleterious street culture he had immersed himself in, his parents reasoned. No one, including Crase, could imagine that in sending him to live in Los Angeles, he would have a hand in expanding the visibility of Hip Hop through his gift of graffiti writing. This young Central American kid from the Bronx became a dispenser of Hip Hop cultural capital, which helped adapt Hip Hop visual aesthetics to a West Coast context. In Los Angeles, he became a participant in a scene, The Radio Club, where a unique cluster of artists and creatives would recognize the potential in each other. There, local creatives had a chance to meld their own performativities with East Coast cultural repertoires.

Arriving in Los Angeles in 1983, Crase had an experience that paralleled that of Markski, described in Chapter 4, in which the Los Angeles area felt like alien territory. The difference in racial dynamics between his neighborhood in New York City and his new neighborhood in Los Angeles stood out to him. In particular, Crase was unaccustomed to how in his new neighborhood, Black Americans and Latinos generally did not belong to the same social circles. The family that welcomed Crase to California lived in the Los Angeles neighborhood of Hollywood, and fifteen-year-old Crase was enrolled at Hollywood High School. At his new school, he noticed racial divisions in the types of aesthetics embodied by Black Americans and Latinos. His fashion drew the attention of other young people, given that most Latinos did not dress as he did. He noticed that a number of Chicano young men at his high school, for example, traditionally wore khaki pants and flannel shirts. His African American classmates, Crase noticed, did not wear this type of clothing.

While mutual recognition could be a life-giving experience for young creatives like Crase, misrecognition was dangerous. At one point, Crase was questioned by a Chicano gang member who lived in the apartment building where Crase was staying. "Where you from?" the gangster asked him. Crase explained that he was from New York City. "Are you Puerto Rican?" the gangster pressed further. "No, I'm Guatemalan," Crase clarified. The gang member wanted to know why Crase dressed in a way more aligned with Black Americans and insisted Crase not to dress that way. Crase retorted, "What are you going to do about it?" The gangster stepped away, but Crase realized he would have to watch his back. As he also learned from his Black friends at school, the colors he wore in public mattered in Los Angeles. Unknowingly, he sometimes wore red in Crip neighborhoods, and blue in Blood neighborhoods.

Crase's new urban location situated him strategically in relation to Los Angeles's major thoroughfares, allowing him to quickly familiarize himself with the central corridors of the city and observe the broader social dynamics therein. As he recalls, "I used to live on Normandy, right off of Melrose." He also remembers that "the buses were clean. No one was writing on them," which he saw as a major contrast to the graffiti-laden trains of New York. As a graffiti writer, Crase especially noticed the difference in graffiti styles. As he recounts, "Chicano graff was different from New York City graff. You know, it was a big difference. And I noticed it was more like gangbang writing, you know, the Old English lettering compared to New York style, it was more funky, while more colorful. So, you see that a lot. But it was funny because you still didn't see mix [of different races]. It was like there was no mix between either race. It was 'you do yours, I do mine.'" The Chicano graffiti that Crase saw represented a type of social boundary expressed through visual aesthetics—a distinction between Blacks and Chicanos.

Mutual Recognition of Hip Hop Creatives

Crase's new location in Los Angeles eventually placed him in contact with others that were familiar with New York City Hip Hop culture. Through instances of mutual recognition, these new acquaintances attempted to draw out Crase's giftedness as an artist. Crase retells a chance encounter that took place at a Los Angeles liquor store a few weeks after his arrival in California, wherein he was introduced to other young people immersed in Hip Hop culture:

> It was about 7 o'clock at night, and I was hungry and wanted to go get something to eat. I told my dad's friend, the people I used to stay with, "can I go get some sodas?" He told me "just make sure that you don't jaywalk," because the first week, I did it in front of a cop! I didn't know you couldn't jaywalk. That was the joke. So I went into the store and I'm getting my stuff. And I had a pair of red suede Pumas with the fat laces. And Suga Pop came in there with Oz Rock, some other guys and his brother, they used to call him Elf. And they walked in and they're checking me out. I'm looking at him, and I'm like, "What's up with you?" he goes "Yo, where you from?" I go, "I'm from New York." He says "Where?" I say, "Bronx."
>
> I noticed he had something on his jacket, on his windbreaker. He took it out and I was like "What'cha doing with those Zulu beads?" He had Zulu beads from Zulu Nation. He said "I'm down with Rocksteady," and I was like, "Word?" We started talking and I told him how I just moved and you know, write graffiti. He's like, "yeah, you bomb?" I was like, "yeah." He said, "Yo, man, you gotta go to this club man. It's called the Radio and it's, you know, It's Hip Hop. You know, we have pretty much everything breaking." He goes, "just like the Roxy's or 1018."

Crase's encounter turned out to be with renowned B-boys Suga Pop, Oz Rock, and their friends; their invitation to a club called The Radio proved to be an important opportunity for Crase. The mutual recognition that took place was an important catalyst in allowing the encounter to produce meaningful exchange. It was a game-recognize-game moment. In particular, the outward appearance of the young men encountering each other in this instance helped to facilitate their awareness of Hip Hop cultural capital. Crase was immediately struck by the fashion aesthetic that these young men represented, as it reminded him of what he was used to in the Bronx. Apparently, they too noticed that his fashion sense reflected New York City sensibilities. What piqued Crase's interest was his recognition of the beads that Suga Pop was wearing. Zulu beads were black beads worn on a necklace typically with a medallion bearing the Universal Zulu Nation insignia. The Universal Zulu Nation, founded by Afrika Bambaataa, originated in the Bronx, where Crase was from, and the sight of the Zulu beads immediately transported Crase back to his home neighborhood in the Bronx. His focus was fixated on the beads.

Suga Pop and Oz Rock, Crase discovered, played critical roles in disseminating B-boy knowledge in Los Angeles in part because of the connections they had to

New York City. Both of them functioned as translocal brokers in the Los Angeles scene and in disparate locales globally. Suga Pop grew up in a Samoan household in New Zealand. He followed a migratory stream that initially touched down on locales familiar to Pasifika peoples (Henderson 2006). Moving from New Zealand to Hawaii, Suga Pop excelled at dancing. In his teens he moved to Los Angeles, where he interacted with the Samoan community in the Harbor area. There, he advanced in the regional street dance styles popular among Samoans, namely popping and locking. According to Henderson (2006), who documents the place of Pasifika people in street dance and Hip Hop, he also expanded his dance knowledge under the tutelage of members of the famed Electric Boogaloos. Soon, his dance skills would take him beyond the usual Pasifika migratory routes. Pursuing his interests in dance, Suga Pop headed to New York City. In New York, he allied himself with the Rock Steady Crew, and quickly advanced in his breaking skills. Along the way, he passed on some of his popping knowledge to locals. As Henderson (2006) notes, New Yorkers had been exposed to the Electric Boogaloos via the television show *Soul Train*, and had adapted their own version of the dance style, which they dubbed electric boogie. Suga Pop, having learned from dancers at the core of popping dance styles, participated in a dance exchange, sharing with New York locals his knowledge, and gaining knowledge from them. When Suga Pop returned to Los Angeles, as mentioned in Crase's retelling of his encounter, Suga Pop was already affiliated with Rock Steady and had likewise gained ties to the Universal Zulu Nation.

Oz Rock, too, was a key translocal broker in the dissemination of Hip Hop culture. Adolfo "Oz Rock" Alvarez, of Cuban American background, grew up in Providence, Rhode Island. From Providence, Oz would travel into New York City to visit family. While spending time in New York, Oz saw breaking for the first time (Ming and Corbeil 1991). Having a knack for dancing, he soon joined a B-boy crew called the Dynamic Rockers. As his skills expanded, and ever ambitious, he transitioned into Rock Steady, the premier breaking crew in New York City at the time. Oz perfected his craft in New York City, and initially kept his skills within the Northeast region of the United States. When some of his Rocksteady crewmates were featured in the film *Flashdance*, Oz got an inkling that his dance skills might be a ticket to more. He auditioned for a sponsorship by the Nike corporation that would allow him to tour the country and showcase his dance skills. He was selected by Nike after his impressive audition. Under Nike's sponsorship, Oz toured around the United States performing his breaking skills, and eventually arriving in Los Angeles to perform. Once in Los Angeles, Oz decided to try his hand at bringing his talents to the Hollywood screen. He informed the dance crew he was touring with that he had decided to remain in Los Angeles. Oz's vision to participate in Hollywood productions paid off, earning him spots on television commercials; a made-for-television movie, *The Pilot*; the television show *St. Elsewhere*; and the film *Body Rock*. Yet, Oz's influence went beyond New York, Los Angeles, and Providence, Rhode Island. He was also a key figure in the breaking scene in Miami, Florida, helping to form a link between the three primary sites of initial Hip Hop dissemination for Latines—New York, Miami, and Los Angeles. Later, his status as a B-boy superstar would take him to the Philippines to promote the movie *Body Rock*.

Important doors would open for Crase through his introduction to these key figures of Hip Hop and through his invitation to the Radio Club. The mysterious Radio Club sounded interesting to Crase, but he was still unsure whether he wanted to venture out into the city given the racial politics he had observed. Crase was encouraged to visit the Radio Club again, through an experience of mutual recognition at his high school. Word got around that Crase, as do many graffiti writers, carried a black book where he produced graffiti writings and shared them with others. OG Chino, for example, was enrolled at the same high school and was inspired after seeing Crase's graffiti black book. Soon after his encounter at the liquor store, Crase got to know Trevor, a new friend at school who also saw the black book. Through Trevor's crew, Crase was introduced to Aaron Ferguson, who went by the name Graff1. Graff1 was one of Los Angeles's first homegrown graffiti writers. He participated in an exchange with another graffiti legend, Shandu, at a famed graffiti spot, the Belmont Tunnel. This instance of cocreation, Crase explains, was mythologized as one of LA's first graffiti battles. Crase and Graff saw each other's work and mutually recognized each other's talents. Crase told his new friends about meeting Suga Pop and Oz Rock. These connections further energized the sense of mutual recognition. Soon, Crase found himself being picked up by his new friends and heading over to the MacArthur Park neighborhood of Los Angeles where the Radio Club was located.

A Space for Mutual Recognition

"The Radio," alternately referred to as "Club Radio," or "The Radio Club," was a critical site for Hip Hop's development in Los Angeles; it became a site of mutual recognition for local and translocal creatives. The founding of The Radio, in most publications, has been associated with Alex Jordanov; people who visited the Radio remember Jordanov's prominent presence at the club. Known as Super AJ, or sometimes just AJ, Jordanov is an avant garde artist, DJ, and journalist of ethnic Russian origin who relocated to the United States from Paris, France, in the 1980s, at nineteen years of age (Le Flambeur 2019). Jordanov arrived in the United States to try his hand as a music writer, and soon after enrolled at UCLA. Through a friend named Bernard Zekri, who arrived in Los Angeles to do work for Jean Karakos, owner of Celluloid Records, AJ was introduced to the Hip Hop scene in New York City. Zekri took AJ to New York just as Hip Hop was showing up at clubs like the Roxy, and AJ witnessed Hip Hop's expansion there (Le Flambeur 2019). Celluloid Records, it turns out, worked with the likes of Afrika Bambaataa, Grandmixer DST, and Fab 5 Freddy on some of their earliest projects. Inspired by what he saw, AJ envisioned how this scene might be transplanted to the Los Angeles context. This vision would birth the Radio.

Jordanov had several friends whom he partnered with to found the Radio, including Myriam Sorigue, KK Barrett, and Trudy Arguelles. The group of associates had experienced Hip Hop in New York City and recognized the creative potential in the arts movement. They established a site of underground creativity that drew local creatives and provided a platform for New York–based artists. Trudy Arguelles, whose surname harkens to her father's Spanish roots, remembers when her then-boyfriend, KK Barrett, shared his excitement with her over a genre of music that he had newly been introduced to, called Hip Hop. "It's going to be bigger than punk!" Arguelles recalls KK telling her. Comparing Hip Hop to punk was no small matter for KK and Trudie. The two creatives were among the leaders of the punk scene in Los Angeles, in the 1970s (Armendariz 2015). They understood what it was to be part of an underground subculture and saw the potential for Hip Hop to rally a following as an underground scene.

In an interview for the Dublab podcast (2020), KK and Trudie describe the beginnings of the club:

KK: In 1983, I was looking for a different kind of music. And me and Alex Jordanov, my partner, and Trudie, and Alex's girlfriend Myriam, started a club called Radio, which was a Hip Hop underground club. After hours from 2am to 6am on Friday nights.

Trudie: It was a great club, where it became very popular. It was only open on Friday, and one of the reasons it was so popular was, we were determined to let all ages in, because a lot of the greatest performers coming up were young kids. And as part of the agreement with the landlord was that after every show after every evening we had to completely clean the place, including outside and inside sweeping and mopping, and everybody would chip in to help us, because it would take quite a while.

As Arguelles notes further in email correspondence with me:

Hip hop was new and fresh. I had been to a new club called the Roxy in New York which was like a roller-skate disco club where Africa Bambaataa was DJing and that was maybe my introduction to hip-hop. When we met Alex Jordanov in LA, he knew about the performers from his friend who owned a hip-hop record company who was French like Alex and Miriam. Through this connection Alex was the one that secured the bands to perform at Radio. Often they stayed over at Alex's apt on Santa Monica Blvd as well.

Arguelles adds that some of the groups even stayed with her and KK. She and KK had grown accustomed to this type of arrangement when they helped spearhead the LA punk rock scene. Just a few years earlier, performers from the punk scene making their way through the Los Angeles circuit would often show up at their doorstep unannounced, knowing they could have a place to stay there. Many of these early punk rockers were New Yorkers, thus Trudie and KK were used to this East to West exchange.

Given their understanding of how subcultures functioned, in light of their experience in cementing the LA punk rock scene, KK and Trudie, along with their associates, recognized that the most appropriate space to build a Hip Hop following in Los Angeles would be an underground club. Along these lines, as Trudie notes, when she had been to the Roxy in New York City, she had observed how much of the creativity came from the younger constituents. If this underground club was to capture the true spirit of the movement, it would have to allow for younger people—younger teens—to attend. In order to open the door for teens, the club would have to eschew serving alcohol, which the founders elected to do.

The Radio opened its doors in the MacArthur Park neighborhood of Los Angeles, an area centrally located in the city's urban corridor. The neighborhood was fast becoming a hub for Central American immigrants and refugees, and as such was dubbed "little Central America." The club was located in a refashioned theater with a front stage where most of the chairs had been removed in order to create an expanded dance floor for club-goers. The founders initially energized the club scene by hosting artists from New York City (Viator 2020). In particular, they took advantage of ties they had to Hip Hop artists in New York, and were able to draw to their Los Angeles stage the likes of Run DMC, Grandmixer DST (Hess 2009), and the Cold Crush Brothers, among others. It made sense that creatives such as Suga Pop and Oz Rock, who had spent time in New York, and had honed their talents there, would be drawn to a club like the Radio.

Jordanov and KK also recognized the potential of providing a platform for local artists who were embracing Hip Hop culture. The two of them would visit record stores in various parts of Los Angeles to scope out the records that were gaining an audience locally. They were especially vigilant in scouting for local talent that approximated what they had seen in New York City. As KK shared with the *LA Times* (Spurrier 1983), "When we go into black neighborhoods and record stores where we're finding a lot of our rappers, the kids we talk to are thrilled by this." The formula that brought people to the Radio, KK explained further to *LA Times*, was "new talent and new records."

At VIP Records, in South Central Los Angeles, they came across a record titled "Coldest Rap/ Cold Wind Madness," by a young artist named Ice-T. Jordanov and KK were immediately impressed by Ice-T's skills on what turned out to be his first record. Soon after hearing his record, AJ and KK called Ice-T and invited him to perform at the Radio. After Ice-T's performance, they invited him to stay as the house emcee, or as Ice-T describes it, as the stage manager (Yang 2020). The club managers would pay Ice-T $30 a night, and Ice-T became a fixture of the club (Dublab 2020). As Jordanov explains in an interview with Vice (Belhoste 2015), "Ice-T established himself as MC, he animated the evenings."

According to house DJ, Chris "the Glove" Taylor, in an interview with Michael Khalfani (2017a), the Radio received a large influx of visitors when it made the front page of the *LA Times* Calendar section, in August of 1983. The *LA Times* feature of the Radio begins with the following statement:

> Clubgoers who haven't had enough by 2 a.m. can head down to the Radio (2400 West 7th St. 463-2209), a six-moth-old dance club run by Alex Jordanov and KK, a former member of the influential L.A. punk band the Screamers.
>
> These days KK's tastes run more to funk than punk and the Radio has become a magnet for late-night fans of rap, scratching and break-dancing. Many of the records played at the Radio come from obscure New York independent labels.

The scene began to expand, not only in that more local artists were participating in the scene but also in terms of the various styles and aesthetics represented by the creatives who set foot in the club. New wave music was hitting the airwaves and was being mixed with early Hip Hop, accompanied by a punk aesthetic in some cases. Artists such as Malcom McLaren, Adam Ant (Yang 2020), Michael Jackson, Chaka Khan, Prince (Jordanov 2017), David Lee Roth, and Bono (Le Flambeur 2019) came to the club. Matt Groening of *The Simpsons* fame, became friends with Jordanov and visited the club (Le Flambeur 2019). Anthony Kiedis of the Red Hot Chili Peppers worked the entrance (Le Flambeur 2019). Roger "Orko" Romero, who frequented the Radio, was especially struck by how integrated the crowd was, in contrast to the type of segregation he observed in the surrounding areas of Los Angeles: "Coming from LA, where it is segregated, then you go into a room and it's all kinds of people! There were punk rockers, rock-a-billies, whites, cholos, Asians, little kids! And it felt like everyone was an artist."

One particular account has achieved mythical status among aficionados of the early scene—Madonna's live performance at the Radio (Kelly 2004). According to Trudie, Madonna's first performance in Los Angeles was at the Radio. The DJs at the Radio played her records, even though they were rarely played at local radio stations, if at all. Trudie explains that, "Madonna was just there to come and hang out and have fun, and people probably didn't even know who she was there, but they all knew her song. But I kind of pushed her, I goaded her on stage and said, 'Oh, you got to sing with Ice-T and that was a fun night'" (Dublab 2020). Ice-T remembers sharing the stage with Madonna in more problematic fashion. According to Ice-T, during a conversation with podcast host Ben Yang (2020), known as Ben Baller, "During her show she was touching me and singing and I had a girlfriend who got really pissed that this white girl was touching me on my chest!"

Developing the Elements of Expression

One of the reasons the Radio Club was pivotal in the development of the West Coast scene is because of the way it provided a platform for the various Hip Hop elements to be recognized by a broad array of creatives, and to solidify their performative conventions. According to Radio Club participant Aaron "Graff1" Ferguson, in an interview for *LA Taco*, "People came from San Diego, San Bernardino from all over" (Fujita 2013). DJs, for starters, played a critical role in setting the tone for the scene. Based on Roger "Orko" Romero's recollection, the club initially lacked variety in DJs. The club expanded when the managers recruited DJs. Among the DJs that spun at the Radio were such names as Chris "the Glove" Taylor, Afrika Islam, Egyptian Lover, Chevy Shank, Booker T, and Suave, the latter three being part of the Shake City Rockers. The Glove and Egyptian Lover were West Coast–based. Afrika Islam and the Shake City Rocker DJs came from New York and settled in Los Angeles. Hen Gee and Evil E were also in rotation. Attendees such as Robert "Ace Rock" Aceves recall the way the DJs spun various types of music, including funk, rap, and New Wave.

Chris "the Glove" Taylor, in an interview with DJ Tony Alvarez (2020a), describes the scenario in the following manner:

> At Radio, the only people who ever DJed there, other than a celebrity DJ, was Shake City Rockers, which is—shout out to Booker T, and Chevy Shank, and Suave, all them cats—they were like the bane of my ass at that place Bro. they always wanted to DJ but it was like "Bro, I'm here I come in at 11:00 and that's it. Y'all can DJ before then or after I leave at 5:00 but I'm rocking this muthafucka." So whenever I'd go to the bathroom or something they'd slide in. But then it was me, Shake city, they were the openers, and then Egyptian Lover.

The Glove goes on to note that he and Egyptian Lover were the only DJs originating in the West Coast who had advanced DJ skills in that scene. Nevertheless, they were mixing in the line-up with other DJs originally from New York City. While the Glove's description denotes a sense of friendly competition, he also suggests a degree of mutual respect that existed across this bicoastal representation of DJs.

One of the DJs, DJ Chevy Shank, was among the orchestrators who brought together a group of young creatives who became one of the first West Coast B-boy crews—Shake City Rockers. Shake City Rockers, or SCR, played an important role in the dissemination of Hip Hop culture in Los Angeles as the crew was committed to performing the elements of Hip Hop with excellence, and they drew significantly from homegrown talent. As Crase's talent was recognized, he became an affiliate of SCR. According to Crase, Ice-T maintained an association with SCR (see McKenna 1984). Crase joined SCR upon frequenting the Radio, and there found a sense of belonging. SCR included members that were Black American and Latino, though the group was largely initiated by Black American members. Other Latino members, alongside Crase, included Ricky Rick, of Argentine origin; Jimmy Jam, of Chicano background; and Roger "Orko" Romero, of Nicaraguan origin.

Among these Latino SCR members, Orko is arguably one of the most recognized names, particularly in light of his activity and contributions in the B-boy world. Orko was known for unique variations of the head spin move on the floor. He was especially celebrated for his power moves and would go on to gain fame in New York City in the B-boy community there. He and acclaimed B-girl, Honey Rockwell, from the Bronx, would meet and marry, continuing on a legacy of breakin through providing instruction to others. Crase became an important connection between this crew of B-boys that formed on the West Coast and the Hip Hop communities of New York City. Crase helped organize a visit of these young men to New York City, and was able to introduce these West Coasters to the East Coast scene.

Another crew that arose at the Radio was known as the Radio Crew. The Radio Crew was a group of performers who frequented the club and periodically performed at other venues. The most decorated member of the Radio Crew today is Ice-T. Other members included The Glove, Egyptian Lover, Greg Broussard, and Alex "Super AJ" Jordanov (last.fm n.d.). A record released by Rayco Music and Rainbow TV Music titled *Breaking and Entering* (The Radio Crew 1983), containing songs from the film *Breakin' 'N' Enterin'*, is attributed to the Radio Crew and lists several crew members as contributors, even naming several songs after the likes of The Glove, Super AJ, and Egyptian Lover. Some dancers, such as Ace Rock, were affiliated with the Radio Crew as well. Ace Rock collaborated at the Radio with another dancer who rose to fame, Gerardo Mejia. Gerardo, known for his 1990 hit single "Rico Suave," was a respected underground street dancer before becoming a popstar. Signaling his street dance connections, he appeared with another lauded street dancer, Greg "Coco" De la Luz, on the 1988 film *Colors*. According to The Glove (Taylor 2018), the Radio Crew was formed for the documentary *Breakin' 'N' Enterin'*, produced by Topper Carew (1983), as a way to spotlight the distinct artists who were spearheading the West Coast scene (Viator 2019). The interjection of mass media into the scene precipitated the way collaborative formations began to take shape. The Radio Crew tended to consist of members older than those from SCR.

Public Recognition

The Radio Club caught the attention of documentary filmmaker Topper Carew, who was attempting to capture Hip Hop culture outside of New York City. The Radio was chosen by Carew as the site of a documentary called *Breakin' 'N' Enterin'*, a film attempting to document the establishment of Hip Hop in Los Angeles. The tour guide for the film was Ice-T, who by now was gaining a substantial amount of public visibility. The film featured a number of up-and-coming starlets, and a handful of seasoned performers who would contribute to the West Coast scene. Dancers such as Boogaloo Shrimp, Shabadoo, Pop N Taco, Ana "Lollipop" Sanchez, The Blue City Crew, Suga Pop, and others, made appearances throughout the documentary. While the film featured disparate locations around Los Angeles, the Radio Club was a key locus of activity in the film, not only for filming purposes but also as a point of connection for many of the artists in the film.

The public profile that was achieved by Club Radio, after its feature in *Breakin' 'N' Enterin'*, prompted further media attention. Cannon Films decided to produce a movie primarily centered on activities at the club in 1984. The film *Breakin'*, directed by Joel Silberg, was among a cluster of films that aimed to be the first Hip Hop blockbuster made for the big screen. The film was especially competing with Harry Belafonte's *Beat Street*, set in a Bronx backdrop. The *Breakin'* film crew rushed through the process and the film met its production timeline, beating *Beat Street* to the big screen. Months after the film's release, a second installation of the film franchise was already in production, *Breakin' 2, Electric Boogaloo*. The films featured a significant number of artists, particularly dancers, who were active participants at the Radio Club, many of whom appeared in the earlier documentary.

The three films associated with the Radio Club location, the documentary and the two feature films, played an important role in disseminating Hip Hop culture into the West Coast. At points, the film misses the mark in representing the West Coast scene. Timothy "Popin' Pete" Solomon, of Electric Boogaloos fame, discussed in a podcast interview, for example, how some of the writing in the film script misrepresented the way young, urban Angelenos spoke at the time (Silver 2020). Indeed, the use of the term "breakin'" in these West Coast films is misleading. Breaking as a dance form is generally not well represented within these films, save for a couple experienced dancers who perform the style with skill. The street dancers in the film were more familiar with, and better representatives of, West Coast associated dance styles such as popping, robotin, locking, and whacking. Nevertheless, the films did promote a particular vision about how Hip Hop culture had a place in the West. Furthermore, by combining these West Coast styles with breaking, a thoroughly Hip Hop element, the films helped to move along a process wherein West Coast forms of performativity would be subsumed under the larger umbrella of Hip Hop. By gaining a stamp of approval from major media outlets, it also precipitated a sense of mutual recognition across bicoastal stylings of dance aesthetics.

The diversity of the people featured in the film also provided a particular take on Hip Hop in Los Angeles. The film intimated that LA Hip Hop was a multicultural movement, a space that was welcoming to all (Viator 2019). Alongside Black American and white artists, Latines were prominently featured among the artists, especially dancers. Dancers such as Pop N' Taco, Vidal "Lil Coco" Rodriguez, Ana "Lollipop" Sanchez, Hugo Huizar, Robert "Ace Rock" Aceves, Viktor Manoel, and Adolfo "Shabadoo" Quiñones (Johnson 2016), were all of Latine heritage. Furthermore, the members of the Blue City Crew were of Samoan heritage, based in Los Angeles's Harbor area, and had ties to Suga Pop (Henderson 2006). To some extent, when it came to diversity, these films did reflect actual artists in the West Coast scene, with a few exceptions. The Radio, as it turned out, was one of the spaces within which these artists were interacting and recognizing each other's talents. In this case, Hollywood was drawing from the scene itself, and was likewise projecting that image onto the world stage. To Crase, the colorlines in Los Angeles were salient. At the Radio, however, and through Hip Hop, these lines were less prominent. According to these films, Hip Hop offered a possibility for a diverse set of people to create together. Even when Hip Hop was presented as something fueled by competition, the groups competing against each other were often interracial; the colorline was not the primary division in these films.

The making of these various films generated another byproduct: Creatives now had additional incentive for perfecting their craft, considering that they might be featured in some type of film or TV spot to be consumed by the masses. Dancers, in particular, found opportunities to be featured in film and television. Michael Jackson, for example, featured various Radio Club dancers in his videos. Captain EO, a key attraction at Disneyland, featured a video with Popin Pete,

Pop N Taco, Skeeter Rabbit, Hugo "Mr. Smooth" Huizar, Donald Devoux, and Jazzy J Boog Soulfire. Likewise, the time and energies it took to produce these films made an additional contribution: Artists were spending time with each other perfecting their crafts and standardizing their skills. Indeed, video footage from a 1983 episode of ABC's *Eye on LA* (Shake City Bboys 2023), featuring dancers auditioning for the film *Breakin'*, emphasized that now B-boys and B-girls from a wide array of backgrounds could make a career of their skills. One Black American dancer in line to audition stated, "It's not a stereotype dance that Blacks and Mexicans can only do it. No, anyone can do it." These experiences of professionalization were solidifying standards for these young urban artists in reciprocal ways. They were learning from each other and establishing norms in the field; they were being socialized to perform for an audience beyond their peers in the cypher. As Lakewood (2022:55) notes, for performers, these instances "heightened the experience of spectatorship and extended parameters of the visual field beyond their immediate circle."

The Reach of the Radio

In her historical presentation of the rise of gangsta rap in Los Angeles, Viator (2020) argues that the Radio Club presented an inauthentic glimpse into Los Angeles Hip Hop. The club manager, Alex Jordanov, as Viator notes, was a transplant who came from Europe to Los Angeles and worked to establish the Radio Club as a beachhead of New York City Hip Hop culture. Ice-T was an excellent partner in this endeavor, given that Ice-T himself had ties to the East Coast, and readily moved across coasts (Marrow and Century 2011). Various New York–based artists and cultural innovators came through the Radio Club, and some stayed for an extended period in Los Angeles. This was no minor detail, with the likes of the "Son of Bambaataa," Afrika Islam, making his presence felt in Los Angeles in collaboration with Ice-T. Viator argues that the true foundation of West Coast Hip Hop was not the transplanted facsimile of Bronx-style Hip Hop available at the Radio Club, but rather the local-born mobile DJ scene that drew thousands of predominantly Black young people, as best exemplified by Uncle Jamm's Army. The Radio Club, according to Viator, primarily put Black performers on display as a way to cater to well-heeled white audiences interested in an authentic urban experience.

While Viator makes a convincing case about the importance of the mobile DJ scene, the reach of the Radio Club was also significant. Questions about the authenticity of the Radio Club notwithstanding, the Radio Club was an important meeting site for many of the movers and shakers of the early West Coast scene. Ice-T's memoir, in conjunction with subjects' recollections, suggests Ice-T and

Afrika Islam's activities at the club were central to the larger vision of launching a West Coast chapter of the Universal Zulu Nation. While this vision did not take off, at least not in formal affiliation with the UZN, Ice-T did form a strong base of artists through the work he was doing at the club. Moreover, his Rhyme Syndicate network emerged in part from the connections he sustained at the club. And even as the club did often showcase East Coast artists, it also provided a space wherein local artists engaged with visiting artists.

Important synergy was generated through these creative encounters, predicated on a recognition of intelligibility across creative styles. That is, creatives recognized the potential in bringing distinct creative stylings together. As Robert "Ace Rock" Aceves describes, when discussing his season at the Radio Club, "I was there for the marriage between West Coast street dance and Hip Hop." Some of the best dancers who performed the locking and popping dance forms, two styles associated with Los Angeles, were present at the club (Chang 2005) and had the opportunity there to blend their homegrown styles of dance with the New York City styles being introduced to them. Likewise, DJs and emcees from both coasts were coming together. As the *LA Times* Calendar (Spurrier 1983) notes about the club, "both local and New York rappers and 'mixers' (who blend sounds by manipulating records on two turntables) drop by to lend their talents."

Furthermore, the club holds an important place for the development of Latine Hip Hop artists. Various Latine artists visited the Radio Club, and some performed there. Among these, one of the most prominent was Kid Frost. Frost, who became an associate of Ice-T, performed various times at the Radio Club. DJ Pebo Rodriguez, who DJed at various clubs throughout Los Angeles, remembers visiting the Radio Club after finishing one of his gigs in Hollywood. He specifically stopped by the Radio Club at 4 am to watch Frost perform. Pebo, along with his associate Dave Storrs, who also visited the club, went on to produce records for both Kid Frost and Ice-T in 1984, and worked with Chris "the Glove" Taylor in producing music. Pebo and Storrs founded ElectroBeat Records, one of the first labels to produce records for early LA Hip Hop artists.

Despite the fact that the mobile DJ scene drew a critical mass distinct from the Radio Club's constituency, many artists from these scenes did overlap. Chris "the Glove" Taylor, was an important bridge between mobile DJ crew Uncle Jamm's Army and the club. Indeed, Ice-T and Kid Frost at times performed with Uncle Jamm's Army as well. So, while the capacity of the Radio Club to capture Black Los Angeles's attention was truncated, its place as a site of performative innovation, creative networking, and local/regional organizing, is of utmost importance. Ice-T (Marrow and Century 2011) suggests that his involvement in the club is what ultimately opened the door for a greater number of Black creatives to frequent the club. According to Ace Rock Aceves, Ice-T's presence also brought in more of Brown Los Angeles: "I didn't go until Ice-T and the Glove started showing up so I wasn't there before whatever kind of punk rock and stuff AJ had going on there. I didn't see that. The only reason why people like us started going is because we heard a buzz on the streets that Ice-T and The Glove had a little spot where they were getting down at. That's how the whole thing started."

Many have visions of the club that involved multiethnic diversity. Club founder Trudie Arguelles-Barret remembers the club as a place that reflected the population of Los Angeles. In her words, "Radio was about 1/3 white, 1/3 black, and 1/3 Latino. Latinos were regulars. Also, we had Filipinos and Asians; basically, it looked like the residents of LA." Trudie's words coincide with the description provided by Chang (2005), which alludes to the participation of African Americans, Latinos, Koreans, Filipinos, and Samoans. Crase remembers that when he first started going to the club, it was mostly white and geared toward a punk rock crowd. He says he saw it shift and become more multiethnic. With the increased presence and visibility of Black DJs such as DJ Chevy Shank and Chris "The Glove" Taylor, "The crowd started to mix, Black, white, Samoans, and Chicanos. That was the unique part. I never saw any fights." It is important to note, then, that the space was evolving as distinct groups started to recognize the potential of the space, and extended welcome to each other there. The presence of Black creatives, then, not only appealed to whites but also helped draw in a more diverse crowd of brown and urban creatives.

Recognition through Visualized Memories

An important artifact of the *Breakin'* film franchise would later have an effect on the way the club is remembered. The directors of the film hoped to convey a Hip Hop feel by presenting New York style graffiti at various points in the movie. Local creatives in Los Angeles, in 1983, were taking notice of New York–style graffiti, with some beginning to develop their skills, but Hollywood was not yet tapped in to that local street scene. Ice-T knew about Crase's talents in graffiti because of Ice-T's connections to members of the Shake City Rockers. When Ice-T was asked to be in the film, he reached out to Crase to provide authentic graffiti art for the film's backdrop. Because of Ice-T's referral, Crase was given the opportunity to audition as a graffiti writer for the movie set. Crase remembers the selection process vividly (Marquez 2016):

> After school, I went to the audition. Once I arrived, Ice-T introduced me to the people. They asked if I could do a piece on an 8×10 plywood canvas.... I did and they liked it. A week later, I got the call that I got it. To be part of that movie was a big accomplishment.

Crase asked if he could bring a friend to help him in the project and recruited Aaron "Graff1" Ferguson to assist in the endeavor (Image 5.1). The two of them created several pieces for the film.

For a particular club scene in the film, the backdrop was to conspicuously display the name "Radio Club." Crase and Graff1 were commissioned by the directors to handle this expansive piece. Part way through completing his piece, the writers were told to halt their work. The word "Radio" was mostly complete, and "Club" had been outlined. The club managers prohibited the film directors from including the club's name in the film as the managers had not been paid for use of their club's name. The directors resolved the situation by asking the writers to alter the name of the club in the signage. As Crase recalls, he had been watching the movie *Tron* the night before, and the film sparked an idea. The writers altered the piece to read "Radio Tron," covering the outline of "Club" with "Tron." As Graff1 recalls in an interview with podcast host Ronek, "We were thinking, 'Okay we can't use the club, let's go into the future.' So the movie was in the future, so we put 'Radio Tron.'" Under pressure to produce, the young men dipped into their imaginations and transported the locale into the future.

The name Radiotron would be associated with both the film and the club for years to come. In the film, Radiotron became the name of the club where various scenes took place, especially dance scenes. The name, however, survived

Image 5.1 Crase, Kid Flare, and Graff1, during the making of *Breakin'*. (Reproduced courtesy of Byron Marquez)

on in the lore of the club and of another establishment that would meet at the same building. Radiotron would be the name given to the Youth Break Center, a community center that held meetings there during the week and provided creative space and activities for young people in the area. In the memories of many Angelenos, because of the film, the name Radiotron would be conflated with the Radio Club. The Radio Club and the eventual Radiotron, however, functioned as separate establishments.

Conclusion

The Radio Club ceased to operate in the building soon after the film was released. I received various stories explaining the closure of the Radio Club. Some attributed the end of operations to a rise in rent at the building. Jordanov indicates that the owner had wanted to expel them from the building for some time and that police consistently burdened club operations (Le Flambeur 2019). Others said that once the film was released, the owners desired for only the legend of the club to live on. Crase compares the fate of the Radio to the fate of the Roxy in New York in that once both clubs were featured in the films *Breakin'* and *Beat Street*, respectively, they lost their mystique and transitioned to a different format. Trudie and KK, in their interview with Dublab (2020) clarified that the club lived on for a period at another location, their warehouse. While there, the legality of the club was further brought into question, and the authorities shut it down. I return to questions about the club in the next chapter.

What remains true in my analysis of oral histories and in my review of existing accounts is that the Radio played a critical role in the establishment of the West Coast scene by providing a space for East Coast translocal cultural brokers to share their gifts and talents especially with local creatives in the city. This was ground zero for the convergence of groundbreaking creatives from these locales to meet, and numerous brown creatives were part of this encounter. There was a mutual recognition of the potentiality in building a West Coast scene. At the Radio, East met West, and people caught a vision for how Hip Hop could bring people of different backgrounds together. It was also a place where legends were able to establish themselves as key purveyors of the culture. The Radio, often conflated erroneously with Radiotron, lives on in the memories of some of the earliest Hip Hop heads of Los Angeles. It was a site of resonant activity where innovators experimented with what Hip Hop could be on the West Coast. Next, I turn to the emergence of Radiotron, which shaped a new wave of local talent and fostered an expansive homegrown Hip Hop culture among a younger cohort of creatives.

6
Radiotronic Waves

"I just wanna know if this is real," Gabriel stated in a hushed tone. Sporting a black, loose hoodie, glasses, and glancing side to side ever so slightly, Gabriel put a flier down on the table before me. "Is this really happening?" he continued, pointing to the flier. The flier advertised the inaugural gathering of Saint City Session, an open space of Hip Hop creativity in Santa Ana, California. Described as an "urban arts sanctuary," a team of local creatives formed Saint City Session in 2006 for Hip Hop heads to develop their creativity in a communal setting. I sat at a table welcoming guests the first night of the event when Gabriel arrived, clenching the flier he received at Santa Ana College. Gabriel was a graffiti writer, I learned. He was thoughtful, respectful, and carried himself in a vigilant manner, as if ready to bust a tag on a wall. Gabriel was our first arrival. As indicated in the flier, we had open walls for artists to paint on. We hosted the event inside and around the social hall of First Baptist Church of Santa Ana. Several dozen teens and young adults joined in that first evening looking for a place of their own.

In the two subsequent years that I volunteered with the Saint City Session team, I learned that our model resonated diachronically with the legacy of Radiotron, a critical hub of Los Angeles Hip Hop that ran from 1983 to 1985. This resonance surfaced on a specific Saint City Session night in the inspiring speech of a special guest. Our guest, Julio "Lil Cesar" Rivas, spoke about Radiotron, a community center he attended as a teen, and whose legacy he furthered years later. Also known as the Youth Break Center, Radiotron offered ongoing workshops in the Hip Hop elements as well as club nights for youth to enjoy. Many found their place at Radiotron, and solidified their Hip Hop identities there. Lil Cesar described Radiotron as a life-giving space that helped him to excel as a B-boy. Years later, Lil Cesar created another space, also named Radiotron, where B-boys and B-girls continued to develop their crafts. He and his spouse, Norma Umana, also founded the Hip Hop School of the Arts in Pomona, California, sustaining Radiotron's legacy for several years there.

In the time of sky-rhyming, an emerging cohort of young Los Angeles creatives began to find their place in Hip Hop. The Radio Club, Radiotron's precursor, was one of the first sites identified with Hip Hop in Los Angeles. Key members of the West Coast Hip Hop vanguard emerged from the Radio Club as their artistic sensibilities converged with those of visiting outsiders. Nevertheless, not all Radio Club participants identified with Hip Hop and many of the leading figures that emerged from Radio Club embodied preexisting channels of resonance. At Radiotron, on the other hand, a younger cohort emerged that primarily identified with Hip Hop. Radiotron became a hub for the younger edge of a West Coast Hip Hop generation, and represents a distinct contribution in Hip Hop's Los Angeles adoption. The Radio Club welcomed underage visitors alongside adults, however, Radiotron ran daytime programs that fostered a space primarily populated by teens and youth. In this chapter, I turn to the accounts of various creatives who participated in the life of Radiotron, especially Carmelo Alvarez, Radiotron's founder. Just like Gabriel in the opening vignette, many young creatives came looking for something real at Radiotron, and found it.

Making Power Moves

About one hundred demonstrators marched on Los Angeles City Hall, on August 14, 1985, hoping to reclaim their place. The building that housed the Youth Break Center, also known as Radiotron, was slated to be demolished in order to accommodate a parking lot and a new commercial development. The owner of the building, Jack Huntsberger, sold the property, leaving the youth center few options. Many of the young creatives who were regulars at Radiotron gathered that day, under the leadership of Carmelo Alvarez, this time claiming space on the steps of City Hall, seeking options for their center. According to KCAL-TV Channel 9 news reporter Jim Murphy, "None of the city council members came out to listen to the protesters or to offer them encouragement, but they had the most unusual protest we've ever seen" (RadiotronEvent 2009). Carmelo Alvarez organized this "most unusual protest" to reflect the energy that drew youth to Radiotron. B-boys and poppers like Oz Rock, Heckle and Jeckle, Handyman, and Lil Cesar, proceeded to create a cypher of protest outside of City Hall, with onlookers taking in the spectacle. A sampling of the most talented young dancers in Los Angeles moved one by one across a checkered linoleum floor, laid out on concrete. One protestor held a sign that read, "Let us dance."

Breaking in front of a center of power was itself a bold move—a power move (Osumare 2007). Indeed, "power move" was the term B-boys and B-girls used to classify the more acrobatic maneuvers in their repertoires. On that day, they were exercising power in more ways than one, as both a "performative and sociopolitical dynamic," as Halifu Osumare (2007:3) argues. Moreover, breaking in public increasingly represented an act of resistance, with young people being criminalized for it. Cities were passing ordinances forbidding the act. A place like Radiotron became all the more important to young creatives who sought spaces to develop their creativity.[1] Furthermore, MacArthur Park, the neighborhood where Radiotron was located, posed a variety of dangers to area youth. The neighborhood was well underway in fulfilling the description that urban theorist Mike Davis provided for it a decade later (1995): "Nearby MacArthur Park, once the jewel in the crown of LA's park system, is now a free-fire zone where crack dealers and street gangs settle their scores with shotguns and Uzis. Thirty people were murdered there in 1990." Young people in the area faced a double-edged sword of criminalization and street violence in their own communities. These forces culminated in the 1990s with the Rampart Scandal, in which the Rampart Division of the LAPD received national attention for practices of corruption, unwarranted violence, and narcotics dealing, among other things. Carmelo Alvarez recalls that the Rampart Division was feared among young people during the Radiotron years.

For Carmelo, this demonstration was not merely an attempt to evoke a bureaucratic response, though certainly one was sought out. In reference to the protest, Carmelo told Miriam Hernandez of KCOP Channel 13 news, "I made a commitment to serve God in any way that I could." For Carmelo, his protest was a divine imperative. This request to the city was itself an act of mountain-moving faith. Carmelo was asking the city for a plot of land where they could move the building to. He had been given the rights to the physical building that housed Radiotron, though not the land. An *LA Times* (Gollner 1985) article cites Olivia Mitchell, director of the mayor's Office of Youth Development as indicating that, "It would take one to two years for city officials to review the request and decide whether to lease land to the center. 'They think that bureaucracy can move (quickly), which it cannot,' she said. 'Each of the processes takes time and he (Alvarez) would just not get it (the land) fast enough.'" To Carmelo, too much was at stake in terms of the lives of his young people. As he told Channel 13 news, "I have a choice, either I let them go out there in the street and take their chances or I take my chances and allow them to be in here [at Radiotron]." From Carmelo's standpoint, he could not give up on this place.

Few groups of creatives understood the weightiness of having a place like Radiotron as those who were part of the Central American diaspora. MacArthur Park was undergoing a major transition, as refugees and immigrants from Central America settled in the neighborhood. It was quickly becoming one of the most prominent Central American enclaves in the nation (Mackey 2018; Tate 2013). As various collaborators that I spoke with recalled, young Central Americans faced a unique set of challenges in Los Angeles. On the one hand, place-making in Los Angeles involved dealing with trauma from the past, particularly for those

---

[1] See Magaña (2020) for a helpful discussion of counterspace. Radiotron in many ways functioned as a counterspace.

who experienced the violence of civil war, and the hardships of migration. On the other hand, place-making involved adapting to the new surroundings in the inner core of Los Angeles. Existing gangs, established in Chicano barrios, posed safety threats to many newly arrived migrants. Indeed, as some collaborators pointed out to me, the formation of the infamous MS13 gang began out of a desire to protect vulnerable Central Americans from existing gangs. For many, Radiotron became their place of refuge as participation there involved habitation, habituation, and a respite from "topophobia" (Forman 2002:28).

Wilber "Wilpower" Urbina, found his place at Radiotron. As a B-boy, Wilpower loved to practice B-boy power moves at Radiotron. He was also part of the diaspora that was newly relocating to the Westlake neighborhood around Radiotron. In 1979, his family migrated from El Salvador to Los Angeles. Wilpower was eight years old. Since then, Wilpower had encountered bullies in his surroundings. He describes himself as being somewhat undersized as a youngster, but quite fast. He had to be fast. As he moved into his teen years, he discovered Radiotron, only four blocks from his home. As a B-boy, Wilpower felt empowered. Dancing provided him with new opportunities to carve out a place for himself. At Radiotron he learned to do moves that built up both his confidence and his physique. He excelled at his craft. Soon, he noticed that peers that bullied him in the past, now respected his skills. This mattered to Wilpower, who remembers not having people of his background to look up to in Los Angeles. Specifically, he sought role models from El Salvador to be inspired by, but local media rarely spotlighted his coethnics in positive ways. Through Radiotron, he became that to other people. B-boying at Radiotron helped him make a place for himself in Los Angeles.

Lil Cesar, also from El Salvador, offers additional insights regarding Radiotron's significance. When he first came to the United States, in 1981, at the age of twelve, Lil Cesar discovered his family had fled the ravages of war only to encounter violence on the streets of Los Angeles. As Lil Cesar explained to Katie Madden of *La Verne Magazine* (2014), "Radiotron impacted my life because, you know, as a youngster, I had a place where I could train and practice. My surroundings were really a challenge. There were so many gangs, and it was a challenge not to get into that, but hip hop really pulled a lot of kids, not just myself, away from gangs and gave us a purpose." Fleeing from violence and facing violence did not preclude Lil Cesar from wanting the social ties that most teens seek. And yet, as an English-language learner, he found it difficult to communicate with certain peers in Los Angeles. Breaking offered an alternative mode of communication. In the process of increasing his language proficiency, Lil Cesar found that he could also communicate with his peers through dance. In dance, he experienced a form of acculturation into his receiving context. Eventually, he spearheaded one of the most decorated crews on the West Coast and beyond, the

Air Force Crew, known for their "air moves." He and Wilpower from El Salvador, Orko from Nicaragua, Little Luis from Guatemala, and other crew members, such as DJ Hazze, became international celebrities, making power moves around the world. Some Air Force Crew members got to perform before the Queen of England at Buckingham Palace, for example. They first needed to survive the streets, and Radiotron offered sanctuary in that era.

Radiotron's function as a place of refuge reflected Carmelo's personal history, including his struggles and victories in life and the arts. Carmelo understood the urgency of creating a place where young creatives could express themselves. He himself had been the product of such spaces. At the age of fifteen, Carmelo had the opportunity to receive some of the best tap dance training available in Los Angeles (Image 6.1). While attending Barnsdall Junior Arts Center, he met Chester Whitmore, who invited him to join his tap troupe. Chester took Carmelo to the Inner City Cultural Arts Center, where he introduced Carmelo to his mentor Fayard Nicholas. Carmelo eventually obtained a paid internship at Inner City Cultural Arts Center under the direction of Bernard Jackson. During that time, he was trained by LA cultural legends such as Rose Portillo, George C. Wolfe, Tomas Benitez, and James Burke. Memories of Bernard Jackson's work at the Inner City Cultural Arts Center especially inspired Carmelo. Jackson had founded the Inner City center after the Watts Rebellion (Oliver 1996). Carmelo's vision crystallized at this Center. He decided he would one day found his own arts center, which would provide creative opportunities in underserved communities.

Creativity as a Calling

In learning about the life and afterlives of Radiotron, I found the center's impending demise presented a galvanizing effect. The fight to keep Radiotron alive conveyed its importance in the lives of many creatives in Brown Los Angeles and in the region broadly. Creatives were not just fighting for a center, they were fighting for their lives. This connection between life and creativity was embedded in the very story of Carmelo Alvarez, Radiotron's founder and director. Indeed, he had to fight his own battle to stay alive in order to one day establish Radiotron. The twists and turns leading up to the start of Radiotron foreshadow what the youth center would become. I turn now to a decisive moment in Carmelo's personal narrative.

Carmelo gripped the fence of the freeway overpass, allowing his upper body to hang over the edge. Taking a deep breath, he absorbed the Los Angeles skyline and watched the headlights below whiz by. From his perch on Sunset Blvd, he contemplated whether this should be his final day alive. Carmelo felt that the

Image 6.1 Carmelo (R), and cousin, Bobby Blanquez, tap dancing at a family wedding. (Reproduced courtesy of Carmelo Alvarez)

entertainment industry had rejected the talents and abilities he embodied. He had labored to break into film, and encountered a racist ethos not willing to embrace diverse Mexican American stories. He had taken concerted steps to develop his art—theater, dance, visual arts—surrounding himself with as many art masters in the field as were available to him. Intentionally, he had avoided the gang life surrounding him. He was in his twenties and had yet to find a sustainable life. Without the support of his family, save for his mother, and rejecting the stereotypical roles being offered to him, Carmelo wondered if his creative endeavors were worth pursuing. Closing his eyes, Carmelo saw the light of the candle that his mother burned every night since he left home at seventeen years of age. He cried out to God, "What do you want me to do? You give me a talent, but I can't eat from it!" A response cut through Carmelo's inner core: "Use your gifts to save the children." The phrase was simple. The words stilled the din that had overtaken his mind. "I can use my gifts to help children," Carmelo began to tell himself. He pulled himself back over the freeway wall, now free to go.

Carmelo felt a peculiar urge to walk over to his old neighborhood on 11th and Union, close to downtown Los Angeles. As he trekked back to his familiar stomping grounds, a place where he had hung out with his homeboys as a teen, a particular building caught his attention—the Red Shield Community Center run by the Salvation Army. Carmelo knocked on the door at the community center. The Salvation Army captain who ran the center opened the door. "How can I help you?" he asked Carmelo. "I'm here to work," Carmelo interjected, barely waiting for the man to finish his inquiry. "We don't have a job for you," the bewildered captain responded firmly, scanning the young man before him and the street beyond. Carmelo insisted, "Well, I'm here to work. You know, whether you pay me or not, I'm here to work. I'm looking for a job and I'm here to give with my talents. My gifts." Something in Carmelo's response, perhaps his confidence, piqued the captain's interest. He questioned the lean young man with dark wispy hair, "What do you do?" "Well, I can teach dancing, acting, and art," Carmelo offered. A quizzical look overtook the captain's face. He nodded, and said, "We're opening a performing arts center. We just built the brand new building right here." Not missing a beat, Carmelo said, "Let me work for a week. And if you like my work, you hire me." The captain paused to think about the offer.

A week later, Carmelo, was officially given the title of performing arts supervisor for the Red Shield Youth Center. He started teaching dance and theater, and putting on plays with children who were enrolled in afterschool programs. That fateful night, he felt that his purpose had been elucidated, but did not expect that the door would be opened so quickly. It was 1978, and for Carmelo, it was the first in a series of projects wherein he successfully established creative spaces for young people to flourish through the arts. These experiences would resonate in the West Coast scene.

Carmelo honed his craft as a youth arts director and was appreciated by local youth. Nevertheless, he endured taunts by gang members and opposition from organizational leaders. He ultimately pushed creative boundaries by putting on a Bible-based play with a cast of Chicano gang members. Carmelo was fired for his creative risks, but the youth of the community threatened organizational leaders until Carmelo was reinstated; their efforts worked. Eventually, his time at the Salvation Army center drew to a close and he continued working in performing arts. Carmelo relocated to New York City and for three years sought arts-related opportunities there. In New York he managed a coffee house showcase event and produced Off Broadway plays. His time in New York City continued to spur his desire to mentor others in the arts, and he acquired additional skills along the way. During that time, he caught glimpses of Hip Hop culture on the streets. He recognized it as an underground arts movement, having yet received scant attention by the media. Increasingly, he felt the urgency of mentoring youth through the arts.

Keys to the Building

In 1983, Carmelo moved back to California, to the MacArthur Park neighborhood of Los Angeles, to pursue his dream of opening up a youth arts center. A group of funders from Carmelo's network had gathered funds to launch a youth center and saw Carmelo as an ideal director for the project. They invited Carmelo to lead the way. Carmelo rented an office space in the MacArthur Park neighborhood from which to launch his performing arts center. He obtained nonprofit status as the California Academy of Performing Arts. Along the way, he met Cynthia, who came to work for his fledgling organization. They eventually married. She played an important role in establishing the organization. Carmelo began to reconnect to contacts in the dance and theater world, aiming to offer classes for youth in the center. Unfortunately, the initial youth organization that Carmelo led was swindled by someone purportedly there to help, and Carmelo was left without funds to pay the rent for his office. He approached the owner of the office buildings to inform him of their trials, and was met with a surprising response.

The owner of the building that Carmelo rented from, Jack Huntsberger, was interested in helping Carmelo. Referencing one of the properties that he owned across from MacArthur Park, Huntsberger informed Carmelo, "I have this little theater in the back and it'll be perfect for you." The facility sounded precisely like the type of space that Carmelo could use. Huntsberger produced a set of keys as he spoke. "But there's a club that meets there on Friday nights, from 11pm to 5am. You'll have to get rid of them, and the building is yours," the owner added. Carmelo was naturally intrigued by the opportunity but the scenario seemed complicated. Huntsberger was essentially asking Carmelo to manage the building but to terminate Huntsberger's contract with the club managers, whom Carmelo had yet to meet. The club managers, from what Carmelo knew, had no idea of Huntsberger's plan to remove them from the property. Keys in hand, Carmelo resolved to visit the club on Friday night and better assess the situation.

Carmelo scanned the building at 715 South Park View, across the street from MacArthur Park, noting the high arch framing the front door entrance and its tall, rectangular windows. It was past midnight and the sounds of electro funk reverberating through the building walls suggested the club was in full effect. It was 1983 and electro music had taken off in Los Angeles. Reluctantly, Carmelo went through the front entrance and began walking up the stairs that led to the main theater area where a stage and floor served as the primary dance area for the club. Passing people along the way, he immediately sensed that this was not the crowd he was used to seeing in the area. Crash! A glass bottle shattered near Carmelo as he ascended the stairs. "Fucking Mexican!", he recalled hearing from overhead. "There's Madonna!" he heard someone else exclaim. Madonna was then on the verge of releasing her first album and was making waves in the area.

Upon reaching the dance floor, Carmelo noted that the focal point of the club was Ice-T, the emcee for the Radio Club. Carmelo observed as Ice-T called the crowd to wave their hands in the air, and directed them to move in various directions. Periodically, Ice-T rapped for the crowd. While many people danced at the club, Carmelo also noticed dancers came to the stage at various points to showcase their talents. Carmelo observed that some dancers were extremely talented in what he recognized as popping and locking dance styles. He also caught glimpses of breaking, which he had observed during his stint in New York City. He noticed various participants attempting to learn this style. Carmelo was spellbound by the sight that he witnessed. As someone with vivid memories of "the hippies movement from the sixties," Carmelo immediately made a connection between what he remembered from back then and what he was witnessing now. This was a movement on the verge of reaching a tipping point, Carmelo surmised. A movement drawing people together from such disparate walks of life was powerful and had the capacity to spread to an even broader constituency. This was art, Carmelo reflected. And though some of the participants were outsiders to the city, he also noticed plenty of young, working-class people of color participating in the scene, and showcasing their talent.

The assignment of removing the club from the building seemed problematic to Carmelo. He felt uneasy about shutting down a creative space, while he worked to open an arts center. The solution, Carmelo reasoned, was to allow the club to stay, and use the space on designated weekend nights, but to allow the art academy to operate in the building during the week. Carmelo negotiated with the building's owner, Mr. Huntsberger, and got permission to extend the club's contract. They would be allowed to stay and exist in the building if a certain percentage of their rent went to support the youth center. Carmelo informed the club managers that the club would be sharing space with the youth center, but was met with contention from the managers, who wanted to operate in the space independently of another organization. Carmelo also learned that they had been in negotiations with Cannon Films to produce a film, a project that might be complicated by the presence of the youth center. The club promoters decided to move their operation to another site.

The Youth Break Center

"Hey Mr., can we break in there?" Carmelo was surprised to find a young man, known in the neighborhood as Gizmo, at the front door of the building, with several friends in tow. "Can we break in there?" the young man persisted. Carmelo was no stranger to knocking on doors and seeking opportunities. He thought about it for a few seconds. "Sure," Carmelo replied. Carmelo was in the process of opening the youth center, after all, and these were youths! That very moment, in fact, Carmelo had been contemplating how to advertise for his center. Perhaps these teens could help. Without much fanfare, the California Academy of the Performing Arts had participants.

The young men were known as the Hungry Breakers, Carmelo discovered. They had been breaking in the park across the street for money. The year was 1983, and the park was not a safe place for children and teens. Carmelo recognized that this was an opportunity to create a safe place for these teens. As they began to congregate within the new youth center to practice their breaking skills, they quickly began to tell their friends about the space. Soon, teens from around the city were coming to the youth center to practice their skills. Carmelo seized the opportunity to mentor these young people in the art expressions that they were familiar with. He began to create session times for the teens to practice their particular Hip Hop elements of choice. There was a notable interest in breaking, given the attention breaking was receiving on the big screen. A space for graffiti was also designated, in the building's upstairs. Rather than doing graffiti out on the street, creatives had the opportunity to do it lawfully at the building. Carmelo designated particular walls and spaces as areas where budding artists could produce works of art. These art sessions became part of the center's afterschool programs.

Carmelo was not alone in his endeavors. His mother, Sofia, who had always believed in her son's gifts as an artist, volunteered to help out at the newly opened youth center. Initially she drove to MacArthur Park from her home in Whittier. When her husband, Carmelo's father, found out that she was assisting Carmelo at the youth center, he took the car keys from her, restricting her ability to drive to Los Angeles. Not willing to give up, Sofia would take the bus from the city of Whittier all the way to MacArthur Park, over an hour each way, to volunteer at the center. She typically ran the snackbar at the center. Teens nicknamed her "Mama Breaker." Sofia played an important role in the local legitimacy of the center, as parents started to wonder about what their children were doing in the building. In one memorable incident, the mother of a young graffiti writer stormed into the building and demanded to see what her son was doing there. She was greeted by Mama Breaker. Mama Breaker calmed the woman's concerns and indicated that the students were safe at the youth center.

Michael Mata, a youth minister from the First Nazarene Church of Los Angeles, visited the youth center, having heard about it from neighborhood teens whom he mentored. Mata recalls the energy that he observed at the youth center:

> You got the graffiti artists. You had the breakdancers, you had some rappers, right at the beginning of rap, you know, rapping there. It attracted a lot of people from different parts of the city. There were probably some better performers, you know, some people who became stars, if you will, celebrities came out of that. There were people that remember, "that was where I started" or "that was where I became exposed to being free, to kind of being free and creative." And Carmelo created that space that was very energetic, respectful, for young people. Really, he was helping young people develop in the direction they wanted to go with their art.

Mata's recollections were consistent with Carmelo's own articulations of his approach to working with students in his center: "I would always find every kid's gift. Like, the way God used my gift to help kids. I would also have the gift of finding kids' gifts. And I'd put them to work doing that." Even the center's name reflected the preferences of local youth. As youth watched the *Breakin'* movie, and continued frequenting the youth center that had "RadioTron" emblazoned within its walls, the youth became enthused that their center was THE Radiotron. The teens asked Carmelo if the name of their center could be "Radiotron." Carmelo obliged their request, contacted Cannon Films, and got permission to use the name, which maintained a resonance of the Radio Club and *Breakin'* film confluence.

Even as teens started to come to the youth center, the programming of the center lacked teachers seasoned in the Hip Hop arts. That dilemma was quickly resolved with the unexpected arrival of David Guzman, a Nuyorican young man who made his way West in search of a job opportunity in entertainment. Guzman likewise sought safety, after receiving threats on the streets of New York. Having undergone arts training at a prestigious performing arts high school in New York City, Guzman had skills as a choreographer which belied his young age. Coming from the South Bronx, and known there as MC Sin, Guzman was rooted in the soil from which Hip Hop sprouted. Guzman was friends with Afrika Islam, a key leader in the Universal Zulu Nation (UZN), an organization central to the expansion of Hip Hop. A respected DJ in the Bronx, Afrika Islam, knew Ice-T. Having visited the Radio Club on various occasions, Afrika Islam settled in Los Angeles and traveled back and forth to New York City.

One night, a group of creatives, including Guzman, met at The Roxy, the famous New York City nightclub featured in the film *Beat Street*. There, Afrika Islam introduced Guzman to Ice-T, and Guzman learned about the Radio Club. Through their conversation, Guzman understood that if he came to Los Angeles, he had a job waiting for him at the Radio Club. Only seventeen years old, Guzman soon decided to seek out the opportunity at the Radio Club. He made his way to the MacArthur Park area, expecting to find Ice-T, or Alex Jordanov, one of the club managers he heard about. Instead, Guzman was met by Carmelo. The club, it turned out, was no longer operating at that address. Carmelo invited Guzman into the building, where the two conversed. Guzman shared about his background in Hip Hop, dance, and rapping. Carmelo recognized that Guzman possessed qualities that youth in the community could benefit from. He offered Guzman an opportunity to work at the youth center. Guzman agreed to help develop youth arts programs. He was allowed to live in the building and was given an office there.

Guzman added his own flavor to the youth programs at the center. For starters, the name of the center became the "Youth Break Center." The name conveyed that the center offered a break from the streets and also offered a space for breaking. Given his background in the arts, Guzman designed additional classes for students. Guzman recalls, "I was teaching Taekwondo, teaching rapping, and I was teaching DJing." Guzman had the knowledge to teach many of these classes himself, but also brought in other creatives to teach. As word of the center's programs spread, various talented young adults showed interest in helping with the programs: "I got Animation to teach pop locking, and then I got Oz Rock to teach breaking," Guzman explained. Both of these artists were among the top in their dance styles (Ming and Corbeil 1991), still lauded by my collaborators, having since passed away. The center started charging fifty cents daily for participation in the programs.

Radiotron at Its Peak

As Radiotron gained publicity, more people walked through its doors. Two types of visitors frequented the center: Weekend club-goers and weekday program participants. With the Radio Club discontinued, Radiotron opened its own club night, a showcase night hosted on the weekends. Guzman helped grow out weekend showcase nights, collaborating with DJs like Captain Rock and Antron; the nightclub ambience welcomed five hundred to a thousand people.

During Radiotron's second year, renowned radio station KDAY partnered with Radiotron to host weekend club nights there. Famed West Coast DJ, Tony G, of Cuban descent, became the house DJ for these weekly club nights (see Coleman 2016). Creative competition was an aspect of the center's culture. Attendees participated in battles and contests, with showcase nights providing teens a platform to practice and improve on Hip Hop skills (Image 6.2). The event was not limited to teens from the youth center, but regulars helped to promote the event. Initially, the Radio Club crowd, and the Radiotron crowd were distinct. As these events grew in popularity, however, some familiar faces from the Radio Club visited the weekend showcases. A number of young artists have memories of these showcase nights, and of the battles that took place.

Zender remembers being invited to Radiotron by members of his B-boy crew. At the time, Zender lived in the city of Maywood, east of Los Angeles. A precocious teenager who navigated the old disco scene with older friends, and frequented house parties along the eastern edges of Los Angeles County, Zender had fond memories of when breaking first came to his town. The friends he gathered with to break in Maywood began to talk about a place where they could compete against other crews. This group of teens packed into a car and drove to MacArthur Park, thinking they would get a spot at a Saturday night B-boy battle. To their surprise, the venue was packed, and there were nearly a thousand young people on the dance floor. Zender did not get to showcase his skills, but he was hooked on the Radiotron experience. The prospect of competition was a major draw at Radiotron.

Darlene Ortiz found refuge from a difficult home life at Radiotron. She initially found respite from her woes through Hip Hop, especially as a B-girl. After forming a dance crew with Nereida and Lourdes, two Puerto Rican cousins who arrived at her high school from Brooklyn, Darlene started to network through dance competitions (Ortiz and Cuda 2015). At one competition that she and her crew won, she met Oz Rock, who was judging the contest. Oz Rock introduced her to Radiotron, and that opened a whole other world for her. She would make the trek from Riverside County all the way to MacArthur Park, to sharpen her skills. Video footage from Radiotron reveals Darlene skillfully rhyming alongside a sharp-delivering Jazzy D, house emcee at Radiotron. Carmelo recalls the footage, stating, "That is the night when she and Ice-T met." Ice-T approached Darlene that night about having her appear in a music video, though later admitting no such video was in the works yet. Darlene, in an interview with Reggie Ossé (2015), explained that Ice-T saw Radiotron as a "kiddie club." Accustomed to the Radio Club, Ice-T noticed Radiotron skewed younger. From that encounter, a romance sparked between Darlene and Ice-T. Arguably, the two would become Hip Hop's first "power couple" (Diaz 2015). Eventually, Darlene did appear in Ice-T's video, and was featured on his *Power* album cover.

Image 6.2 Lil Cesar practices head spins at Radiotron. Pieces from Soon, Risk, Prime, and others graced these walls. (Reproduced courtesy of Cesar Rivas)

Meeting Ice-T altered Darlene's trajectory. Nevertheless, she herself was a performer in her own right, and valued Radiotron because she had a creative outlet there. Likewise, as she describes in her personal memoir, Carmelo was a father figure and looked out for her (Ortiz and Cuda 2015).

Numerous artists recall their involvement with Radiotron as pivotal to their Hip Hop identities. Shawndel "Jazzy D" Rosa, for example, recalls his commitments in setting the tone for the Radiotron club nights, significantly shaping the culture of the venue. After serving as the Radiotron MC, he worked with "The Unknown DJ" and Radiotron DJ Tony G to release a record in 1986, "Wack Girl," on the famed Techno Hop Records. DJ Tony A Da Wizard, known for producing the Roadium Mixtapes along with Dr. Dre, and later working with rapper Hi-C, recalls observing Tony G's DJ skills at Radiotron (Alvarez 2020c). As noted, DJ Tony G was a key creative influence among participants. Sugar Style, a group of Chicano and Black American artists, who released an early West Coast rap record, "It's Sad," in 1985, mention Radiotron in their album dedication: "The song 'It's Sad' is dedicated to the kids who took my car's battery from the parking lot next to Radio Tron." Artists such as Myka 9 (Hall 2015; Stewart 2019), Click the Supah Latin, Xololanxinxo, Mellow Man Ace, Cut Chemist (Mao 2006; Mullen 2000), Hines Buchanan (Sonksen 2012), Arnel Calvario (Quijano 2014), DJ Miguel Gutierrez, and various others, have all at some point publicly declared the importance of Radiotron in their artistic development. References to Radiotron abound among Los Angeles Hip Hop artists, indicating that the center provided a space for them to test their talents and learn from others.

Even many who never visited Radiotron recalled its place in the cultural memory of Los Angeles. Artists such as DJ Rhettmatic (Sonksen 2015), DJ Ralph Medrano (Ramirez 2019), B-boy Don Sevilla, and Akwid, none having visited, highlight Radiotron's prominence during their youth. DJ Rhettmatic of the Beat Junkies, for example, names Anthony "DJ Antron" Mabin, known then as DJ Scratchmatic, as one of his inspirations in both name and turntablism. Mabin, a DJ fixture in Los Angeles, won a DJ competition hosted at Radiotron and became a regular for Radiotron showcase nights (Brown 2019). Rhettmatic, too young to attend Radiotron himself, knew of it and of the DJ tradition that emerged there (Sonksen 2015). DJ Ralph Medrano, in similar fashion, reminisces in an interview with OG Huskey Radio (Ramirez 2019) about how knowledge of Radiotron was widespread: "I was like 11 years old bro so I wasn't able to make it to those parties but I was able to place myself in the situation where I would hear everybody's story, I would hear about how it would go until 5 in the morning." Summing up his notions of Radiotron, Medrano proposes, "I say don't try to capture Radiotron, let Radiotron capture you" (Ramirez 2019).

Creatives who attended afterschool programs at Radiotron formed unique bonds there. Many of these students emerged as key performers in the scene as well and were often B-boys and graffiti writers. World-class B-boys known for their power moves, such as Wilpower, Lil Cesar, and Orko eventually traveled the world to share their craft (Chow 2023).[2] Some of the top graffiti crews also had ties to Radiotron (Martínez 1993). UTI, for example, had a number of members who connected at Radiotron, as did K2S and TGO. Steve Grody (2006), who documents the rise of graffiti in Los Angeles, cites Radiotron as one of the primary locales of graffiti innovation. Grody (2007) quotes prominent graffiti artist Crime, highlighting Radiotron's place in the scene:

> Radiotron [an all-ages club where kids could break-dance and hear rap] by MacArthur Park, was where we [breakers] used to hang out, and that's where many of us became friends. After being individuals, we (Crime, along with Shandu, Primo Dee, Risco, Dave) formed L.A. Bomb Squad (LABS) in late '84, the first crew we knew of in L.A, and because we limited the size of our crew, others started to form their own crews.

Crime's words highlight how Radiotron creatives established crews and participated in multiple elements together. One of the key contributions of Radiotron is that it allowed for youths to explore multiple talents and did not restrict them to one form of expression. While some of these artists became known for particular elements, many dabbled in multiple elements. Zender, for example, was invested in rapping in the early 1980s and practiced this skill at Radiotron. Many of these B-boys/B-girls and graffiti writers were among the early recruits to the youth center. As such, Carmelo often has the greatest degree of familiarity with their lives. He mentored many of these teens, and as he helped them identify their skills, he helped them find their places.

One emerging crew were the Radiotron Wizards, B-boys who were especially coached by Guzman. The Radiotron Wizards made their presence felt at the 1984 Olympics, officially performing outside of the primary venue, the Los Angeles Memorial Coliseum. On one legendary night, the Radiotron Wizards battled the Shake City Rockers at The Mix, a club in Hollywood. The Shake City Rockers, who represented a more experienced crew dating back to the Radio Club, faced off with the younger Wizards. The Wizards surprised the crowd when they came out on top. Ultimately members of these two crews would join together as the Airforce Crew, becoming one of the most powerful B-boy crews of the era. They encountered other decorated crews in the scene such as the LA Breakers, started by West Coast founder Disco Daddy. Guzman helped expand the public face of Radiotron through dance as well. At the expansive LA Street Scene festival, Guzman was leading a break performance on stage when a brawl broke out among Bloods and Crips in the audience. Guzman directed the rivals to work

---

[2] Del Barco (1996) argues that B-boys served as Hip Hop ambassadors globally.

out their animosities through dance; as if staging a scene from a Hollywood film, the combatants formed a dance battle (Gault and Harris 2019).

Hollywood started to show up at Radiotron. Guzman remembers that he and other B-boys were invited to Pauly Shore's house to give him breaking lessons. "His mom picked us up so that we could give him breaking lessons. We ended up hanging out with him jumping on his trampoline in his backyard," Guzman chuckled. Guzman himself was still a teenager. He also recalled Vanna White, hostess of the *Wheel of Fortune*, bringing her niece to the center to take breaking classes. Another rising star, Cuba Gooding Jr., took classes at the center. At one point, Carmelo noticed some teen creatives were being offered paid opportunities to showcase their talents. While he appreciated teens being compensated for their skills, he observed that many of them were on the one hand becoming arrogant due to these opportunities, and on the other hand being exploited. One case that stood out to Carmelo was an incident wherein one of the Radiotron students, a Central American immigrant, was paid to dance at a luxurious home in Hollywood and upon arrival was asked to engage in questionable actions. Though Carmelo learned of the incident far after it happened, his concern for participants' well-being heightened. Carmelo considered that Pastor Michael Mata might provide students with a sense of groundedness. Reverend Mata, who had experience working with youth in the city and was a community organizer, offered to help Carmelo in whatever was needed. Carmelo asked Reverend Mata if he could lead a Bible study for the students. For a season, Radiotron students could stick around after their Hip Hop classes and participate in a Bible study.

KDAY, through its performing arts program, established an important partnership with Radiotron that extended both KDAY and Radiotron's presence into the broader community. Rory Kaufman, public affairs director for KDAY, ran a performing arts program that included seventy participants, divided into eighteen distinct youth singing and dance groups (Jones 1985). The young people were largely from South Central Los Angeles and surrounding areas, and performed at events around town, often being compensated for their work. Click the Supah Latin, who was part of KDAY's performing arts program after it transitioned to a different location, fondly recalls how unique and uplifting this program was for the artists and the community. He remembers Rory Kaufman's excellence in mentoring youth in the program. Kaufman did much of the recruiting for the program throughout Los Angeles, and numerous performers were engaged in the Hip Hop elements. As Von Jones (1985:D1) reported for the *Los Angeles Sentinel*, during weekly rehearsals, "the youth explode to the popping rhythms of 'rap' music, and they dance and sing."

Saving the Center

The Radiotron leaders began receiving news that cast doubt on the center's future. According to Guzman, leaders learned that proposed plans to expand the metro system would bring changes to the area around MacArthur Park, potentially affecting Radiotron. It soon became clear that their building was a prime target for developers. Guzman remembers talking to Carmelo about the building potentially getting shut down. A ray of hope broke through when Cannon films reached out to Radiotron staff. Guzman provided a tour to the film directors as they talked about filming a *Breakin'* sequel in the Radiotron building. The directors asked questions about the center's programming and seemed genuinely interested in the impact the center was having on local youth. The directors conveyed interest in helping the center. Guzman and Carmelo made the facilities available for filming, thinking Cannon films would offer them substantial funds and/or creative solutions. Many of the familiar actors from the first film appeared in the sequel. A few additions to the cast, such as Robert "Ace Rock" Aceves, were Radiotron regulars. The film, *Breakin' 2: Electric Boogaloo*, drew from the energy surrounding Radiotron.

Sadly, Radiotron's salvation did not come from the film. *Breakin'*, the first installation, was arguably Cannon Films' last profitable release. The sequel generated far less revenue. The film raised the public profile of cast members, but hopes of saving the center began to dissolve. Adding insult to injury, the plotline of the film involved a youth center that was on the brink of closing, but was saved. The month *Breakin' 2* premiered, in December of 1984, Guzman quit his job at Radiotron. Anticipating the loss of Radiotron, and facing disagreements related to managing the center, Guzman decided to leave Los Angeles. As he had family in San Bernardino and Riverside counties, he decided to move to that area, known as the Inland Empire. In January of 1985, Guzman began teaching youth dance classes for the City of Fontana (Sperling 1985).

News broke that the owner of the building, Jack Huntsberger, had sold the property. Mr. Huntsberger deeded the building, but not the land, to Radiotron. One possibility that Carmelo considered was to secure another property for relocation of the building. As described earlier in the chapter, Carmelo staged a demonstration on the steps of City Hall, seeking intervention from the City Council. By then, the club nights at the building had been shut down due to building code violations. As Carmelo summed up the center's conclusion, "In the movie, the center was saved, but in real life, Radiotron closed." He solemnly added, "I was there when we shut the doors of the building for the last time. As a matter of fact, I was there when the crane and the wrecking ball demolished the building." Watching the demise of the Radiotron building, Carmelo was not ready to give up on the work he had dedicated himself to.

Carmelo's advocacy in the city was not in vain, as city officials eventually offered a solution. Carmelo was granted the opportunity to continue running programs for students across the street from the former building, at MacArthur Park. The MacArthur Park bandshell provided a new home for select Radiotron programs. Some young people that frequented Radiotron continued to participate at the park and some newcomers joined also. As the media's attention began to drift from breaking, a remnant continued practicing the craft. Still, many B-boys and B-girls eventually drifted away. The art would enjoy a resurgence in the following decade. It was no surprise that a number of the dancers that helped to spur breaking's resurgence were participants at the original Radiotron. Indeed, "Lil Cesar" Rivas, one of the rising stars of the early Radiotron days, and his spouse Norma Umana, reintroduced the Radiotron name in the mid-1990s and established a new Radiotron center, working to recapture the spirit of the original Radiotron (Chow 2023). This new Radiotron served as one of the epicenters of the breaking resurgence in Los Angeles and a hub in a global dance wave..

Hip Hop Generations

In the summer of 2019, I attended the anniversary celebration of Radiotron, hosted at the Levitt Pavilion in MacArthur Park. The emcee, Medusa, authoritatively commanded the stage, rapping—and at times entering the dance cypher—constantly reminding the audience of the history being honored that day. Indeed, her versatility on the stage was a masterful culmination of the way that many early creatives participated in all the Hip Hop elements. I watched as numerous other respected figures from the Los Angeles Hip Hop community took to the stage and commemorated Radiotron. The event was headlined by Frost, likely the most recognized figure in the lineup, whose beginnings were intricately tied to Brown Los Angeles. Most participants largely represented underground Hip Hop. Radiotron, it was conveyed loud and clear, was a foundational piece in the emergence of the LA underground scene. Artists from the Project Blowed and Good Life Cafe communities, incubators of Los Angeles underground Hip Hop (Lee 2016; Morgan 2009), milled about in the audience, and some took to the stage. Myka 9, Pigeon John, Rifleman, and Raphi were among those that I spotted.

Radiotron, I surmised, undergirded the underside, perhaps the antithesis, to the Hip Hop genre that LA was most known for—gangsta rap (see Mullen 2000). In Los Angeles, this underside was not merely a waiting room for those hoping to assimilate into the mainstream. Rather, the underground was a space that people worked to sustain and even fought for (J. Lee 2016; Morgan 2009). Moreover, many battled to gain recognition within it. It was a world all its own, which contended for Hip Hop purity and prided itself in honoring the roots of Hip Hop. And truth be told, it was in some cases proximate to gangsta rap, given the relational ties across scenes. Brown Los Angeles had active representatives in this sphere of creativity, and Radiotron was an orienting memorial among these Hip Hop faithful. The perception of Radiotron conjured up by B-boy Roger "Orko" Romero suggests that the site had been sacralized within the Hip Hop memories of many: "Everybody was there. It was like church, Hip Hop church" (Robinson and Robinson 2020). In following up with Carmelo about the history of Radiotron, Romero's description made sense in more ways than one. The degree of familiarity that Carmelo retained regarding the lives of so many Radiotron participants spoke to a "church-like" quality at the site. Radiotron not only impacted those in attendance but also shaped the culture of Hip Hop in the city. To this day, many point to Radiotron as a symbol of Hip Hop authenticity in Los Angeles.

Still, the name Radiotron was not without controversy in the West Coast scene. Not every source I encountered agreed about Radiotron's place in West Coast Hip Hop history. I concluded that diverging accounts about Radiotron are part of the Radiotron story. Radiotron was always a contested space. It inherited its building from another contested institution—Radio Club. Some of the conflicting opinions I learned about relate to the transition from Radio to Radiotron, and whether the club was unjustly removed to make way for the youth center. Disagreements also emerge around the contributions of distinct participants in building up the center into what it became. One detail that remains clear is that Carmelo was/is an ever-constant youth advocate. He was such before the start of Radiotron, during, and after. The trail of evidence, documented in newspapers and film, as well as in oral histories, was significant. As for the center itself, if West Coast Hip Hop commemorated sacred sites, surely Radiotron would be a prominent one—except the site itself is no longer. This was a community housed in a "ghost building" that was eventually demolished. But the resonance of this community lives on today in the skills, the aesthetics, and the pedagogy of many creatives. It lives on in the very lives that found refuge there, and in the individual legacies of those community members that have now passed on themselves. Brown Los Angeles is especially a beneficiary of Radiotron's resonance.

PART III
CHARTING THE RESONANCE
Ebbs and Flows

Chapters in this section trace the decline, preservation, and dissemination of early underground expressions of West Coast Hip Hop amid the emergence of more commercially viable expressions, especially gangsta rap. In the mid-to-late 1980s, the Los Angeles Hip Hop scene shifted drastically and creatives faced threats from heavy-handed law enforcement policies, surging gang affiliations, the crack epidemic, and increasing social stigmas. Many sought to preserve the movement that had provided an alternative to the dangers they faced. Creatives from Brown Los Angeles crossed boundaries of race, class, region, religion, and style to preserve and expand the movement — and to preserve their own lives.

7
Crossing Freeways with Flyways

Frank Contreras was not able to attend Radiotron, but during those years he was busy experimenting with music at home. Contreras was among a batch of creatives shaping what would become Chicano rap. His eventual group, Spanish F.L.Y. (Foolish Loco Youngsters), expressed pride in their Chicano identity (Holland 2015). For their single, "Eighteen with a Bullet," released in 1990, lead rapper Ese Rich Roc rapped in Spanglish, drawing heavily on the Chicano argot, Caló. Their signature sound relied on oldie melodies stacked on airy, crackly breakbeats broken up with occasional DJ record scratching. The original bandmates, Frank "DJ Tricks" Contreras, and Rich Roc, who started creating together in the mid-1980s, hailed from the Harbor Area, one of the most fertile grounds of Hip Hop talent in the nation (Image 7.1). One nearby city, Long Beach, has especially produced artists emblematic of the West Coast sound. Yet, less recognized are the smaller cities that form a corridor along the 110 freeway, the gateway to the Port of Los Angeles. This cluster of cities such as San Pedro, Wilmington, Carson, Harbor City, and adjacent neighborhoods foster a unique camaraderie of working-class communities whose livelihoods have historically relied on port-related jobs. Frank was a product of the Harbor Area, growing up in San Pedro and moving to Carson, with parents from Wilmington. Frank's father, a percussionist, was one of Frank's first creative influences. Additionally, Frank credits artists from the port region that influenced not only himself but all of Los Angeles. Locals recognize that the talent cultivated in the Harbor Area has crossed boundaries in its expansive resonance.

In the Harbor Area, artists crisscrossed boundaries of race, geography, and genre. For example, the proto–Hip Hop era mobile DJ crew, Uncle Jamm's Army, began in the Harbor Area, and drew crowds from Black Los Angeles as well as from other communities. The Boo-Yaa Tribe, originally known as the Blue City Crew or Blue City Strutters, were Samoan dancers and rappers from Carson who rose to global fame. DJ Tony A, a Chicano from Wilmington, inherited from Dr. Dre the work of producing Roadium Mixtapes, coveted cassettes distributed by Japanese American swap meet shop owner Steve Yano. The mixtapes broke some of LA's most renowned West Coast rappers, and Tony A[1] went on

---

[1] He now runs one of the most popular and informative Hip Hop–oriented podcasts in Los Angeles.

In the Time of Sky-Rhyming. Jonathan E. Calvillo, Oxford University Press. © Oxford University Press 2024.
DOI: 10.1093/oso/9780197762479.003.0008

Image 7.1 Spanish F.L.Y., Frank Contreras (L), and Richard Anaya, 1991. (Reproduced courtesy of Frank Contreras)

to produce his own hit music with rapper Hi-C. Filipino American DJ, Isaiah "Icy Ice" Dacio, also from the area, began DJing local parties and went on to become a highly respected Los Angeles radio DJ. And the list goes on. Even as many Harbor Area creatives faced high degrees of containment tied to economic struggle, this was a space of boundary crossing.

In this chapter, I explore how creatives from Brown Los Angeles crossed boundaries of race and place to expand their prospects within Hip Hop and sustain creative resonances. Crossing boundaries involved creative collaborations and resource transmission across social differences. In the second half of the 1980s, crossing boundaries of race and place posed new challenges. Increased salience in boundaries of race and place altered the West Coast scene. In some Hip Hop contexts, a Black/brown divide became especially salient, with racial politics between Black American and Latine populations influencing societal expectations about Los Angeles Hip Hop. The Harbor Area serves as a key site and helpful starting point for exploring social boundary negotiations in the scene. I examine cases of brown creatives from this region, and look beyond as well. In crossing social boundaries to expand their artistic opportunities, brown creatives expressed a sense of commitment to Hip Hop's maintenance.

Crossing the Border-Islands

While Frank Contreras helped further the sounds and styles of Chicano rap, his formation in Hip Hop involved crossing ethnic and racial boundaries. Prior to his creations with Spanish F.L.Y., Frank spent time collaborating with his friend and neighbor, a rapper and DJ by the name of Marcus Tufono, also known as the Kutfather (Contreras n.d.). Marcus was of Samoan heritage. The two formed a crew called the Super Def Creators, and began flexing their skills at school functions and other small shows. The son of a church choir director (Keogh 2021), Marcus snuck into dance functions to observe some of the best DJs roving the Harbor Area, such as a young Dr. Dre. Frank, at the time known as DJ Rockin Def, experimented with his parents' record collection. The Super Def Creators wrote rhymes and expanded their turntable mastery. The friends collaborated until Marcus and his family moved south to San Diego. Even as their geographies diverged, they both made creative impacts in their scenes. One of the pioneers of Chicano Hip Hop, then, honed his skills through finding creative resonance with a friend from the Samoan diaspora, a different brown diaspora.

The life of Marcus "Kutfather" Tufono elucidates how the Samoan diaspora expanded the West Coast scene's resonance. As documented by April Henderson (2006), Samoans were some of the most prolific disseminators of Hip Hop resonance across geographies, including across oceans. Tufono's family migrated from Samoa to Daly City, California, where Marcus was born. From that Northern California starting point, the Tufono's moved south to Carson, one of the cities in the United States with the highest number of residents of Samoan ancestry; there, Marcus found his love for DJing. After several years the family moved farther south to San Diego, where Marcus continued his artistry and became a professional club DJ. Having made a name for himself as a DJ, Marcus made another major move to a northern coastal city, leaving the southern US borderlands and nearing the northern US borderlands in Seattle. In Seattle, Marcus became a foundational player in the emerging Hip Hop scene. As noted by *Seattle Times* writer Tom Keogh (2021), "Kutfather was also involved in early hip-hop radio shows in the Seattle area, co-hosting KCMU's 'Rap Attack' with DJ Nasty Nes and KEXP's long-running 'Street Sounds' with DJ Supreme La Rock." He influenced the West Coast scene along the migration circuit he moved in, crossing racial boundaries along the way. Tufono passed away in 2020, commemorated by a slew of artists who were inspired by his creative work.

The diasporic trajectory Tufono followed was not unlike that of other Samoans throughout the United States. Other creatives engaged with the Samoan diaspora while developing their crafts. Henderson traces the life of various artists who followed Samoan diasporic routes in their artistic development. Among these, Suga Pop was one of the most recognized in the early West Coast scene, serving as a Hip Hop ambassador who early on exchanged West Coast styles of funk dance in New York City, and brought B-boy moves to the West Coast. Suga Pop, raised in a Samoan household in New Zealand (Henderson 2006), initially followed Samoan migratory routes through the Pacific and eventually joined some of the most decorated dance crews in New York and Los Angeles. Along the way, he expanded creatively by convening with members of the Blue City Crew in Carson, who affiliated with Ice-T's Rhyme Syndicate Network.

As I began to research the place of this brown diaspora from the Pacific, I could not help but reach into my own networks. My partner, Puanani, is Samoan through her paternal family. I contacted several of her uncles and discovered that they participated in Harbor Area proto–Hip Hop scenes. Her uncles Fao and Teleso were lockers, and later poppers, as part of the Midnite Lockers. They regaled me with stories of dance geniuses who traveled from the Bay Area, where boogaloo, robotin, tuttin, and strutting took off, and battled dance aficionados in the recreation centers of Carson, at places like Scott Park and Dolphin Park. The dance styles of the Bay resonated in Los Angeles, in part because of the Samoan diaspora. I also learned about key sites of Hip Hop sociability that drew from the Samoan community. Samerika Hall, for example, a hall in Carson established by the Samoan community for celebrations and gatherings, became a key site for Hip Hop events; numerous artists who toured the West Coast performed at this venue. A number of brown Chicano creatives, such as DJ Tony Alvarez, remember events at this hall. Big John's Hall was another venue serving the ethnic Samoan community that hosted historic Hip Hop events.

Through these creative exchanges, the very boundaries of brown were being blurred. Moreover, various brown and Black diasporas were converging in the Harbor Area through participatory, multidirectional resonances. According to Boo-Yaa Tribe member Donald Devoux (Castro 2014), the Carson Twin Cinema, embedded amid Los Angeles freeway gridlock, attracted dancers from across the region and across backgrounds. Many working-class moviegoers watched Kung Fu flicks at this theater, resonating with early NYC B-boy affinities for martial arts films. So too, Scott Park in the area drew a variety of dancers. Among these was Wilmington local Michael "Boogaloo Shrimp" Chambers, brilliant dancer and key figure in the West Coast scene. Chambers, who has family roots in Louisiana, acknowledges the influence of Samoans in the region (Khalfani 2018); Devoux has memories of instructing a young Chambers in the art of Boogaloo, which Devoux picked up from his Bay Area–based uncles, Jack and Charlie Hisatake (Castro 2014). DJ Tony A credits Chambers with teaching him how to pop. Likewise, Chambers discusses spending summers in East Los Angeles, connecting with the Chicano community there (Khalfani 2018). Filipino American street dancer Jeff De La Cruz remembers picking up dance skills at some of these sites as well, and later collaborating with Boogaloo

Shrimp. These chains of resonance point to connections across Samoan, Black, Filipino, and Chicano creatives. These spaces and moments of Black and brown diasporic convergence expanded Hip Hop's resonance.

Crossing Borders

Mike "Iceman" Rivera helped to expand Hip Hop's resonance across borders, but at first his prospects in the movement were tenuous. Initially, Iceman tried his hand at Hip Hop precursors locking and popping, dance styles that were prevalent in his Wilmington neighborhood in the late 1970s and early 1980s. He was soon moving on to high school when he realized those styles were not going to work for him. "In my neighborhood, people like Lil Coco and Dianne 'Queen Boogaloo' Williams were better than me, so I couldn't be a popper. In the hood where I grew up, people made fun of you when you got beat by a girl or a little kid." For a time, Iceman stayed away from dancing to avoid defeat, especially since it meant potentially getting beat by a child or teen girl. Lil Coco, made famous as a star in the *Breakin'* franchise, grew up near Iceman, and was a real threat. Dianne Williams, known as Queen Boogaloo was unrivaled, and mentored Lil Coco in dance. Iceman had another reason for pause when it came to being a popper. Many of the people in his area who were dancing were gang bangers. He watched steadily as friends from his hood navigated the streets and became entangled in gang life, many ending up locked up, or losing their lives. So he stayed away from popping and locking. But opportunities in dance did not disappear. Another style of dance would grab Iceman's attention—B-boying.

Iceman was initially reluctant to try B-boying, but once he saw it executed correctly, he jumped right in. Finding ongoing inspiration in Oz Rock, and Baby New York, B-boys who migrated from the East Coast to the West Coast, Iceman worked to learn as many skills as he could master. At the time, breakbeats were not plentiful in Los Angeles, so Iceman would dance to funk, electro, disco, and new wave music. Iceman joined a crew called Unique St. Rockers, which built a name for itself by battling in the diverse settings of the Harbor Area, including against predominantly Filipino and Samoan crews. Though Iceman was excelling in this setting, he also wanted his friends to battle against other crews alongside him. That vision hit a wall because the Unique St. Rockers were not open to Iceman's friends joining their crew. Iceman took matters into his own hands, forming his own crew and bringing his friends along. He and his crew practiced incessantly until they got so good that they defeated the Unique St. Rockers in a battle. The new crew was dubbed the Floor Patrol.

One of Iceman's crewmates, Cesar, was an old friend whose family had migrated to Wilmington from Mexicali, Mexico. The family frequently traveled back to visit the border town, and periodically would invite Iceman to join them. In middle school, through the years 1981–1983, Iceman was becoming increasingly independent and ventured out beyond his neighborhood whenever he got the chance. The situation at home was not always easy, and Iceman eventually found ways to escape through dance, and through visiting new locales. He grew accustomed to traveling with Cesar's family to Mexicali. On one occasion, he stayed in Mexicali for a month with Cesar's brother Peter, who lived there, tending to his family's mechanic shop in the city. Iceman was invited to visit Mexicali for a weekend trip, a trip that seemed quite normal by this point. The upcoming weekend trip included three members of the crew, Cesar, Ronnie, and Iceman. The trip was supposed to only last a weekend, but unexpectedly became a much longer, life-changing experience.

When the crew arrived in Mexicali, Cesar discovered that there would be a dance contest at a local carnival. The crew decided to sign up and compete. B-boying was just getting underway in Los Angeles in 1983 but was far less accessible in Mexico, especially in live performance. The crowd and judges were blown away by the demonstration that the Floor Patrol put on. The crew won first prize. While the crew was largely competing for fun and for the thrill of performing in front of a crowd, the energy from the performance overflowed into another important outcome: Young people in the audience expressed major interest in the dance skills performed by the crew. Young people from Mexicali flocked to the Floor Patrol and asked if the crew could teach them how to dance like they had done for the competition.

Soon, the Floor Patrol members were passing on their B-boy skills to young people from Mexicali, hosting sessions at a park there. By passing on his skills to others, Iceman established friendships with others from Mexicali. By now, his stay in Mexicali had extended from a weekend to several weeks. Among those that came by the park to learn B-boy skills, Iceman remembers a young man named Jorge Paez, who would later be known as El Maromero Paez, a professional boxer renowned for circus-like theatrics, acrobatic moves in and out of the ring, and a signature mullet haircut. Paez had a successful run as a boxer, challenging some of the greats of his time. Sharpening his show skills performing in a circus run by his grandmother, he added B-boy skills to his repertoire. During that time, Iceman especially built camaraderie with three B-boy neophytes from Mexicali: Gory, who was nineteen years old; Cali, who was seventeen years old; and Mike, who was sixteen years old. At fourteen years of age, Iceman was instructing dancers older than him, and they respected him for it. These connections also presented Iceman with new opportunities.

The young men from Mexicali excelled quickly, and thus when they learned of an opportunity to try their luck with dancing, they were willing to take risks. The television show *Siempre en Domingo* offered opportunities to showcase talent from throughout Mexico. Members of the newly born Mexicali chapter of Floor Patrol, Patrulla del Piso, thought they had a chance of getting on *Siempre en Domingo*. They planned to travel by train to Mexico City, where the show was filmed. Iceman remembers the train ride in detail, especially watching the Mexican countryside, and seeing some of the small towns along the way. During the two and half days that they were on the train, he got sick. The crew had to venture out from the train in order to find food for Iceman. Iceman recalls that in a deeply forested area near the train stop, there were Indigenous communities and women that would sell food to travelers. He recalls that this food sustained him on the trip and he was able to recover.

Though the idea of appearing on television initially motivated the boys to take the journey, while they were on the train those plans were derailed. The boys befriended a pair of brothers on the train, headed back home to Guadalajara, Jalisco. The brothers from Guadalajara hit it off with the crew, and invited them to visit Guadalajara, offering the crew a place to stay at their parents' home. For the Patrulla del Piso, it was really about the adventure. They decided to visit Guadalajara and see how their dance skills might open doors for them there. After two and a half days on the train, they arrived in Guadalajara.

In Guadalajara, opportunities abounded. Initially, the boys danced at street plazas, where audiences gathered to watch them. For two weeks, they stayed with their friends from the train ride and went out daily to perform on the streets. Soon after, a man who managed night clubs in Guadalajara spotted the boys and envisioned ways to maximize profit through their skills. He gave them his business card and offered them an opportunity to perform at various theaters, clubs, and establishments. The business man began to pay the crew for their artistic labor and provided them with an apartment for lodging. The young men were now making a living from their performances. Once they accumulated funds, one of the first things they did was to go back to the family that first housed them in Guadalajara and pay them for their time there. The family was grateful.

A watershed moment came when the crew was invited to march in a parade in Guadalajara. The boys wore matching outfits that their now boss had acquired for them through one of his business connections, a sports uniform store. Iceman remembers going to the store and looking through soccer uniforms. They selected ones that most closely approximated B-boy gear, warm ups with stripes on the side. The fashion options that Iceman preferred as a B-boy were not available, but the crew did the best they could. When they marched in the parade, their matching soccer uniforms drew negative attention from some teens in the crowd.

Iceman remembers hearing young men yell homophobic slurs at them. Iceman did not immediately catch on to what they were calling the crew, and he yelled back, "What's that?" "You're Menudo!" someone from the crowd mockingly yelled, referring to the Puerto Rican boy band that was then achieving international success. The crew could not stand the jeers. Gory, the oldest of the crew, explained to the hecklers that the crew danced break. The hecklers were skeptical but wanted to know more. With little hesitation, the Floor Patrol broke into a dance cypher. The energy in the crowd changed. Something resonated among the critics. In fact, two of the most vocal critics decided to follow the Floor Patrol for the rest of their parade walk. The critics had become fans. For the rest of their time in Guadalajara, the Floor Patrol had a following, and the most consistent followers were the two mockers. At many of the performances that Floor Patrol had around town, these two young B-boy disciples would follow. Eventually, they became the foundational B-boys in Guadalajara's movement.

One particular memory from Iceman's time in Guadalajara reflects how Hip Hop's border crossing resonance provided grounds for connection in unexpected locales. The Floor Patrol frequented a particular *discoteca* on Wednesdays. One night when they were there, Iceman spotted a young man who expertly performed B-boy moves. The young man looked Mexican, but Iceman wondered where he got his moves from. Iceman approached him and learned he went by the name Lyrical Engineer Genius G; he was from Los Angeles County, Pico Rivera, to be exact. Tony, as he was known by family, had been sent away to Guadalajara because of what his parents considered to be misbehavior and was to stay in Guadalajara for two years. Hip Hop was one of his practices toward staying connected to his community back in Los Angeles. In some ways, his story mirrored that of Markski, who maintained his Hip Hop practices to stay connected to the Bronx. Lyrical G, as it turns out, was one of Markski's disciples in Pico Rivera. He joined the Floor Patrol during his time in Guadalajara. Iceman's story signals how Hip Hop belonging blurred the boundaries of the nation-state and forged binational ties for some creatives.

Black and Brown?

In the years after Iceman returned to Los Angeles, divisions were emerging in the West Coast scene. While Hip Hop previously provided grounds for building across ethnic, racial, and national borders, certain collective boundaries were becoming more pronounced for many urban creatives. In particular, the Black/brown colorline became increasingly pronounced, often in relation to conflicts between Chicano and Black American gang affiliates. The emergence of gangsta rap would establish Los Angeles as a Hip Hop hub and spotlight many of the realities faced by Black Los Angeles; conversely, it was entwined with prison and gang politics dividing Black and brown communities. These dynamics reflected larger forces of de facto segregation and urban disinvestment pitting ethnic communities against each other. Likewise, patterns of militarized policing and mass incarceration (Rose 2008) heightened racialized prison politics, which bled out into the community. At the neighborhood level, resonance channels experienced static when gang affiliations gained currency.

Los Angeles's reputation as a hub of gang violence entered national discourse after a tumult erupted at a popular Hip Hop concert tour on August 17, 1986. With Run DMC headlining, the "Raising Hell" tour did just that. Accounts from concert-goers paint a picture of attendees fearing for their lives amid brutality and pandemonium. The entire Long Beach Arena, the venue that hosted the concert, was in complete disarray. Headlines indicate that about forty attendees were severely injured; witnesses suggest that was an undercount. The incident pummeled Hip Hop's reputation in the eyes of much of middle America (see Brown 2020).

Scholars note the prominence of the Raising Hell incident in fueling antirap discourses (Waksman 2022), with social commentators blaming Hip Hop and ignoring local dynamics at play. Murray Forman (2002:139–140) implicates the mainstream media in neglecting the role of gangs in fomenting the violence, and failing to report that "the violence was spatially motivated, owing to a context in which rap fans of warring gangs converged within a compressed space. Mainstream media and critics also tended to focus on the stereotypical associations between rap music, black youth, and masculine aggression." Based on Forman's analysis of initial reporting, media placed the blame on artists and on Hip Hop music, and ignored the role of territoriality and gang culture that developed locally in the Los Angeles area.

Likewise, reporting tended to cast Black youth and Black masculinity in a negative light, and projected negative perceptions of these dimensions onto Hip Hop. A television news report from West Palm Beach Florida, a city scheduled to host the Raising Hell tour, for example, conveyed such a message within its report (Whitaker 1986). A featured interviewee stated, "Teenage energy period and perhaps black teenage energy in particular, it's very scary for various reasons and I think seeing that and reading reports of that it's creating a real, just a real clamor." Such commentaries fed into tropes of blackness as a threat to American civil society and by necessity cast young Black men as outsiders (Jeffries 2011), implicating Hip Hop as emblematic of Black moral deficiency (Rose 2008). Rarely did assessments address the structural challenges faced disproportionately by working-class urban Black people such as deindustrialization and mass incarceration.

While national pundits railed against Hip Hop, some reports, particularly from local outlets, emphasized local efforts in responding to gang conflict. Evidence suggests that some local outlets generally understood that a gang brawl escalated into pandemonium at the Long Beach concert. The West Palm Beach report previously referenced, for example, mentioned the efforts being made to beef up security in response to gangs. Newspapers such as the *San Bernardino County Sun* (Stephens 1987:42) asserted that gang violence is "a concern during rap music shows, and was the principal problem at the Long Beach Run-DMC concert." The newspaper went on to assure readers that the nearby Orange Pavilion had much stricter security than the Long Beach Arena, about seventy miles to the West. The Orange Pavilion had hosted the same tour without a hitch days before the Long Beach incident. The Sun further implicated gang colors as the primary catalyst to the conflict, narrowing the problem further. If concert venues would strictly enforce against the presence of gang "colors" and "insignia," concerts would more readily remain safe, the *Sun* argued.

With the moral panic over rap music becoming ever more heightened, Run DMC themselves denounced the heinous acts of that night. Russell Simmons, their manager, immediately canceled their subsequent show at the Hollywood Palladium. As Viator (2020) notes, however, there was much work to be done to salvage the image of the group. In a highly coordinated manner, "the trio gave interviews with many of the very same mainstream media outlets they had once disdained. The message, simply, was that it had been gangbangers, not rap fans, doing the fighting" (Viator 2020:102). Members of Run-DMC took verbal shots at everyone from the security staff at the venue, to the Bloods and Crips, to Los Angeles itself for "letting things get to the point where 'gangs are running your town'" (Viator 2020:103). So while critics with national platforms blamed Hip Hop along racialized lines, and local venues zeroed-in on what they understood to be a gang problem, the artists distanced themselves from gang culture altogether.

Counter Explanations

Not everyone gave the same weight to the explanation that Black American gangs were the primary culprits of the melee. Various concert attendees and participants pointed to cross-racial tensions as a catalyst in the chaos. One of the strongest proponents to this explanation was none other than Rodger Clayton, founder of Uncle Jamm's Army. Clayton, who worked as a promoter for the Long Beach "Raising Hell" concert, was on stage attempting to bring peace as the chaos transpired. He described the scene in the following manner for *Rap Pages* (Chang and Nardone 1994:74):

> What has never come to light with that mutha-phukking Raising Hell show, it wasn't gangs in the Long Beach Arena, it was a race riot. Let me tell you what happened. The Long Beach Insanes had stole a Mexican girl's purse, so some

Mexican dudes went upstairs, broke in the broom closet and went down and hit up the Long Beach Insanes. Hit 'em with brooms, mops and some sticks. It was 'bout 10 of them. Then, all the Black gangs got together and they started whupping every Mexican every white boy, throwing 'em off the second level. The news never brought that to light.

I sought and found additional accounts that complemented Clayton's version. One important source was a 2013 video I found on Youtube in which an attendee stood outside of the Long Beach Arena and recorded his recollections of the event. The eyewitness, David Cordova, a rapper known as West Grim, was open to discussing the event with me after I reached out to him on social media. Coincidentally, I discovered he collaborated with Spanish F.L.Y., and is related to Frank Contreras. As West Grim summed up the experience:

The Run DMC concert was my first [concert], though I really didn't grow up in gang culture, so it was a shock. But, I remember it vividly and yes there were southsiders [Chicano gang members] and they were clashing with the Crips from top to bottom. I'll never forget the low rumbling sound of people clashing and running for their lives like a stampede across the arena watching it slowly getting close.

Despite the fear that West Grim experienced, paradoxically he remembers this experience as solidifying his identity in Hip Hop, and continues to write music to this day.

West Grim's video received comments that echoed what he shared with me in conversation as well as what Rodger Clayton shared in print; others too believed that cross-racial tension fomented the magnitude of pandemonium. One commenter, Richard Castrellon, described a confrontation that he witnessed between "the Crips" and "the Hispanic gangs," who broke into an equipment closet seeking makeshift weapons. Another commenter, Todd Sigler, described himself as a "skinny white kid with three of my white suburban friends," who felt that they were "the only white people in that room." He especially felt like a target as he watched "the Crips wearing Raiders trench coats, moving through the crowd and beating people down." He added that, "For years I would think of that night whenever I saw someone with a Raiders jacket on." Conversely, a commenter with username Annadaraban6603 reported an experience of a Crip concert-goer sitting nearby and defending her and her friend when the violence neared. Another commenter with the username Themisianos recalled seeing "a young Mexican gentlemen [sic] laying in a pool of blood," and elsewhere seeing Mexican gang members chasing Black American gang members. Finally, capturing a slice of the distinct gangs in conflict, one commenter observed,

"There were Crips, Bloods, F-Troop [a Chicano gang] from Santa Ana and the Doves from Long Beach, fighting it out." There are many additional details included in the original comments, and most support the notion that this situation became divided along racialized gang lines.

Attuned to the potential danger of this event, local creatives drew on street-level intelligence to understand the situation. Iceman, for example, told me that he avoided the event because word on the street was that gang violence would explode there. Hex related hearing that people were linking up along racial lines to defend themselves. In such a convoluted burst of conflict, it is likely multiple divisions were at play, with minimal organization taking place. At the local level, one of the messages circulating was that the conflict involved cross-racial violence. Moreover, cross-racial violence enlivened by racialized gang affiliations and prison gang politics has been a persistent point of Black/brown tension in working-class communities. The Raising Hell incident emboldened the racial boundaries of West Coast Hip Hop. Furthermore, as noted by Viator (2020), the incident stigmatized the Los Angeles area rap scene. The defining lines of West Coast gangsta rap were being drawn. Perhaps Hip Hop was not the grand unifier that was suggested in spaces such as the Radio Club, Radiotron, and in the *Breakin'* films. At the very least, Hip Hop would become increasingly reliant on street credibility through gangsta credentials (see Rivera 2002), a perspective influencing Brown Los Angeles as well. As Kid Frost stated in his interview with Brian Cross (1993:192), Mexicans were not "really listening to Hip Hop until the emergence of the gangsta rap." Gangsterism had its allure but was laden with racialized politics for creatives.

Racial Crossovers through Radio

Following the Raising Hell incident, the radio station KDAY and its various Black American leaders committed to addressing divisions rooted in gang violence. KDAY's initiatives had important implications for Brown Los Angeles. Declaring a "Day of Peace" on October 9, 1986, KDAY General Manager Ed Kirby organized a live event to address the Raising Hell fiasco. Though Run DMC was prohibited from performing at the city-sponsored LA Street Scene Festival in September of 1986, KDAY featured them live on air alongside singer Barry White, and Olympic boxing gold-medalist Paul Gonzales (Boyer 1986). The celebrities urged gang members to refrain from violence. For two hours, the station opened up their phone lines for conversations about gang violence and the state of their communities. Radio guest Leon Watkins, regional director for the Community Youth Gang Services (CYGS), offered practical solutions to gang members looking to change their lives. According to the *LA Times*, "telephone lines were swamped" (Boyer 1986:1). Watkins's office also received calls that day; at least 500 people called their 231-HELP gang hotline and additional lines. Many callers were gang members seeking to leave their gangs. Watkins hoped that the Day of Peace would offer a season of peace through November and December (Boyer 1986).

KDAY's intervention spoke to the station's influence across ethnic communities. The first station in the United States to primarily play Hip Hop music, KDAY leaders worked to reflect the needs and tastes of the community, and aimed to respond to localized social realities. While their gang intervention efforts primarily focused on addressing violence among Black American gangs, they were also attentive to gang issues in Brown Los Angeles. Their inclusion of Paul Gonzales, for example, signaled an appeal to listeners from Brown Los Angeles and the particular gang-related issues affecting communities therein. The 400 gangs in Los Angeles County, counting 50,000 members in their ranks (Harris 1986), included gangs from different ethnic and racial groups, after all, with many connected to barrios from Brown Los Angeles. Executive director of CYGS, Steve Valdivia, understood KDAY's work as ramping up efforts toward peace, noting specifically that there had been recent successes of peace among gangs in heavily Latine Highland Park, though peace appeared short-lived (Harris 1986).

The Day of Peace brought about some early wins. There were no reported incidents of gang violence that day. According to Leon Watkins, the event inspired a peace treaty among members of the Bloods and Crips (Harris 1986). Many of the young people that drafted the peace treaty were members of the CYGS public works program. Two of the primary stipulations of the treaty were as follows: "1. We the members of the Bloods and the Crips agree to get along with one another, respecting and understanding that we all share a common cultural background. 2. We agree to stop killing each other." As of the *LA Times*'s reporting on November 5t (Harris 1986), the peace treaty only included twelve signatures, but news of the treaty was fast spreading.

To bolster this work, Valdivia announced that his agency would be rolling out the Genesis Project, a jobs program offering alternatives to gangs. A follow-up event was called in November of 1986, sponsored by KDAY, that would include Jermaine Jackson, Jamaal Wilkes, singing group the Whispers, and the LA Dream Team. On June 23, 1987, Run DMC was back in Los Angeles, participating in another panel conversation sponsored by KDAY (Bailey 1987). This conversation was held at the California Youth Authority Southern Reception Center and Clinic in Norwalk, California. Eighty young people, wards of the state, were present to participate in this conversation, which aired live on KDAY. James Hahn, future mayor of Los Angeles, at the time the city attorney, participated in the event. Hahn praised the work of Leon Watkins and the CYGS. Still, Ralph

Bailey Jr. (1987) of the *Los Angeles Sentinel* was skeptical in his reporting, noting that gangs were spreading beyond city centers and jockeying for territory, often related to cocaine distribution. Nevertheless, this meeting, which took place in Norwalk, a city with a significant Latine population, continued KDAY's presence in Brown Los Angeles.

Looking back, Greg Mack's hiring as music director at KDAY in 1983 marked an important step in the station's inroads into Brown Los Angeles. Having worked for radio stations in Texas, Mack arrived in Los Angeles with an attentive ear. He incorporated Hip Hop music into the rotation of his last station in Houston, and is credited with shifting KDAY's musical format into one primarily consisting of Hip Hop music (Alonso 2020). KDAY became one of Los Angeles's most competitive stations when Mack enlisted some of the top DJs in the area. Initially, Mack attempted to recruit Rodger Clayton of Uncle Jamm's Army fame, but was rebuffed. For a time, Clayton's Army did contribute mixes to be played on air, but after a falling-out with Mack, took their services to a competitor (Patrin 2020). Through his connection to Lonzo Williams, Mack brought the World Class Wreckin' Crew, with Dr. Dre and DJ Yella, into KDAY's rotation. This skilled DJ team set off the "Traffic Jam" format, wherein LA listeners were treated to innovative mixes, heavy on Hip Hop, during rush hour traffic. Dre's mixtapes, sold at the Roadium Swap Meet, gained iconic fame. With Dre's mixtape and DJing endeavors soaring sky high, he quit KDAY, leaving a gap in the programming. Through the recommendation of Kid Frost, whom Mack met through networking, Mack was introduced to DJ Tony Gonzalez. Mack was astounded by Tony G's talent and hired him to spearhead his new format. He hired two additional luminary DJs in Jammin Gemini and Joe Cooley. These three formed the foundation of the KDAY mixmasters.

Mack was not able to pay his DJs for their services on air, but they were able to promote their work through their aired mixes and were paid for doing live events around town. For a season, that held the DJs steady, but they began receiving other lucrative job offers, such as touring with artists. Mack amassed a deep cadre of DJs to offset shifts in the DJ rotations. The extended group of DJs recruited on Mack's watch included several with ties to Brown Los Angeles. Along with those already named, the mixmasters included DJ Aladdin, DJ M-Walk, DJ Tray Ski, DJ Romeo, DJ Battle Cat, DJ Ralph Medrano, DJ Julio G, Hen Gee, and Jammin' James. Among these mixers, DJ Julio Gonzalez, was Mexican American and Puerto Rican; DJ Ralph Medrano, aka the Mixican, was Mexican American; and Hen Gee was Honduran American, all with unique ties to Brown Los Angeles.

Mixmasters from Brown Los Angeles were performing a type of crossover on the airwaves, crossing ethnoracial boundaries through DJing. KDAY's outfit of mixers had an array of programmers and performers that understood the diverse tastes of Brown Los Angeles, along with understanding other distinct sectors of the region. Julio G and Tony G, the former having modeled his name after the latter, had an important influence on the programming aimed at Brown Los Angeles, and would eventually shape the sound that became LAtino Hip Hop. While most of these DJs were selected through a live audition process, DJ Julio G, was selected by Tony G, after Tony observed Julio's DJ skills in live performance. Julio G went on to become one of the key Hip Hop curators in Los Angeles radio. Likewise, Ralph M and Hen Gee curated signature sounds that distinguished them from other DJs in the scene. The DJ lineup was so celebrated that listeners from distant locales would labor to capture even the spottiest transmissions, such as future Los Angeles radio personalities the Baka Boyz, tuning in from Bakersfield (Muñoz 2015).

KDAY's platforming of creatives from Brown Los Angeles extended into KDAY's events throughout the community. Often, this involved strategizing over which event locations allowed for reaching particular audiences, keeping in mind racialized gang territories. Casa Camino Real in downtown Los Angeles became a key site for converging crowds from Black and Brown Los Angeles (Abrams 2022). In terms of gang affiliations, it was considered neutral territory. This became ground zero for a burgeoning ethnoracial crossover movement. Still, some creatives from Brown Los Angeles recall having negative experiences when crossing racialized gang boundaries for KDAY. Click the Supah Latin recounts instances when he performed around town with KDAY's performing arts programs and his beatboxing talents were met with resistance because of his Latino ethnicity. He succeeded in winning the crowds over with his talents. Kid Frost recalls a situation where he, Ice-T, and Tony G were performing for a KDAY event at the opening of a Church's Chicken. The event ran amok, when "the Crips and Bloods went at it real bad" (Coleman 2016). So while the crew performing was multiracial, gang lines often limited Hip Hop's spatial presence (Forman 2002). Nevertheless, creatives from Brown Los Angeles were sometimes the face of KDAY; their platforming by KDAY conveyed that creatives of Brown Los Angeles *could* represent Hip Hop in Los Angeles.

Conclusion

Converging diasporas in creative hubs of Los Angeles amplified Hip Hop's resonance in the region. The case of the Harbor Area is an ideal instance of how creatives working across distinct resonance channels, often rooted in their own diasporas, generated expansive opportunities for creative expression. For many creatives, this involved crossing local, racial boundaries. For others, it involved crossing national boundaries. Nevertheless, the heightening of racial boundaries, especially within Black and brown creative scenes, coincided with expanding gang affiliations, and further segmented the West Coast scene. While initially energized by the boundary crossing opportunities that Hip Hop afforded them, many creatives began encountering a highly compartmentalized scene, which decreasingly valued the forms of expression that they had grown to love. Some of these creatives continued to cross boundaries and helped build bridges amid moments of violence and tension. It is important to note that even in cases of cross-racial violence, intervention often consisted of cross-racial coalitions of Black and brown leaders confronting the issues at hand. And even when creatives from Brown Los Angeles were on the microphone, often it was Black leadership or Black collaborators who were helping to build the platforms, such as with KDAY. The collaboration across groups never ceased to be crucial. Those who succeeded the most were often the ones that understood how to navigate the social boundaries ever present in the scene.

8
The Stage and the Crossfade

When thinking of Hip Hop collaborations, I would not have predicted seeing these two acts performing together:

> It's Ahmad, with the homie Dax Reynosa
> Armageddon's getting closer
> So Jurny keep your lyrics in a holster
> Got Satan running cuz we're coming against him and ain't supposed to

Ahmad and LPG (Dax and Jurny), two acts that contributed to the soundtrack of my teen years, were on stage doing a song together. The song was a prereleased version of "World War III," a cut on LPGs 1998 album *360 Degrees*. Ahmad rose to fame in 1994, when his single, "Back in the Day," had multitudes feeling nostalgic for an imagined stress-free childhood. Ahmad himself was still a teen when that song was released, signaling just how quickly the stresses of adulthood could overtake countless Black and brown kids in the hood. Though some labeled Ahmad as a one-hit wonder (Gary 2010), in the late 1990s underground heads knew that Ahmad was still excelling at his craft. For example, his freestyle performance on the *Wake Up Show*, popular for spotlighting underground artists, was an all-time favorite; it stayed in my memory for years even after I lost the cassette tape I recorded it on. Yet, even before that radio appearance, I heard rumors about Ahmad doing Christian music. I did not expect that soon after hearing this news, a mere three years after his hit song, I would see him at a mostly Latino Pentecostal church rhyming alongside Dax and Jurny. He had gone from rapping about life back in the days to rhyming about Armageddon, atop a Pentecostal altar turned concert stage. As I chronicle in this chapter, the factors that brought about this moment were products of a long-standing pattern in which Pentecostalism amplified Hip Hop's resonance in Brown Los Angeles and far beyond.

The performance with Ahmad and LPG took place at an event called "The Spot," hosted by Canaan Fellowship church. Organized by DJ Roman Gallegos, the pastor's son, the event essentially turned the Uptown Whittier neighborhood church into a night club geared toward underground Hip Hop heads. Dance cyphers and freestyle rhyme exchanges took place in impromptu fashion, along with open dance floor times more typical of a dance club. At various points, the crowd's attention was directed to the stage so scheduled artists could perform live. Between 1997 and 1998, I attended several of these events. In some respects the event was not explicitly Christian, playing Hip Hop records recognizable to a wider audience. In other ways, it was a Christian event, especially given that all featured artists identified as Christians at the time. Among these, many were active in the LA underground scene, frequenting spots like the Good Life Cafe, Project Blowed, Club Unity, Club Elements, and Foundation Funkollective. Still, for many of these artists, their primary platforms were churches, and often Latino Pentecostal churches.

"The Spot" was part of a larger network of sites and events, a scene, that straddled the worlds of underground Hip Hop and Christian Hip Hop (Gault and Harris 2019). The expansion of "Holy Hip Hop" in Los Angeles, as Zanfagna (2017) argues, was itself an underground phenomenon. It was a response to seismological and sociological earthquakes and sent its own sonic shakes through the cityscape. The scene I encountered was bustling in the late 1990s, spilling into the early 2000s, often represented by events taking place every weekend throughout the greater Los Angeles area and involving substantial participation from Brown Los Angeles. This hybrid scene of the late 1990s, I came to learn, emerged from boundary blurring work that took place in an earlier era, starting in the time of sky-rhyming. In this earlier era, crucial creative energy was generated within certain Latino Pentecostal churches that operated as "fluid sets," allowing boundary-crossing cultural performativities for outreach purposes (Hodge 2010:208). As West Coast Hip Hop was being defined, and the first iteration of a Los Angeles scene died down, one scene that began to emerge was tied to these religious spaces serving urban communities. At this moment, churches were poised to offer something unique to those who had lost the creative spaces that shielded them from the outgrowths of structural inequality.

Scholars of Hip Hop and Christianity often examine how Hip Hop has been adapted by Christians to spread the gospel, the good news (Gault and Harris 2019; Pinn 2007; Zanfagna 2017). In this chapter, however, I also examine how Hip Hop was spread through the Christian message. In particular, I contend that the creative resonance emerging in these congregational spaces helped to preserve the underground resonance characteristic of early Los Angeles Hip Hop. This was particularly "an ethos of the subaltern," which Anthony Kwame Harrison describes as featuring "maverick sensibilities of those who assert agency from positions of social marginalization and oppression" (2019:1). The impetus of Pentecostals to reach racially marginalized urban populations partly facilitated this subaltern resonance. Along with preservation, innovation was taking place in these spaces, as new artistic adaptations emerged, often motivated by outreach efforts. Simultaneously, dissemination took place, as creatives went forth to spread their message, and shared Hip Hop along the way.

Paradoxically, these performative church stages became spaces of both redemption and rebellion. Even as these spaces were meant to provide participants with access to the sacred, their underground, subaltern ethos blurred the boundaries between sacred and profane (Hodge 2016; Zanfagna 2017). This blurring of boundaries allowed for ongoing resonance across explicitly and nonexplicitly religious expressions. As Alex Nava (2022:20) notes, in Hip Hop the sacred and profane are "less parallel streets than crossroads." Here, acts of creative redemption became acts of creative transgression. As I chronicle in this chapter, through spaces of creative transgression, churches serving Brown Los Angeles came to amplify Hip Hop's resonance. These churches contributed to the conditions that gave rise to the scene I witnessed a decade later and made Hip Hop believers out of a wide array of creatives.

Found at the Altar

Accepting his girlfriend's invitation, David Guzman, aka MC Sin, began attending church at Harvest Christian Fellowship. The pastor there, Greg Laurie, customarily had an altar call, inviting attendees to give their lives to Jesus Christ or renew their commitments to God. Guzman approached the altar again and again, several weeks in a row; he felt the Spirit moving in him. On one occasion, he went forward to the altar and felt an inner voice saying to him, "You need to rap for Jesus!" He understood that God was speaking to him. When troubles at Radiotron emerged, Guzman had wrestled with what to do next. He ended up in the Inland Empire, in San Bernardino and Riverside counties. The church he attended, Harvest, was emblematic of Southern California's Jesus Movement, which originally drew hippies into its fold. The church had sprung from the ministry of Pastor Chuck Smith, a one-time member of the Pentecostal denomination the International Foursquare Church who founded the Calvary Chapel church network. When Guzman first attended, he noted it was a predominantly white church within a suburban environment, but the testimonies of many congregants resonated with him. He saw that many were "recovering stoners," and recalled his own past: "When I went to junior high I was part of the stoners. I was a wannabe stoner! So I went to church with these recovering stoners! I started to get saved."

Guzman continued seeking ways to maintain his livelihood through his Hip Hop talents, now in the Inland Empire (IE), 50–60 miles from Los Angeles. The IE was brimming with creative talent and opportunities. Guzman described with excitement how, "a new club was opening in Riverside called Club Metro. For the grand opening they hired me to open the club. The one night a week that I did was a Hip Hop night and I brought in the Airforce Crew." The Airforce

Crew, B-boys that Guzman worked with at Radiotron, included Lil Cesar, who had helped David in running youth programs. David gladly explained, "They all came from LA for the grand opening. They did a Hip Hop show for us. As a matter of fact we did a contest and those guys won! Everybody thought I rigged the contest. Lil Cesar, Oz Rock showed up. Orko. They were my boys." The participation of these B-boys allowed Guzman to relive his time at Radiotron.

Despite some successes, Guzman struggled with substance abuse. On one fateful Sunday, after going up for the church altar call, it occurred to Guzman that perhaps he would find support from some of his new church acquaintances. As he pondered this idea, his sight fixated on the church's sound engineer. Immediately after Sunday service ended, Guzman darted over to the sound booth. As Guzman recounts, "I'll never forget, I told the sound man, 'man, I like your beat. I like what you guys are doing. And I heard a voice when I was here at church that I'm supposed to rap for Jesus.' And so he takes me to the back room where he's going to show me something."

The sound engineer invited Guzman behind the stage to a sound equipment storage room. Along the way, he asked Guzman his name. "My name is MC Sin," Guzman replied. The sound engineer looked at Guzman with a smirk, and unphased reached into an equipment closet and handed Guzman a four-track recorder, which Guzman could use for a home recording studio. David, quizzically, stared at the device. "'You need to go rap for God!,' he said to me. I'll never forget that. He didn't even know me!" On a subsequent Sunday, the sound engineer took Guzman to the church bookstore and gave him a cassette of a group called the Rap-Sures. He described them as a white rock band from Newport Beach, California, who had rap songs on their album. Guzman appreciated their attempt at Christian rap, but he mostly enjoyed the rock music on the album.

Guzman continued seeking Hip Hop–related opportunities that appeared at odds with his newfound faith commitments; these opportunities eventually forged an important connection. He had the opportunity to collaborate with members of 2 Live Crew during their formative stage in the Riverside area, before they reached stardom and moved to Miami. Fortuitously, Guzman was then given the chance to serve as MC for a show headlined by the band War. He was invited to promote the event on local radio. As David spoke on the radio show, he felt an urge to talk about his spirituality. That night, he identified himself as a Christian Rapper on the air.

The phone at the station started ringing almost immediately. The incoming call was from a young rapper named Christopher Cooper. Cooper had difficulty speaking, as he was recovering from an assault-inflicted brain injury. He had recently gotten out of a coma, and a portion of his face was paralyzed. Cooper resonated with Guzman's vision of Christian Rap. He too said God had called him to be a conscious rapper that talked about God. The two decided to connect.

Cooper was hoping to record his first demo. Guzman had the equipment to do just that. They met up after their radio show conversation, and the demo became reality. The demo, and his skills on the mic, would position Cooper to become a leader in Christian Hip Hop.

For the time being, Guzman, who by now had changed his name to MC Scroller, planned to start a Hip Hop crew, called JC and the Boyz. JC stood for Jesus Christ. "I had this vision because I was following what I knew from the Bronx. Everyone ran with a crew! Most emcees didn't rap alone," Guzman explained. The name JC and the Boyz was in some ways a promise that Guzman was making to himself to build a community of creatives, "But I didn't have any 'Boyz,' it was just me!" he mused. Now he had a partner to rap with. Cooper had other partners he was rapping with already, and they called themselves Soldiers for Christ. Guzman saw an opportunity to combine forces, so he brought Cooper and his crew into JC and the Boyz. Along the way, David invited other creatives, like twin brothers Robbie and Noel Arthurton, who were emcees and dancers, to join the crew. The pair had come to California in hopes of making it in the entertainment industry. At one point, they connected with Kid Frost, but that collaboration fizzled. This supercrew of emcees represented various different backgrounds, including Black American, Puerto Rican, and Mexican American.

The Role of Pentecostalism

Pentecostalism is one of the fastest-growing religious movements in the world, historically finding resonance among working-class, marginalized populations. The movement narrates its genesis back to an upstairs room in Jerusalem wherein the followers of Jesus Christ unexpectedly began to speak in a variety of tongues, given utterance by the Spirit of God, or Holy Spirit. According to Christian tradition, the incident occurred during the Jewish celebration of the Feast of Weeks, dubbed "Pentecost" in Koine Greek, with Jews from the broad reaches of the Jewish diaspora converging on Jerusalem for the holiday. Onlookers were bewildered yet drawn to this spectacle of speech, as they heard their own disparate languages spoken by Galilean Jews. The Apostle Peter emerged to interpret for the spectators what the unfolding scene represented, explaining the event as a fulfillment of prophecy.

Modern Pentecostalism is linked to the Azusa Street Revival, which took place in Los Angeles in 1906. The Revival transpired in a former horse stable in Los Angeles, but began at a prayer meeting at a house on Bonnie Brae Street, about a mile from the location that would house Radiotron seventy-seven years later. The gathering was led by a Black preacher, William Seymour. Racial, linguistic, and socioeconomic lines were blurred, though not without opposition.

The Revival, which lasted for years, challenged the racial capitalist order of its day (Day 2022). As Keri Day argues (2022), many of the practices that emerged from the revival are resonant of the spiritualities cultivated by enslaved peoples of African descent and their descendants, with Black women playing an important role therein. Mexicans were active participants in the revival services (Sanchez-Walsh 2003; Espinosa 2014; Ramírez 2015), and many went on to become Pentecostal evangelists among compatriots in the United States, in Latin America, and beyond. Puerto Ricans working the sugarcane fields in Hawaii encountered outgrowths of the revival through preachers in Hawaii (Espinosa 2014), and some converted to Pentecostalism; many returned to Borinken and to the contiguous United States, where they spread Pentecostalism. Mexican and Puerto Rican converts amplified the resonance of the movement, in some cases working together.

In the time of sky-rhyming, some Pentecostal churches were welcoming of Hip Hop creatives, reflecting distinct resonances between Hip Hop and Pentecostalism. As Emdin (2017:110) proposes, Hip Hop "derives many of its contemporary forms from models developed and practiced in Black Pentecostal churches." The resonances between Black Pentecostalism and Latino Pentecostalism (Ramírez 2015), in turn, contributed to Hip Hop's resonance in Brown Los Angeles. In my own experience, an Afrodiasporic movement originating in the Bronx, New York, made sense to me, in part, because of Latino Pentecostalism. Through Pentecostalism, Latinxs engaged with traditions rooted in Black American spirituality. Pentecostalism also functioned as a cross-coastal channel of resonance for Latine collaboration. It is no wonder that while the lifeworlds of many creatives were crumbling in the mid-1980s, with some creatives literally losing their lives in those years, people of diverse backgrounds found refuge in Latino Pentecostal churches.

The Cross and the Switchblade

The Victory Outreach church movement was a key link between Latino Pentecostalism and Hip Hop. Victory Outreach, started by Pentecostal pastors Julie and Sonny Arguinzoni, was one of only a few churches welcoming expressions of Hip Hop in the 1980s. Julie is Mexican American, and Sonny Italian–Puerto Rican. When the couple met as students at an Assemblies of God theological school, the Latin American Bible Institute (LABI) in La Puente, California, both had recently overcome drug-related struggles. Julie struggled to intervene in her brother's drug addiction. She attributed her own religious conversion to the testimony of her "converted ex-addict brother" (Hansen 2018). Sonny's issues with substance abuse were more personal.

Precursors to Pastor Sonny's story are captured in the book, *The Cross and the Switchblade*, an autobiography cowritten by Reverend David Wilkerson (Wilkerson, Sherrill, and Sherrill 1963). A film adaptation of the book starring Pat Boone and Eric Estrada aided in the proliferation of Wilkerson's story. The book and film portray Pentecostal preacher Reverend David Wilkerson's evangelistic work among gang members in New York City. The dramatization of Wilkerson's story, according to Orsi (1999:11), falls within "the popular American genre of Christian narratives of city redemption." Orsi proposes that these accounts flatten the experiences of urban community life, misrepresenting the racialized experiences of residents, and overlooking lived religious practices in the community. While Orsi's observations serve as a cautionary note against the evangelical tendency of casting cities as centers of vice and perdition, it is also important to consider the lived religious experiences of urban dwellers who joined Wilkerson's ministry. Wilkerson's ministry resulted in the founding of Teen Challenge, a faith-based organization dedicated to treating people with substance abuse issues.

Given his struggles with substance abuse, Sonny Arguinzoni found help at an early iteration of Teen Challenge. As a heroin-addicted teenager in New York City, his hometown, Arguinzoni had hit rock bottom. At Teen Challenge, Arguinzoni encountered evangelist Nicky Cruz, who himself had converted through the evangelistic work of Wilkerson. After experiencing a religious conversion through his interactions with Cruz and Wilkerson, Arguinzoni came to Los Angeles County to attend the same Bible school that Nicky Cruz had attended, LABI.

In 1967, Julie and Sonny founded Victory Outreach Church, which Hansen notes was "a ministry dedicated to addicts" (2018:70) from the start. Their church ministry eventually birthed a church and rehabilitation network extending throughout the United States and beyond. In a 1999 interview, Arguinzoni stated that 90% of the movement's pastors were ex-addicts (Hansen 2018:71). Victory Outreach's rehabilitation model shared many similarities with the Teen Challenge model. Along with a focus on drug rehabilitation, the target audience throughout the Southwest tended to be Latino and Chicano (Vigil 1982), though some congregations were multiethnic. The movement's Pentecostal roots are represented by its lived theology, the founding pastors' training,[1] and the founding pastors' conversion experiences.

The Pentecostal commitment to evangelism using expressions that are intelligible to targeted audiences is a critical aspect undergirding Victory Outreach's incorporation of Hip Hop into its public outreach (León 2004). With its readily

---

[1] The Assemblies of God is the Protestant denomination with the largest number of Latine members (see Espinosa 2014).

transportable, easily adaptable forms of expression, the Pentecostalism of Victory Outreach melded itself to the urban expressive cultures of the communities that it was embedded within (Flores 2014). Based on the stories of Victory Outreach members, this process of Hip Hop adaptation was largely organic, emanating from members themselves, not from a grandiose strategic plan hatched by a board of distant leaders. And leaders themselves were likely to be in tune with the streets, as most had come from the streets. Moreover, most of the Hip Hop performers at Victory Outreach had sufficient street credibility to be taken seriously. If any church could pull off having Hip Hop at the pulpit, and gathering an audience for it, it was Victory Outreach.

A Chicano Rap Gospel

As I sought to understand how Hip Hop started showing up at Victory Outreach, several people pointed me in the direction of Danny Lara, one of the youth leaders at the church since the early 1980s who continues to work as a minister. Pastor Danny speculated that he was likely the first person to rap on stage at Victory Outreach, in the early 1980s. While nailing down the exact date of this occurrence is difficult, the means by which Danny Lara was inspired to rap provide some clues as to when Victory Outreach welcomed its first rapper to the pulpit. "I learned to rap from Ice-T," Danny asserted. I thought that Danny meant that he learned to rap by listening to Ice-Ts records, but learned instead that Danny claimed a face-to-face interaction with Ice-T:

> My friends and I would go over to Venice Beach and we'd see Ice-T rapping there with some of his crew. One time I went up to him and started talking to him. Ice-T hadn't gotten big yet, so we just walked up to him and had a conversation with him. I asked him what it is that he had to do to make his raps. I wanted to know how he came up with his lines and how he put it all together. So Ice-T pulls out this paper bag and then he starts to write on it. He showed me how he would write out his rhymes, line by line, and then come up with a full verse. I watched him do it and then I went right home and started doing it for myself.

This story suggests that Danny learned to rap circa 1983, given Ice-T's frequenting of Venice Beach at the start of his career. With this new skill, Danny soon became the house rapper for Victory Outreach events. In establishing this newfound identity, as an emcee, Danny tested out various stage names: "I started with the name DLJ, which stands for Danny Loves Jesus. But I wanted a different name that was harder, so then I started going by the name Homeboy Sermon."

Homeboy Sermon is the name that several collaborators associated him with decades later, suggesting that the name stuck. His new skills became especially helpful for some of the outreach-oriented events that Victory Outreach was known for.

As part of the youth leadership team, Danny had influence in the lives of many young people. He was a mentor and a role model to members of the youth group, and also was successful at reaching young people on the street and inviting them to attend church events. His outreach efforts were especially targeted at young people involved with Los Angeles urban culture. Danny explained that it was not actually his rapping that drew large numbers of young people with an affinity for urban culture to the church. Instead, he clarified that, "I had guys coming from all over LA to Victory Outreach. It started with me recruiting dancers for the *Duke of Earl*." *The Duke of Earl* was an elaborate theatrical performance produced and presented at Victory Outreach. Dancing, not rapping, was initially the main artistic expression of interest for many young people during that period.

Danny's mention of recruiting dancers for *The Duke of Earl* reflected a particular commitment that was characteristic of Victory Outreach: Victory Outreach excelled at drawing from cultural expressions that were familiar to urban, mostly Chicano audiences (Flores 2014). *The Duke of Earl*, for example, was a play that Victory Outreach produced to reach young people especially drawn to Chicano street culture. The play depicted the struggles of Chicano gang life and presented stories of life transformation among those who chose to accept the evangelical gospel message (Sanchez-Walsh 2003). Hip Hop would eventually be incorporated into these stage performances. This implementation of Hip Hop elements meant that Hip Hop was being juxtaposed alongside an older Chicano cultural performativity, noted by Arlene Sanchez-Walsh as reflecting Chicano street culture from as early as the 1970s—pre–Hip Hop in Los Angeles.

This implementation of Hip Hop performances in Victory Outreach's theatrical productions seems to have followed the pathway expressed by other Los Angeles Chicano creatives for whom West Coast funk culture served as a precursor to Hip Hop culture. West Coast funk culture provided a cultural repository deemed acceptable by many Chicanos for expressing a sense of ethnic authenticity, given the longstanding investment of Chicanos in funk culture (Vincent 2014). For a production intended to portray a raw and authentic image of street life, funk culture would have proven just right. And as for the integration of Hip Hop into the Chicano-centered performances at Victory Outreach, the initial reliance on funk culture would have been a logical pathway. Danny's recollection of events suggested as much, noting that the first dancers he recruited were poplockers, a decidedly Los Angeles expression tied to funk culture. Eventually, other elements of Hip Hop, such as DJing and breaking would be integrated into these plays. To this extent, based on her research in the 1990s and early 2000s, Arlene Sanchez Walsh notes a clear integration of Hip Hop into Victory Outreach's performances. As she states (2003:146), "Victory Outreach, in particular, seeks not only to validate Hip Hop culture but also to rescue the gang member from his or her vanquished status in American culture."

Even as Hip Hop and proto–West Coast Hip Hop were being blended into recognizable expressions of Chicano street culture, reflecting modes of cultural confluence that were certainly happening on the streets, Hip Hop itself was being altered at Victory Outreach. Moreover, even as Chicano culture was being influenced by Hip Hop, new iterations of Hip Hop were being generated. This is likely an adaptation that Zanfanga (2017:7) references in her study of Christian Hip Hop in Los Angeles, when she states, "the gangsta rap that many gospel rappers previously performed is informed by the *cholo*-inspired attire, tattoo art, and lowrider culture of Southern California Chicanos, revealing how black and brown diasporas also find their overlap through holy hip hop." Danny specifies that regarding the way Hip Hop was being integrated, "we put an oldies feel to it." That is, Danny and his emerging group of performers integrated the familiar sound of oldies into their performance. Danny himself would eventually have the opportunity to rap during some of the *Duke of Earl* performances. When asked what instrumentals he would use to rap over, he indicated that he employed, "oldies instrumentals."

The blending of rap and oldies is a trend that McFarland (2008) has noted as being especially prevalent within Chicano rap music. McFarland points to popular songs produced by Tony G and Julio G which draw from oldies as songs that are highly recognized by Chicanos. Tony G, in particular, sampled oldies as part of his production repertoire. The work being done at Victory Outreach, as described by Danny, possibly foreshadowed the well-known musical projects produced by Tony G, Julio G, and other producers in this Chicano rap tradition. Danny's accounts are from the early 1980s, suggesting Victory Outreach functioned as a space for urban cultural experimentation, all for the cause of reaching young people for Jesus Christ. Through their theatrical productions, the stage was being literally and figuratively set for the emergence of a particular stream of Hip Hop. While I do not argue that these productions at Victory Outreach were the ultimate origins of Chicano Rap, they certainly made a contribution to the subgenre.

Lest we consider that the cultural innovation taking place at Victory Outreach was restricted to a narrow, localized scene, that of the Victory Outreach congregation, Danny made it clear that Victory Outreach's evangelistic efforts were widespread. "We went all over Aztlan," Danny indicated. "Aztlan" is a term that rose to popularity within the Chicano movement of the 1960s and 1970s. As delineated by Lomelí (2017:2), during the emergence of the Chicano movement, "Chicanos felt the need to belong somewhere, and Aztlan became the closest thing to a physical reference of origins." Danny's reference to Aztlan pointed to the evangelistic tours throughout the Southwest that the Victory Outreach teams would go on, taking their plays and performances on the road. The use of the term "Aztlan" also points to the understanding of this movement taking place especially within Chicano spaces.

This blending between Hip Hop and Chicano street culture was not always a smooth process, as attested to by Danny himself. The image that Danny represented became a contested territory as demand for his rapping ministry started to rise. Homeboy Sermon was not only a rapper but also a preacher, after all. "They would get two for one," Danny explained, noting that Victory Outreach pastors respected him both as a rapper and as a preacher. He recalls that one of the Victory Outreach pastors that he was working with tried to shape the image that he portrayed on the stage and pulpit: "This pastor tried to tell me how to dress if I wanted to be a rapper," Danny remembers. "He had me dress like a locker—like Rerun used to dress on that TV show, What's Happening! I told him I don't want to wear those bright colors." The particular style that the pastor told Danny to dress in points to the early era of rapping that Danny was making an excursion into, and also highlights the particular reference points that were at the pastor's disposal. Danny preferred what he deemed to be a more Chicano-oriented style of dress.

Opportunities continued for Danny to use his talents within the Victory Outreach network, and also on street platforms throughout the Los Angeles area. On various occasions, Danny had the opportunity to open up for evangelist Nicky Cruz, immortalized as the central character of the film *The Cross and the Switchblade*, and a leading figure in the Victory Outreach movement. Danny also recalls going to rap on the streets of East Los Angeles, on Whittier Blvd. He would play his instrumental tapes through a boombox and rap his lyrics on the street to whomever would gather. Danny hoped to gather others in his rap endeavors, with one particular project, a mixtape called "That's What Time It Is!" providing an opportunity to gather other talented rappers in the area. In part, the project allowed Danny to draw people out of the woodwork. In order to recruit other talented Christian rappers, Danny and his associates "threw a call out." They spread the word through their networks and people began to contact them about participating in the mixtape. Not all were invited onto the project, though, as "the ones that were good we had them go into the studio," whereas those less talented were turned away.

The studio that Danny and his associates had access to, a studio in the Frogtown neighborhood of Los Angeles, was used by other artists, some who would rise to fame. Danny claims an especially poignant memory of running into members of the group N.W.A. at the studio as N.W.A. had been finishing up a recording session at the studio. "We started talking to some of the guys from

N.W.A.," Danny adds. "We ended up sharing the gospel with them, and we told them about the type of music we were doing," Danny continues. He recounts that Dr. Dre told Danny and his partners, "'That's a cool concept that you guys have.'" Danny lamented that Dre did not understand that what they stood for was not a "concept," but rather a commitment to serving God.

The gospel encapsulated in Chicano Hip Hop packaging that Danny was sharing moved him even farther out than he imagined, geographically speaking:

> We had the chance to go all the way to New York. People at first told us you aren't going to do well here. You guys are West Coast. All the guys from the West Coast would brag. But we weren't like that. Later, they told me that I was the only one that they liked. Because I would share my testimony with them, and I'd talk to them. I remember a guy from the Latin Kings got saved. After he got saved, I gave him my jersey that I was wearing. He couldn't believe it.

These opportunities were focused on spreading the gospel message, but they also involved experiences of cultural exchange. Danny was sharing what he knew from Los Angeles, and the forms of sharing the gospel developed at his home church in Los Angeles, with young people in disparate locations throughout the United States. Still, the greatest task that these ministers had before them was to care for the many marginalized young people who came through the doors at their churches. Many of these youths sought life-giving resources and were living on the edge.

Turning Tables

One of the leading figures of that era at Victory Outreach, Youth Pastor Pepe Montenegro, aka Pastor Peps, recalled that their youth ministry experienced a rapid phase of growth during the time that Hip Hop creatives were showing up. One particular exchange with a creative stood out to him. Pastor Peps remembered how the aroma of fresh donuts at the Winchell's donut shop sweetened the mood while he embarked on a potentially intense conversation with a new church attendee. A young man, encouraged by his girlfriend to speak to Pastor Peps about spiritual matters, sat with Pastor Peps at Winchell's. Eddie, the young man, thus far had a generally positive experience at the church. Nevertheless, the more he got involved at the church, the more he felt unsettled. The Christian tradition that Eddie had been raised in, and the form of Christianity he was experiencing at Victory Outreach, did not feel compatible to him. In Pastor Peps's words:

> He was still a little rough with Christianity. One day at church he pulled me aside and he said, "Hey, I want to talk to you about this." So he had his Catholicism that he wanted to run at me. And so, he and I sat with his girlfriend at the Winchell's donuts right there on Coberta and Workman Mill Rd. We sat there in the corner. We did some apologetics. As we went through the conversation, he accepted the Lord that day at Winchell's. I led him to the Lord.

The concept of accepting the Lord denoted an experience of spiritual conversion among Victory Outreach regulars. Indeed, testimonials of religious conversion were part and parcel of the Victory Outreach culture, a church noted for accounts of radical religious conversion experiences among young people often involved in gangs, crime, and/or substance abuse (Flores 2014). If anything, this particular testimony, of Eddie's conversion, was quite tame. He was not a hardened gang member, a drug addict, or a criminal with a long rap sheet; he had a car, a job, and was in a steady relationship. As Pastor Peps remembered him, he came from a nearby suburb, was outgoing, and had a strong entrepreneurial spirit. What made Eddie's testimony stand out was not that he had hit rock bottom, but that he had a particular set of skills that were especially valued at Victory Outreach: Eddie was a DJ.

The youth group at Victory Outreach was mesmerized by the innovation that Eddie exhibited when he was first allowed to DJ at church. Eddie introduced the ministry of vinyl to the altar. Mimicking the motion of a DJ scratching records, Pastor Pepe imitated the sounds Eddie produced on his turntables: "Je-sus, Je-Je-Je-sus, Praaaaise the Lord!" The youth group crowd had never heard anything like this. They had heard Hip Hop, but had not heard someone making Christian pronouncements by scratching records. The first time the church heard this, Pastor Peps recalls, "We were all blown away! Like, 'Yeah, do that!'" The number of young people attending the youth services swelled by the hundreds as representations of Hip Hop culture became more frequent at the church. DJ Dove is the name that Eddie Valenciano would be known by. He contributed to an expansion of Hip Hop in the church around 1986, before the concept of a Hip Hop church had been packaged and marketed (Miller 2012). He also became one of the most successful producers of early Christian Hip Hop artists in the Los Angeles basin, eventually starting his own label, Holy Terra Records.

A Holy Hip Hop Hub

A variety of creatives started showing up at the doors of Victory Outreach and ultimately gave rise to the concept of "Holy Hip Hop." Guzman arrived after receiving a flier for an event there. The church was hosting a youth talent night where participants could sign up to showcase their talents. Guzman showed up eagerly on the night of the event and scoped out the place. A couple hundred young people, mostly teens, were energized by the upcoming performances. Guzman signed up to rap. Quickly, he realized that he was not the only rapper in the house. Dax and Jurny took to the stage and rocked the crowd; they were extremely talented, by David's estimation. A showman himself, Guzman also took to the stage and flexed his skills. Soon after, he connected with his fellow MCs. Without hesitation, Guzman pitched the idea to Dax and Jurny that they join him as part of JC and the Boyz. However, Dax and Jurny informed him of their own crew, LPG, and that they would keep their own association. Guzman wondered why they held onto their name, the Lord's Personal Gangsters, and suspected the influence of gangsta rap played a part. Nevertheless, David remained in communication and collaboration with Dax and Jurny.

Soon, David was inviting other MCs and other acts to visit Victory Outreach. Chris Cooper, aka Super C, aka Sup the Chemist; the Dynamic Twins, composed of Robbie and Noel Arthurton; and MC Peace, a Puerto Rican MC and producer extraordinaire from the Bronx, were among the squad. A number of these emcees had East Coast ties. Super C, the Dynamic Twins, MC Peace, and Guzman himself had roots in New York. the founding pastor of the church, it turned out, also had roots in New York. As Guzman excitedly pointed out, founding pastor Sonny Arguinzoni was an Italian Puerto Rican from New York. Guzman strongly identified with Pastor Sonny, and ultimately established ongoing rapport and a close connection with him. The connections kept these creatives coming back, even if they belonged to other churches. Some of these creatives alternated between attending Victory Outreach and Loveland Church with Pastor Chuck Singleton, another key creative hub located in Fontana (Zanfagna 2017).

"Holy Hip Hop" emerged from the resonance generated by these creatives. One creative, Andre Henderson, offered perspective toward Holy Hip Hop's formation. Andre, now a Victory Outreach pastor in South Africa, explained that he arrived at Victory Outreach after moving from San Francisco, California, to Los Angeles to attend college. Andre had few resources in Los Angeles, but he had goals and aspirations. His move to California was a leap of faith, and he was living out of his car at the time. One day, while washing his car in Los Angeles, he received a flier for a youth night at Victory Outreach La Puente. The flier said there would be live rappers on stage; according to Andre, that detail caught his eye. As he recalled, "I was into hip hop, so I thought I would check it out. When I went to the Youth Night, I saw a group rapping called JC and the Boyz (Image 8.1). When I saw them rapping I thought I would like to use my talents for God like that." The event sparked something within Andre.

Image 8.1 JC and the Boyz. (Reproduced courtesy of David Guzman)

For Andre, using his talents was not only a creative decision but a spiritual one as well. As he explained, "I made the altar call." His altar experience solidified Andre's commitment to participate at this church. "That following Wednesday I went to the Youth Night," Andre remembered, "and while going to my car, one of the young people walked with me to my car. When he got to my car, he noticed all kinds of clothes and things in my car. He asked me, 'why is all this stuff in your car?' I eventually told him I was living in my car." The young man saw this as an opportunity to help Andre. He asked his mother about having Andre stay with them. Sure enough, his mother agreed, and Andre had a place to stay.

The young man that reached out to Andre was DJ Dove. Grateful, Andre followed Dove home, and was met by a surprise:

When I went into his room; he had two 1200 Technics turntables sitting in his room. I asked him "are you a DJ?" He said "yes" I said "no way! I'm a rapper," and he said, "really?" That day we started rapping and making beats together. We formed a group called the Victory Outreach Disciples. We started doing concerts together, and we named them Holy Hip Hop Concerts. We did our first Holy Hip Hop Concert in 1988 at the Mother Church in La Puente, California, which seated over 1,000 people. It was so full that we had to do two showings.

The act of kindness on the part of Dove, and the step of faith taken by Andre led the two to form their own Hip Hop group and to push forward the concept of Holy Hip Hop. According to Andre, the concept of "Holy Hip Hop" emerged from his work with DJ Dove. Various others have their own perspectives on the origin of the term "Holy Hip Hop." Chris "Super C" Cooper remembers that the term came from him and DJ Dove, during their season at Victory Outreach. Pastor Peps leans toward the explanation that the term emerged during one of their youth leaders meetings, which Dove would have participated in, as he recalls. While minor details vary, all takes include DJ Dove as a contributor. Dove was in the mix, front and center, in the creation of the term. Pastor Peps adds that he believes the term came from the community, that the concept was tossed around and that the community of creatives landed on Holy Hip Hop.

In constructing the concept of Holy Hip Hop, these creatives were establishing an alternative identity that allowed them to not only stay connected to Hip Hop but also distinguish themselves from aspects of the larger movement that they saw as deleterious. By giving a name to their extended cypher, this also created an opportunity for others to join in and for a distinct movement to emerge. While Christian Hip Hop scenes sprung up in multiple locations, Los Angeles would become one of its primary hubs early on. Given the outward-facing nature of churches like Victory Outreach, Holy Hip Hop became intertwined with the message that these creative evangelists preached.

Crossing Boundaries

In providing a creative sanctuary, Victory Outreach also functioned as a lab where creatives tested the boundaries of faith and artistic expression. One important way the boundaries of faith and creativity were tested was through the preservation of a particular aspect of Hip Hop: battling. Danny Lara, who did much of the recruiting of young people for the shows and performances that Victory Outreach sponsored, incorporated battling into his recruitment. Danny was himself attuned to the dance styles of the day and dabbled in popping, for example. As creatives with a variety of Hip Hop talents came to the church, he began to incorporate their skills out on the streets, for recruitment. Pastor Peps remembers that the church would invest in shiny fliers, "like the world, just like party fliers. We even had our own artist that would actually draw some stuff." With flyers in hand, teams would go to spots that attracted young people.

A major music festival, called the Rock of the '80s, in Pico Rivera, served as one of the recruitment grounds. Pastor Peps adds, "we would go there to the actual parking lot, and we'd go in line, and we'd go as close as we could to the entrance and pass out our flyers. And then we had a testimony. We'd have the flier, but then we'd also have a testimony, real quick, BOOM! I was partying. I came out of this. Boom! So we passed out thousands upon thousands at this thing." Danny was central to the recruitment initiatives and he would bring talented dancers to battle people at these sites. Dax and the cousins were part of the team that Danny worked with. Danny would approach potential recruits at these sites and events and would challenge them: "If you guys lose you have to come to our crew." And just like that, many ended up at Victory Outreach. The youth group grew through these ongoing Hip Hop confrontations.

Dax Reynosa had much to say about negotiating the boundaries of Holy Hip Hop and engaging in battles. As Dax explained it, for his crew, the motivation to rap at church was largely pragmatic. Dax was not trying to be a "Christian rapper."[2] There were few stages, according to Dax, that allowed Hip Hop creatives to hone their craft through live performances during the early 1980s, religious or nonreligious. Dax recalls that in his early teen years there were school dances where some young Hip Hop creatives would gather and begin rhyming: "We started rapping in circles or cyphers, and, and then beat boxing." Neighborhood community centers also sponsored teen dances, and these spaces presented Dax with opportunities to cypher with others. When Dax first started rapping, these were the most accessible spaces that gave Dax and his peers some type of audience to perform in front of, albeit in an informal and often spontaneous way. However, as gang banging began to increase, Dax remembers that these opportunities started to dry up, until they were no longer available in his neighborhood.

Thankfully, there were opportunities farther out, and Dax honed his skills through participation at the Radiotron Youth Center; his experiences there influenced how he approached his participation at Victory Outreach. He recalls riding his bicycle and taking public transit to the inner-city hub that drew creatives from far and wide. Participating at Radiotron required an investment, and Dax and his crew were willing to give it. Dax remembered energetically some of the high-profile attendees that he encountered there: "I'd go to Radiotron and Pauly Shore was there! Pauly Shore used to go to Radiotron! Cuba Gooding Jr. used to be a Radiotron! Dre was there, he was in the World Class Wreckin Cru! Myka 9 would go. Jewish kids from the rich neighborhood would ride their bikes down there."

Radiotron was important to Dax not only for furthering his rhyme skills but also because it allowed him to practice the other elements of Hip Hop. B-boying was an especially integral part of the Radiotron community, for example, and

---

[2] Zanfagna notes that many early Christian-identified rappers in Los Angeles eschewed the label of Christian rapper; she attributes this to the fact that many of these artists were rappers first, before they identified saliently with Christianity. Dax differs from many of these artists in that he grew up attending church, as the son of a minister, and still did not want to be labeled a "Christian rapper."

Dax took advantage of opportunities to expand his B-boy repertoire. Battling was often part of honing his skills, and Radiotron offered opportunities to battle creatives from throughout the Los Angeles basin. Moreover, at Radiotron, Dax grew accustomed to interacting with creatives from a wide array of backgrounds. Yet, Radiotron ended in 1985, again reducing the opportunities for Dax and his crew to continue to hone their skills. The expansiveness of Hip Hop, and the opportunities it afforded to bring participants together across the wide cityscapes of the LA Basin infused Dax with a type of Hip Hop cosmopolitanism. Though Hip Hop for Dax was grounded in his immediate environment, it was also a doorway into an expansive social world.

Ironically, even as the rise of gang banging posed threats to the viability of some youth-friendly Hip Hop venues, Gangsta Rap was rising to prominence as a subgenre that was emblematic of LA Hip Hop. This presented a perfect opportunity for Victory Outreach in relation to the type of outreach work they were doing and it also presented an opportunity for Dax. The advent of gangsta rap brought various streams of cultural and creative resonance into alignment within the outreach events that Victory Outreach hosted targeting young urban Black and brown crowds. The long-standing affinity for funk and soul music, for example, functioned as an aesthetic channel of resonance for many Victory Outreach attendees, as well as for potential attendees. Realities of Chicano gang culture were also front and center for much of Victory Outreach's target audience. The growing demand for gangsta rap was prominent among this audience, and church leaders began to recognize this as an opportunity. At that juncture, Dax and his family members had been attending the Victory Outreach mother church, as it was not far from their home. Dax's father had been a pastor in the Foursquare denomination, and began to attend Victory Outreach with his family after transitioning away from his pastoral role. As Dax became increasingly involved with the youth ministry, some of the leaders became aware of his Hip Hop talents. Soon, Dax was invited to share his skills on the stage. Dax especially credits Danny Lara for giving him a chance to take to the stage. Church carnivals were one of the first spaces where Dax was invited to rap on stage.

Dax's skills brought important benefits to Victory Outreach. As Dax explains, the major production of the *Duke of Earl*, which had introduced many members of the larger public to Victory Outreach, was in need of revamping. This production and its various outgrowths were presented to thousands of attendees, and continue to be part of the Victory Outreach culture. Even many non-Christian and unchurched people in the barrios of the greater Los Angeles area are familiar with the productions put on by Victory Outreach. Dax remembers that Danny Lara, who was one of the youth leaders at the time, had been tasked with updating the play, which had been written in the 1970s. There would be a *Duke of Earl* part two. Dax specifically pointed out that the play "needed to be brought up to date to be more youth-friendly. Danny Lara asked my cousin and I to help bring it up to date. It was a big deal that in the party scenes there were now poppers and breakers. We helped bring that in. So not only did we write the intro rap, we also were in the play, in the party scenes." As Dax pointed out to me, he and his cousins Jurny and Vince helped to write a rap that was performed at the beginning of the entire production. Furthermore, Dax and his cousins acted in several scenes of the play, especially in a party scene. The scene included dancers, and Dax and his cousins drew from their talents in that arena as well. A video clip from one of the Victory Outreach productions of the *Duke of Earl* shows Dax rapping on stage alongside Danny Lara. His cousins Vince and Jurny were on stage as well. In that brief clip, dated circa 1987, Dax demonstrated poise and skill that surpassed his young teenage years. As one of his eventual associates, emcee Propaganda, noted about the video clip, Dax's execution was "flawless."

Dax's trajectory was moving beyond the church productions, though. He and his cousins were growing up with the larger scene and momentarily had found a niche, the church, where they could flourish. Yet, just as the scene was expanding, the cousins were also expanding in their creative sensibilities and sociabilities. For Dax, it was important that he and his crew not be pigeon-holed into a limited Hip Hop subgenre. As he explains, "Well, we got lumped into that gospel world, but we're not respected there. Cuz now, in the late '80s, Leimert Park's coming up. Freestyle Fellowship is there, they're not called Freestyle Fellowship yet. Now there's rappers and there's B-boys, it's massive, it's LA wide, and now it's getting worldwide because of NWA and everybody else. But LA is on the map because NWA is dope." Los Angeles was capturing the attention of the world, and the cousins were caught on the underground side of the movement's ever-increasing resonance. The way that Dax knew to build mutual recognition in the scene was to battle.

While Dax was committed to rocking whatever performance stage he was on, his motivation to perform was not solely to win souls in a traditional evangelistic sense. Rather, his motivation was to win souls over spiritually through the vision of Hip Hop that he held (Pinn 2007). And winning souls over, for Dax, sometimes meant gaining a win over an opponent through battling. As Imade Nibokun Borha (2013) aptly titled her thesis about Dax's supercrew the Tunnel Rats, Dax was a proponent of a "Battle rap gospel." Creatives in these scenes were resonating with what the cousins were generating: "So, we're respected by the Aceyalones, the Myka 9s, the Erules, the dudes who were the dudes out here knew us. Why? Because we would battle and because we're battling them. We would battle the dopest dudes from Pasadena, or wherever. We were the only Hispanics—only ones doing it. There were none, zero others. It was me and my cousins," Dax recounted. The cousins were expanding their networks through battling. And as wars were raging on the streets, through their rhymes the cousins were taking names and saving lives.[3]

The habitus that Dax began to embody within the burgeoning underground Hip Hop world did not shut off when he entered into the Christian arena. This was despite the fact that Danny Lara used to get on his case for going to clubs and battling. "Did you preach the gospel?" Danny would ask Dax. Dax was there to expand his skills, though. In fact, Dax recalls that when he was approached by David Guzman to join JC and the Boyz, at Victory Outreach, Dax said, "That sounds stupid. But we can be cool, and we can battle you." And they did stay cool. The crews, by then LPG, and JC and the Boyz, found ways to collaborate. Eventually, some of the members of JC and the Boyz became associates to Dax's supercrew, the Tunnels Rats. Dax, his sister Zane, and his cousin Jurny appear on records with the likes of Sup the Chemist, Peace 586, and the Dynamic Twins, who were all part of the JC and the Boyz crew. Many of the most recognized artists from the Los Angeles Christian Hip Hop world became associates of Dax and his crew. Dax's calling card, battling, helped to simultaneously maintain a boundary of respect, and a spirit of collaboration. The crews that emerged from this scene helped to spark a national movement, a subculture of Christian Hip Hop, but they continued to test the boundaries locally of what it meant to be West Coast Hip Hop.

Conclusion

Similar to the account of Pentecost in the Christian Scriptures, and early accounts of the Azusa Street revival, a type of centrifugal movement emerged from the Hip Hop Scene. Creatives had a wide network of stages, altars, and platforms that they visited and toured on a national level to spread the particular Hip Hop gospel they embodied. Victory Outreach was not the only site of Christian identified Hip Hop in the 1980s. Groups like 12th Tribe came together in the San Fernando Valley, and the Set Free Posse traveled throughout the LA basin setting up street shows. Both of these latter crews had prominent footprints in Brown Los Angeles. Still, as documented by Chris Cooper (2013) in his autobiography, Victory Outreach churches were among the first to offer young artists opportunities for interstate tours. Victory Outreach, then, offered an especially expansive platform through which to spread Holy Hip Hop. These far-reaching moves were formative moments, where creatives battled economic inequalities,

---

[3] Dax and his crew present a helpful counterexample to the "completed fact" theology presented by some Christian rappers, as critiqued by Alex Nava (2022:34). The cypher affinities of Dax and his crew point to a more dialogical engagement with Hip Hop, where, while pronouncements may come across as completed, they are part of ongoing conversations.

racism, and authoritarian personalities to get the respect they deserved (see also Borha 2013). Many aspects of these moments were discouraging, and frustrating for this early batch of creatives, but they soldiered on. Through these trials, these creatives were ultimately forced to make decisions about how they related to the movement that they helped to form.

While Christian Hip Hop is a subgenre of Hip Hop, many of its early proponents were tied to the broader Hip Hop scene and to forms of Hip Hop innovation. The boundary-blurring moves of these creatives problematize facile enclosure of the genre "Christian Hip Hop" and resonate with the more intersectionally robust "Christians and Hip Hop" proposed by Gault and Harris (2019:5). An examination of these converging resonances suggests that what was identified as Christian Hip Hop, more than a subgenre limited to Christian churches, acted as a platform of Hip Hop performance generally—and spread Hip Hop while artists worked to convey their gospel message. With time, many of these creatives ventured away from Victory Outreach, and into other spaces. Some would occasionally return. Yet, this work would be followed by the birth of other more recent scenes, such as the scene captured in the scholarship of Christina Zanfagna (2017) from the 2000s or the scene I describe in my opening vignette. Many new creatives would emerge to amplify their crafts on the stage and to call young onlookers to the altar. As for the veterans, many retained the underground ethos they started with, and chose to continue resonating in the catacombs of Los Angeles's underground scene.

9
Sustaining the Resonance

Tricia Rose (1994:4) states that by 1987, "rap music had survived several death knells." This sentiment was echoed by a number of creatives I spoke to and was conveyed in reference not only to the music but to Hip Hop culture as a whole. The scenes that creatives had immersed themselves in and fashioned their identities around, were either fading away or changing beyond recognition. When Iceman returned from Mexico, for example, he discovered a B-boy culture that was malnourished and in fast decline. Several months after returning from Mexico, by 1986, Iceman lamented, "no one was breaking." According to Iceman, Hip Hop had saved his life, and now the place where many Hip Hop creatives had found solace was disappearing. What would become of Iceman and others now that the scene was moving in a different direction? Various creatives offered perspective as to what was happening with Hip Hop—specifically the grassroots, underground iteration that they belonged to—in the late 1980s. Underground Hip Hop would have to cross from death to life, in order to continue providing a lifeline to these creatives. It appeared that the time of sky-rhyming was a fading memory.

Creative and Social Death

Some creatives spoke harshly of this late 1980s as a time of death and decline, conveying a sense of losing their movement. Graffiti innovator Hector "Hex" Rios remembers the loss he experienced witnessing the changes undergoing the scene. In reminiscing, he emphasized two trajectories that many Hip Hop creatives, especially men, moved toward. According to Hex, one pathway was that "All these dudes went to gangs, slanging, rolling. Everyone was going around with uzis, that was the latest trend. There were [Hip Hop] crews, but there were just remnants." The gangster lifestyle had its allures, which often included access to drugs, or profits from drugs. On the other hand, Hex noted that other creatives gravitated toward the night club life, which was largely bereft of the forms and expressions they had helped to build. He explained, "A lot of these guys went into the disco scene. They weren't breakin anymore. They were dating cha cha girls. They were going to clubs." This latter group was typically entering adulthood and settling down. This also points to the gendered nature embedded in Hex's observations: Many of the key creatives driving the scene were young men who now sought other scenes of sociability; some scenes they sought out had more gender balance than the prior Hip Hop scene, with more women visiting these clubs. For Hex, both options led to the same conclusion: "Everyone here has backstabbed Hip Hop."

Gremz shared many of Hex's views, but in his initial analysis of this era emphasized another factor affecting the decline of the scene: The music and entertainment industry. Similarly to Hex, Gremz noted the major draw to the disco scene, which Gremz asserted was highly influenced by the popularity of freestyle music. As documented by music scholar Amy Coddington, crossover radio stations succeeded by putting their ear to the streets, and paid attention to what urban Latine people listened to. At LA's Power 106, "playlists were aimed at women ages eighteen to thirty-four." Radio executive Jeff Wyatt based his playlists on what he "heard while strolling the Santa Monica pier"; he claimed that he took notes at the beach of what tapes the "Hispanic kids" were playing, and advised other programmers to "be damned" with what was popular nationally because "it doesn't make a lot of sense to care about anything but your audience" (Coddington 2021:43). The music that Power 106 played, "included up-tempo R&B music (by artists such as Club Nouveau and Cameo), dance-pop derived from disco (by artists such as Samantha Fox and Cyndi Lauper, whom Pareles described as 'Madonna wannabes'), and freestyle (by artists such as the Cover Girls and Exposé)."

Before hitting the radio waves, these music formats were often experimented with in clubs. KDAY radio programmer Greg Mack, and radio DJ and producer Tony G were key figures in this move (Abrams 2022). Tony G was instrumental in drawing crowds from Brown Los Angeles to club nights at Casa Camino Real, where KDAY was appealing to diverse communities. DJ Pebo Rodriguez attested to these trends in musical tastes as well, noting that Latine audiences were especially responsive to disco and freestyle; as noted, radio programmers were acutely aware of the broader appeal of these genres across genders. While there were women who participated in the Hip Hop scene, the spotlighted figures tended to be men. The emerging freestyle music format was far more inclusive of women, and perhaps even dominated by women, both as consumers and as artists.

Neecee, introduced in Chapter 4, described loving disco and freestyle music alongside Hip Hop. Some creatives found ways to combine these genres rather than separate them. Neecee and her sister Lilah would perform their Hip Hop–style dances to freestyle music at the club. As Neecee describes, "Well, as you know, disco was coming out, and some of the girls used to go down to the clubs. We'd dance to Debbie Deb, Lisa Lisa, 'Look out Weekend.'" While these songs had come out a couple of years prior, Neecee, who continued frequenting clubs, persisted in mixing Hip Hop dance with freestyle music. This suggests a gendered nature to genre preferences. To Gremz and other men, the scene had shifted away from the original elements. Yet, freestyle and its accompanying genres found an audience in spaces that had substantial representation from women, and some of these women also identified with Hip Hop.

Especially impactful, for Gremz, these years from late 1985 until the early 1990s marked a stark divergence between commercial rap and underground Hip Hop. Hip Hop had largely been grassroots to creatives like Gremz. Now, the grassroots was going underground. And while Gremz noted that some conscious voices received support from the industry, it was generally the industry, not the streets, that was shaping the direction of the movement. According to Gremz, "people had whatever the industry made available to you. The industry killed Hip Hop in a big way." One of the important outcomes of this shift was, "the end of crewism and the beginning of companyism," according to Gremz. The impetus to work in resonant fashion within a crew setting was disappearing. Incentives were now in place to aim for individual stardom.

Unseen from the Scene

Creatives started to disappear from the streets, in more ways than one. While the movement in its prior iteration was dying, some creatives faced both physical and social death (Patterson 1982). One of the most direct modes of social death was incarceration (Jeffries 2011). Through this type of social death, creatives were alienated from their creative communities and from their support systems; their rights were severely restricted and their creative rites significantly restrained. I was astounded that numerous of the creatives I interviewed and studied did time in prison. While Hip Hop had saved Iceman's life, that salvation seemed to be short-lived. Due to drug charges, Iceman was incarcerated for a year. He claims he gravitated toward friends with gang ties due to the decline of his Hip Hop community. Gangs had always been there. Ace Rock, featured in Chapter 3, also served significant time in prison. The fresh-faced youngster who appeared in the *Breakin' 2* film now posed in photographs as a hardened gang member doing time. He recalls trying out the club scene prior to becoming enmeshed in gang life, and being ridiculed by people when he attempted to create dance cyphers as was customary a couple years prior. Zender, too, did time, as did various others.

For some, the outcome proved even more limiting. Social death led to physical death. As some got caught in drug addictions, claiming their hoods, or dealing with mental health issues with little recourse or guidance, death took them from the scenes that they once enlivened. The consequences of involvement with gangs and drugs were increasingly harsh, given what was happening during that period in Los Angeles in relation to laws and enforcement. In 1986, Ronald Reagan passed the Anti-Drug Abuse act, which heighted punitive measures for those involved in drug-related offenses, and also expanded on the categories of offense. Los Angeles became ground zero for this particular battle in the larger War on Drugs. According to historian Donna Murch (2015:164),

> By 1990 drug offenses were 34.2 percent of new admissions to California prisons and 25 percent of detainees in the Los Angeles County Jail, which contained the world's largest urban prison population. The carceral effects were not, however, equally distributed. Numerous studies show the extreme racial disparities of mass incarceration and the war on drugs, and California arguably led this national trend. By the year 2000 the combined numbers of blacks and Latinos were over 64 percent of the total population of the CDC [California Department of Corrections].

The stakes were high as creatives were forced to venture beyond Hip Hop's momentary safety net. Many felt that their sense of identity and agency was being disintegrated. Gremz described the period as, "that time of not knowing who you are, what's going on, the identity crisis, changing what you do." People began to go underground, the "die-hards," according to Gremz. With crews less prevalent, some still held on to hope. Gremz remembers this as a period "when people start to go searching for each other, or trying to bring things back, or keep things going, and you hear these stories of nobody being around, and whose the ones that are going to carry the torches, and even that was considered passe." The analogy that Gremz presents is that "Hip Hop culture was introduced to the world as a very sharp sword and we turned it into a letter opener." In this time of transition, many did not make it out, while others chose to look elsewhere. Some remained rooted by looking toward other geographies.

While Iceman was an early Hip Hop escapist at the height of the West Coast scene, others found pathways of escape during the decline of the scene they knew. Hex could not stand to watch the movement he helped build in Los Angeles die before his eyes. He decided, "I'm taking off to where Hip Hop is still possibly alive, New York," figuring he would find people there still invested in the movement. Prior to that, Hex working a job that drew on his artistic skills, employed by future founders of the Cross Colours clothing brand. At the time, these entrepreneurs, Carl Jones and TJ Walker, ran and owned a company called Surf Fetish, where Hex worked. Hex was designing display backdrops for the company's trade shows and for a season had access to hearty supplies of spray cans. He saved up money and booked a one-way flight to New York City. With little fanfare, Hex says, "I took off, I just disappeared." His primary contact at the time was a foreign exchange student he met in Los Angeles who was now living in New York; Hex stayed with him initially, and found his way beyond that. He ultimately ended up living on the street. He was able to do some of what he planned to do, engage in graffiti writing, and even perform some of his freestyle rhyming on the street, but it was difficult to sustain himself long-term. Nevertheless, for Hex, the move to stay connected to the culture was a life-or-death matter.

Neecee Gonzales took part in a different West-to-East exchange, which she describes in less ominous tones; her experience especially differs from those of the men who described dire situations. In 1987 she went to stay in New York City with a friend that lived in Los Angeles but was originally from New York. For Neecee, the opportunity to stay in New York served to strengthen her identity in Hip Hop. She explains that seeing graffiti as done on actual trains captured her imagination in ways that had not happened in Los Angeles. She also frequented the clubs in the city and was able to expand her dance skills, ever attentive to the nuance of the styles in her new surroundings. Eventually, Neecee would make multiple trips to New York, taking in as much of the Hip Hop experience as she could. Speaking about her and her sister, she declared, "We're West Coast, but we have love for the East, and we brought back whatever we could here [to Los Angeles]." It is notable that rather than fleeing to New York to sustain something disappearing, for Neecee, the trips were about deepening what was still present. To her, there was continuity in expanding her dance skills across club scenes. Nevertheless, she too traversed geographies to sustain her identity.

Gremz escaped with his own agenda. Traveling to New York City, he connected with creatives he had networked with in the past. He was especially interested in identifying those keeping the art of B-boying alive. He recalls walking through some of the housing projects and basketball courts in the city where he had heard B-boys would get busy. He says that there, too, the scene had shifted, largely a casualty of industry tampering. For Gremz, his drive came in part from his ability to sustain creative networks. He had gotten his start early in the scene, and maintained the networks that he and Markski helped build up in Los Angeles. Always looking for ways to connect with those keeping the crafts alive, Gremz found an unexpected way to identify B-boys that were still active.

In high school, drawing from his B-boy skills, Gremz had the opportunity to compete in gymnastics, which at the time were offered at his high school. Gremz excelled at the pommel horse, and competed at a high level, attending regional tournaments and meeting athletes from far and wide. To his surprise, many of the athletes from around Los Angeles that he was competing against in pommel horse were former B-boys. After their competitions, the athletes would generate their own cyphers and resurrect the craft they had spent years perfecting. Gremz continued doing this in 1987 and 1988, the year he graduated from high school. While death of the art and social and physical death threatened some of these creatives, a core group of them held on to the art. In order to hold on, many of them continued to cross boundaries in resonant fashion, sharing the art with others, and attempting to identify those who were still invested in the craft, or had at least retained a recollection of their embodied practices.

Solace in the Music

As gangsta rap was taking off in the West, Afrocentric conscious Hip Hop was also emerging as a force (Ogbar 2007). Though some scholars analyze how this development downplayed Latine authenticity in Hip Hop (Del Barco 1996; Rivera 2003), some creatives from Brown Los Angeles felt a sense of empowerment within this Hip Hop stream (Harrison 2015a). In this era, Koolski, a B-boy from Fullerton, California, was starting to lose his love for Hip Hop. Had it not been for a music intervention he received from a friend, he would not have persisted as a B-boy, ultimately becoming a West Coast affiliate of the prestigious Rock Steady Crew from NYC. As breaking started to decline, he says that he still found ways to dance at "cholo parties," but he also felt a draw toward gang culture. A Black American friend named Rashaun introduced him to conscious Hip Hop music, helping him to see an alternative Hip Hop pathway. Listening to Boogie Down Productions was especially transformational for Koolski. He explains, "I used to think about the lyrics, 'Criminal minded, you've been blinded, looking for a style like mine you can't find it!' I would say that in my head all the time. Rashaun was listening to a lot of East Coast Hip Hop that was coming out back then because his family was from out there. His family there would send him cassettes and they would tell him what to buy here. He would go to Music Plus and buy different cassettes." Had Rashaun not taken the time to introduce Koolski to a more expansive Hip Hop repertoire, Koolski might have joined a gang. He claimed a clearer understanding about the conscious foundations of Hip Hop, and maintained a commitment to the movement.

In similar fashion to Koolski, Delilah Gonzales, introduced in Chapter 4, explains the draw to the music, and in particular to politically oriented lyrics from the likes of KRS1. There was a relatability that she found in this music which spoke to the realities of her social world:

We liked Boogie Down Productions, BDP. The rappers that talked about political stuff, we listened to that because we appreciated what their story was about. I could relate, because what happened in their streets, say on the East Coast, it was happening on the West Coast in our streets too, the survival that these guys had, you know, in single parent homes or hustling on that street to make some money; to put food on the table, moms working all these jobs on and on. Now I'm going to run with the boys and quickly make some money. All of that they were doing on the West Coast too, yes, and if you know that, then you can understand what their grind was. And those lyrics—and I know every lyric to their song, so does my sister—but it hits home like I could still get chills when I hear certain songs because not only does it affect you, the music, but the words. You gotta remember that in the early '80s crack came out so everybody was doing cocaine and crack. Me and my sister weren't doing it, but so many people we knew were.

The music, according to Delilah, raised their awareness about what was happening around them. She and her sister did what they could to speak to their conditions, with their newfound understanding. Delilah and her sister Neecee, however, did not universalize the experience of Black American artists, but rather identified points of resonance with it. They knew there was something unique about the experiences of Black Americans, but also found that these experiences provided them with liberatory insights as Latinas.

Finding a Niche on the Mic

With the decline of a B-boy-centric scene, some creatives dug deeper into the element increasing in popular appeal: emceeing/rapping. Various emcees active in the late 1980s were products of Brown Los Angeles and challenged the racial boundaries of the reconfigured scene. One pocket of creativity that emerged was around Latine-dominant cities to the east of South Central Los Angeles. Cities like Bell, Lynwood, Southgate, and Huntington Park turned out various creatives who played key roles in advancing Hip Hop in Brown Los Angeles and beyond. Even as some neighborhoods in this area experienced high rates of ethnic segregation, various creatives from this area crossed geographic boundaries to boost the signal of their music. Rather than giving up on the changing movement, they shifted their energies to the rap scene.

Among artists from this cluster of gateway cities, Mellow Man Ace, known first as Ase Kool, early on gained notoriety with his bilingual flow. Born Ulpiano Sergio Reyes in Cuba, Mellow released a record with Delicious Vinyl in 1987, "Do This," which spotlighted his English rhymes on the A-side, and his Spanish rhymes on the B-side. The Spanish version would later be reissued in his debut album in 1989, as "Mas Pingon," alongside his hit "Mentirosa," which went gold. Mellow's debut album, *Escape from Havana*, prepared the market for Frost's "La Raza," and sparked Brown Los Angeles's creative imagination. Mentirosa and La Raza shared an important connection: They were both produced by DJ Tony G, one of the primary architects of the Chicano sound that became emblematic of Brown Los Angeles. As previously discussed, Mellow was inspired by Mr. Schick of the Mean Machine, and also drew on his environment concocting his Spanglish rhyme schemes. His community, after all, was a gateway city in more ways than one. It was a gateway into the urban core of the city of Los Angeles, but also a gateway for numerous Latin American immigrants finding their way in the United States for the first time.

Mellow did not rise to fame as a studio-engineered phenom, but rather proved himself for years through the ranks of the house party scene and grassroots gatherings that platformed all the Hip Hop elements. Radiotron director Carmelo Alvarez, for example, remembers that Mellow first picked up the mic at Radiotron. With his brother, Sen Dog, previously Sen Stiff, and T-Tuff, who became Tomahawk Funk of Funkdoobiest, Mellow formed part of DVX (Devastating Vocal Excellence). While some publications claim the group formed in 1988, a flier for an event on July 25, 1987, indicates that the group was performing since then, and likely earlier. Julio G was the first DJ for the group. Damon Trujillo, aka Krazy D, an early member of N.W.A, was an emcee affiliate. B-Real joined as an emcee as well, and DJ Muggs, a teen transplant from New York, was later introduced to the group by Julio G. Julio G became an architect of the Los Angeles sound as an acclaimed mixmaster at KDAY and as a producer. Mellow left the group to launch his solo career. The core members who remained, B-Real, Sen Dog, and Muggs, became Cypress Hill. The circle that formed around this South Gate crew contained some of the most innovative creatives in the Los Angeles Hip Hop scene.

Even as the boundaries between Black American communities and brown communities were becoming more pronounced in the era of gangsta rap, some creatives blurred these boundaries. Members of DVX, for example, challenged these boundaries in Los Angeles as they did not fit neatly into the racial constellations of the area (Ogbar 2007). The Reyes brothers, Senen and Ulpiano, were Afro-Cuban. B-Real's mother was also Afro-Cuban, and his father was Mexican. While B-Real's brother was involved with Mexican gangs, B-Real became involved with a Blood set alongside Sen Dog. Krazy D became the sole Chicano member of N.W.A. He recounts that the N.W.A. song "Panic Zone," was originally written as "Hispanic Zone" (Cizmar 2010). Tomahawk Funk, born Tyrone Pacheco, is Black American and Native American, a member of the Lakota Nation. In joining "Ralph M and Sun," later known as Funkdoobiest, he partnered with Ralph Medrano, or DJ Ralph M the Mixican, and Jason Vasquez aka Son Doobie. Medrano is Chicano, and Vasquez Puerto Rican. Though leaving the group after their second album, Tomahawk Funk was an innovator in the early scene, even concocting Mellow Man Ace's name during a Cypress Street cypher session (Chicago Street TV 2020). Members of this emerging Cypress Street cypher had success on the mic, and blurred rigid boundaries of race, ethnicity, and neighborhood during a period when these lines became increasingly rigid.

Building Peace Movements

Moving to the end of the 1980s, negotiating gang politics became ever prominent for rappers aiming to make it in the industry. In 1990, gangs drew the ire of law enforcement agencies, the attention of media outlets, and the fear of many neighborhood residents. Experts publicly articulated theories about what was causing this spike in gang affiliation, and by extension, gang violence. Steve Valdivia, executive director of Los Angeles County Youth Gang Services, for example, was quoted in the *LA Times* (Sahagun 1990:A1) as saying, "It's become trendy to belong to a gang," a perception that was ultimately harming even youth who were not gang affiliates. Furthermore, the *LA Times* conveyed that "Valdivia also cited a major influx of immigrants from Latin America and other Third World areas 'who have adopted the gang lifestyle and are not as fearful of law enforcement in this country as they were in their homelands.'" These perceptions blamed immigrants from Latin America, and the popularity of gangs, often code for gangsta rap, in heightening gang activity. Such takes were devoid of analysis regarding what drove immigrants to the United States and the structural conditions that drew young people to gangs.

A number of rappers associated with the West Coast movement convened to address the rise in gang violence, particularly gang-related homicides, through their music. This crop of artists included some of the most commercially lauded rap artists of the time, such as King Tee, Body & Soul, Def Jef, Michel'le, Tone-Loc, Above the Law, Ice-T, Dr. Dre and MC Ren, Young MC, J.J. Fad, Oaktowns 3.5.7, Digital Underground, MC Hammer, and Eazy-E. Under the direction of Michael Concepcion, self-proclaimed cofounder of the Crips turned record executive, this assemblage of artists put forth a call for unity in song format. The album, and its namesake hit single, were called "We're All in the Same Gang." According to Ben Westhoff (2016:119), Concepcion "aimed to broker peace between the various warring L.A. gang factions." Though Hochman (1990b) noted in the *LA Times* that not all artists were idealistic about the outcome of the peace efforts made by the artistic collective, the music was eventually credited with helping to orchestrate a gang truce in 1992.

Some brown creatives joined in on the efforts encapsulated in "Same Gang." The compilation album featuring music by the collective billed as the "West Coast Rap All-Stars," included a song by a group called the Latin Kings. The song, "Tumba La Casa," intersected the rise of "LAtino Hip Hop," as well as the wave of West Coast gangsta rap. The style and delivery of "Tumba La Casa" distinguished itself from that of the other songs on the album, largely due to its bilingual content. With an upbeat, funky track produced by Pasadena, California–based producer Broadway, Kool Hec Si, the group's emcee, proclaims that he is making space for people from any "race, or raza." In terms of releasing music on a major label, the Latin Kings may have appeared to be newcomers on that album. Nevertheless, the members of the Latin Kings, Kool Hec Si, who is Puerto Rican, and DJ Fuego, who is Mexican American, had a much deeper history than their contribution to the album reveals.

In many ways, the Latin Kings were an ideal group to bridge the boundaries between Black American and brown Hip Hop, as was emerging in the scene. I spoke to Hector Castro, known as Kool Hec Si, about the origins of the group Latin Kings. The crew name, I assumed, was a reference to the gang Latin Kings. As Hec Si explained, his father was, in fact, affiliated with the Latin Kings in Chicago. Originally, though, Hec Si's group was known as the Puerto Roc Posse, as most of the founding members were Puerto Rican. Given that Hec Si and DJ Fuego stuck together as primary collaborators, and the duo brought on members from distinct backgrounds, Michael Concepcion and other executives found the name Puerto Roc Posse ill-fitting. When they invited the group to contribute to the "Same Gang" project, they suggested the group take on the name Latin Kings. It made sense to Hec Si and he stuck with it.

Hec Si's rise as an emcee came about in the mid-1980s, just as the original grassroots scene was taking a hit and gangsta rap was on the rise. Yet, Hec Si, having been born in the Bronx, had a deep connection to Hip Hop, which seemingly inoculated him from discouragement during changes in the scene. As he described himself, "I fell directly from the tree," referring to Hip Hop's point of origin. Furthermore, Hec Si moved from the Bronx to San Bernardino, California, in 1982. It appeared that San Bernardino preserved some of the creative energy that was dying down in the center of Los Angeles. Hec Si's descriptions of parties and club activities in this outer area known as the IE or Inland Empire, in fact, suggest that places on the periphery of Los Angeles's urban centers were preserving some of the urban artistry. Indeed, the IE gave rise to important groups such as 2 Live Crew, and later A Lighter Shade of Brown, specifically in Riverside. According to Hec Si, there were still active B-boy crews in San Bernardino, far removed from the Los Angeles city center. This was the perfect incubator for Hec Si to sustain his craft as an emcee, and he continued to perform and to battle emcees out in the IE. Being in the IE also gave the crew access to important resources at the local military bases. In fact, Hec Si remembers one of their first producers was stationed at March Air Force base and was originally from the Bronx.

As he reached the end of high school, Hec Si and the Puerto Roc Posse released a song on local label Asgard Records. The single, the original version of "Tumba La Casa," was released in 1988. It was first issued as a cassette tape and later on vinyl. The Puerto Roc Posse, by now, were gaining respect. They had the opportunity to open up for Public Enemy, at a concert in San Bernardino in 1988. Hec Si remembers getting paid $250 by the Boys and Girls Club, who sponsored the event. Subsequently, Hec Si was introduced to KRS1, and had the opportunity to freestyle in front of him. KRS1 appreciated Hec Si's flow. Soon after, Hec Si and the crew caught the attention of Michael Concepcion, who saw potential in the creatives. The youngsters, still in high school, got signed to Warner Brothers records. Working around their class schedules, Hec Si and Fuego often spent weekends in Los Angeles working on music. They would make it back to San Bernardino on time to get ready for school.

The Puerto Roc Posse/Latin Kings were in the running to be the first Hip Hop crew composed entirely of Latine members with music out on a major label. The widely distributed version of "Tumba La Casa," according to Hec Si, was originally recorded in 1988, but did not see the light of day for nearly two years. Though Hec Si and Fuego worked on other projects and even participated in a number of recordings, most of these were never released. The carefully tailored beats that Hec Si was rhyming over were sometimes handed over to other artists that the label had higher investments in. Sadly, as other groups came to the fore in the LAtino Hip Hop stream, the Latin Kings' projects were sidelined on their label. Nevertheless, the Latin Kings had resonated with listeners, as noted in a 1990 article from Florida's *Sun Sentinal* newspaper on "Rap en Español," which celebrates the group's national exposure for "Tumba La Casa." The crew certainly had plenty of talent.

The Latin Kings had survived underground Hip Hop's supposed decline, and had contributed to a peace movement through their music. They had likewise contributed to the innovation in the field and were among the first to champion bilingual rap. Yet, with the disinvestment they experienced, their opportunities languished. While the music of the Same Gang project was helping to fuel a gang truce, Hec Si faced his own personal struggles, and ultimately ended up doing prison time. Through it all, he never lost love for the music and the creative process. When he was released, he was ready to release more music of his own, and returned to his crew and their underground roots. Today, he continues to make music, an emcee through and through. His music touches on themes of unity, peace, and celebration, and he maintains a positive outlook about his craft. "I do it for the love," he asserts.

Returning by Staying

Though his first stay in New York City had been cut short, Hex envisioned himself ultimately going back and settling in New York. A hint of Hex's aspiration to return East was captured in a 1989 documentary, *Bombing L.A.*, produced by Gary Glaser (1991).[1] The film features a clip of Hex describing a particular painting technique that he uses. In the film, acclaimed San Francisco graffiti writer, Rigel "Crayone" Juratovac, describes Hex as being from New York. I asked Hex about that anomalous description. "What happened is that I had just gotten back from New York when he said that. I'm from LA, but I had been in New York, and my plan was to go back to New York." Hex had already built a name for himself as a Los Angeles graff writer, and was one of a handful of graff writers sustaining themselves through the craft. Spending time in New York added to Hex's creative repertoire and to his credentials as an artist. The signs were pointing to Hex's permanent departure from Los Angeles, especially as the scene that he once knew had yet to recover. Gangsta rap, by now, had cemented itself as emblematic of Los Angeles Hip Hop. And yet, something pivoted. Hex stayed in Los Angeles. The *Bombing L.A.* documentary provides clues as to why Hex stayed.

"The graffiti convention is what kept me here in LA. I was ready to go back to New York," Hex explained. He was calculating his next move when he heard about the graffiti convention, later featured in Glaser's graffiti documentary. The event, called "Spray Can 88," was organized by graff writer Frame, along with Carmelo Alvarez, of Radiotron fame, in 1988. Carmelo continued to work in roles that involved cultivating creative spaces for youth in the city. He partnered with faith-based organizations, city departments, and foundations, to empower young people. Spray Can 88 was an event that Carmelo helped sponsor and host at the LA Photo Center. Many of the artists that showed up were teens he had worked with at Radiotron. A number of these artists were now adults, and were themselves ready to mentor an emerging cohort of younger artists. Hex was one of those who was already engaged in passing on creative knowledge to a younger generation. Spray Can 88 sparked further possibilities in him, which eventually crystallized into a clearer vision. Hex felt it—a resonance of what once was.

Something was stirring in the community. According to Carmelo, as stated in the documentary (Glaser 1991), "the number of kids that are now doing graffiti and art seems to be increasing." He explained that the event was something that the artists essentially put together, as spearheaded by Frame. "They have their own network of communicating so they informed each other that this was happening," Carmelo added. These writers had sustained a creative resonance

---

[1] *Bombing L.A.* premiered in 1989, and a VHS version was released in 1991.

from what started half a decade prior. And they were not merely attempting to replicate what they had picked up in the nascent era. Rather, they continued to expand their craft, and were creating increasingly complex pieces. Furthermore, they were clear that their efforts were not motivated by gang ties, despite the fact that gang graffiti was ever present, and tag banging was also emerging as a possibility. These artists, however, largely articulated a love for creativity, originality, and innovation. In this scene, artists like Hex saw an opportunity to build. Soon, new opportunities emerged.

Through re-energized networks of writers, Hex was emboldened to challenge two writers who were garnering much attention in the scene. And what better way to amplify this enthusiasm than through one of Hip Hop's mainstay displays of creativity?—a battle. These writers, Slick and Risk, had recently returned from an international graffiti competition in the United Kingdom, where they had won the top prize. In a BBC report (1989) featuring the two writers, Slick expressed an expansive hope of what this win would bring about: "Hopefully by us winning this, we're taking this, like, the crown back to LA for a while, and then we'll get more enthusiasm and maybe this will be like a worldwide event in a couple years you know like Olympic event or something. You know, that would be cool." Implicit in Slick's words was a vision that enthusiasm from artists in the Los Angeles scene would contribute to a worldwide movement; his Olympic wishes proved prophetic, but for a different element—breaking. Hex had likewise begun to believe that Los Angeles could be an important hub of the Hip Hop elements. He postponed his return to New York when Slick accepted his call to battle.

LA Times reporter Denise Hamilton (1990a, 1990b,1990c) covered the rivalry between Hex and Slick in multiple articles in January 1990. The battle had two installments, given that the first confrontation in the Fall of 1989 had no clear winner. The second faceoff, held in early 1990, became a highly publicized affair. The designated art canvas was the back of a Levitz furniture store that ran along the Los Angeles River, on the city borders of Los Angeles and Glendale. The occasion proved to be an opportunity, as proposed in Hamilton's articles, to argue for the artistic legitimacy of creatives like Slick and Hex, and to distinguish their work from that of taggers, who sprayed fast scribbles of their names in typically unlawful manner. Slick even mentioned that he was reluctant to use the term "graffiti" to describe his work, because of the baggage the term carried (Hamilton 1990a). With coverage from local network television, and the eyes of graffiti writers fixed on this epic battle, Los Angeles graffiti was surely gaining widespread notoriety. For the second confrontation, judges were put in place to declare the victor. In the end, Hex was judged the winner.

The event served a purpose beyond pitting two artists against each other. This was an event that continued to establish Los Angeles as a critical site of innovation within graffiti lore. And beyond graffiti culture, this was trumpeted as proof that "In the past year, Los Angeles has become the acknowledged Center of Hip Hop" (Hamilton 1990a). Hex affirmed this aspirational status, now seeing Los Angeles as a hub of Hip Hop creativity. His plans to return to New York were postponed indefinitely. Instead, Hex began to mastermind a different plan. One that would solidify, within Los Angeles, a hub of creativity that harnessed the resonance of the early years.

A New Point of Connection

In 1990, Hex opened The Hip Hop Shop. Commissioned by shop owners to paint graffiti on the walls of their flower shop on Melrose Ave, Hex received an additional proposition from the owners. They invited Hex to rent half of their facility and use it for his art. Hex agreed. Unbeknownst to him, the owners would vacate the building and notify the owner that Hex was taking over the space. Hex decided to keep the building for himself and immersed himself into fashioning what became Los Angeles's first Hip Hop shop, a space that sold Hip Hop clothing, supplies, and other paraphernalia and hosted events for Hip Hop heads. He went to work, creating a space that would appeal to the aspirations of Hip Hop creatives. One of the distinguishing features of this space was that Hex's own art was emblazoned on the interior and exterior walls of the building. Many people began to recognize the shop for its artwork.

From the store, Hex began marketing his own urban clothing brand—Fat Cap. The brand largely drew on graffiti culture, while more broadly signaling its connection to Hip Hop culture. Soon, Hex was distributing the brand extensively throughout the region. Hex drew from various channels of life experience to ensure that the brand succeeded. His experience working for Surf Fetish, the brand founded by two of the owners of Cross Colours, provided Hex with valuable experience and knowledge. Hex had knowledge of clothing design and had gotten an inside look into running a company. He likewise recalled his years at home, wherein he would sometimes go to work with his father at his garment district jobs or attend meetings for the garment workers union. These experiences shaped Hex's creative imagination, his business skills, and his sense of labor organizing. Running his own business was a natural progression. With his brand and his shop attracting followers, Hex was approached by one of his former Surf Fetish bosses, who invited Hex to come work for Cross Colours. Hex was so involved in his own business that he turned down the opportunity.

The Hip Hop Shop (Image 9.1) attracted creatives seeking opportunities to build community through their participation in the Hip Hop elements, especially those who had been part of the earlier scene. Hex offered some of them

Image 9.1 Hex's Hip Hop Shop. (Reproduced courtesy of Hector Rios)

jobs. Markski and Gremz worked at the store. Gremz began to host open sessions for breakers on Wednesdays. Iceman appeared on the scene, after hearing from a friend, "People are breaking again at the Hip Hop shop!" B-boys like Lil Cesar, Orko, and Wilpower made their way back to the dancefloor at the shop. By then, Wilpower had become the first professional skater from MacArthur Park, appearing in publications like *Thrasher Magazine*. Gremz recalls that the Wednesday sessions were a key meeting point for B-boys and B-girls. The shop became one of the primary hubs for reviving the seemingly lost art of breaking.

As I examined old flyers from events hosted at the shop, I recognized a veritable who's who of the emerging Los Angeles underground scene of the 1990s. One of the workers at the Hip Hop Shop, a young emcee named Rakaa, of Black, Korean, and white ancestry, forged important connections while at the shop. He linked up with a young emcee known as Evidence, and participated in freestyle cyphers hosted at the shop. The two formed the group Dilated Peoples, eventually adding Filipino American turntablist, DJ Babu. Groups such as Freestyle Fellowship, and artists such as 2Mex, of Project Blowed fame, graced the mic at the shop as well. One flier listed an artist by the name of Will One X, whom Hex indicated was Will.I.Am of the Black Eyed Peas. Will was prolific in the underground scene before becoming a superstar. Melrose Avenue became a hub of Hip Hop activity. A number of artists had attended Fairfax High School down the street from the Hip Hop Shop.

Hex's plan to reconnect to New York City ultimately happened in an unexpected manner. By now, Hex's name had gotten around to the networks of Hip Hop creatives that were attempting to revive the scene. A number of key figures from the New York scene started to reach out to Hex. Members of the

Rock Steady Crew made appearances at the Hip Hop Shop. The shop became a touchpoint for Hip Hop purists, including those from New York. According to Hex, "I didn't have to go to New York. New York came to me." Hex was living out his plan "to bring back the power of the purity of Hip Hop." At one point, Hex caught wind that Afrika Bambaataa wanted to invite him to join the Universal Zulu Nation (UZN). Though various West Coast creatives had joined the Hip Hop association, Hex did not think it would be an authentic move on his part, as a West Coast Mexican American artist. He, nevertheless, continued to collaborate with the UZN for a season.

The shop had gained notoriety among respected Hip Hop figures, in the Los Angeles underground scene, and on the streets. Nevertheless, in the midst of the Los Angeles uprising, Hex feared for the safety of his business. There were buildings in the vicinity that experienced defacement, damage, and loss of inventory. The Hip Hop Shop distinguished itself by the graffiti on its exterior and Hex wondered if it would become a target. It appears that the reverse happened. The Hip Hop Shop remained unscathed, a testament to the respect it had earned in the community. Truly, it lived up to Hex's vision for it to be a haven, as one *LA Times* writer noted (W. Wilson 1992). For dehydrated seekers of Hip Hop culture, the shop was an urban oasis.

Conclusion

Creatives who were invested in preserving Hip Hop found a variety of ways to maintain the grassroots, underground nature of the movement. For many, preservation was a life and death struggle. Hip Hop came to represent their sense of resonance with the world, and its absence indicated a type of dissonance in the world. As the scene shifted, some sought to preserve the movement by going back to the source in New York City. Some found solace in the socially conscious, Afrocentric turn in the movement. Others immersed themselves within a particular niche of the movement, namely the work of emceeing. And through emceeing, some challenged the racialized expectations of the shifting scene, and some sought a way to make peace with the world. Finally, some invested in rebuilding that which had crumbled, attempting to resurrect the scene they had lost. In avoiding death, of the movement and of self, creatives found ways to sustain a sense of purpose through creative expression.

Conclusion

Rebirths

In documenting the Christian Hip Hop scene in Los Angeles, Christina Zanfagna (2017) notes that the Los Angeles uprising of 1992 marked a season when many artists were reorienting their lives toward new possibilities amid structural oppression and natural disasters. For Dax Reynosa, too, this season was a defining time. Dax spent the 1980s honing his skills on the mic, performing at live events and gatherings. His group, LPG, consisted of him and his cousin Jurny, and included affiliates such as his sister Zane. After a decade of performing, in 1992, Dax contemplated retiring from music. For him, Hip Hop died at this point. The West Coast scene had shifted; gangsta rap reigned supreme. Dax grew tired of the judgment, internal conflicts, and general trajectory of the once resonant environment of Christian Hip Hop he helped build. The time of sky-rhyming had given way to some battles that were welcomed, and many others that were not. A decade after he started, he was ready to walk away from it all. He spent that year discerning his next steps and considering whether there were a way to sustain the resonance from a decade prior.

Soul Drop

Toward the end of 1993, Dax received a phone call from Hex that reinvigorated his vision. Hex proposed a convening of underground artists at his Hip Hop shop. Hex had seen the possibilities in the scene but sensed the need to safeguard the scene from succumbing to commodified agendas. This vision resonated with Dax. For urban creatives like Dax and Hex, the demise of Hip Hop was a life and death matter. Reinvigorating the scene meant infusing life into the cityscape for a new generation of creatives. "He booked us to come and perform at his shop," Dax explained. "I started to call a bunch of people I knew to promote the event. People showed up," he remembered.

The event, called Soul Drop One, impacted the scene (Image C.1). The multiracial assemblage of Black, brown, white, and Asian American participants included veteran and new-generation performers, some still in their teens. The energy from the performances was palpable. As participants spilled out into the

Image C.1 Flier for Soul Drop One, 1993. (Reproduced courtesy of Raphael Henley)

street, Dax had an idea. The imperative that Dax had felt in the early days was fresh in his being that night. Dax made various targeted invitations. He waited until most had left, and as many artists milled around and socialized, he invited a select group to his home. Most accepted the invitation. At home, he pitched an idea to those present. Dax cast a vision for creating a supergroup. His idea translated into the birth of the Tunnel Rats, a crew that gained an underground and a national following (see Borha 2013).

The Tunnel Rats would bridge various scenes. Many knew them as Christian artists, because they maintained ties in their rhymes and hooks to the Christian message that had shaped them. Much of their national touring took place through their association with Christianity. On the other hand, in Los Angeles, they were also known as underground artists. More than simply yearning for a nostalgic return to the Bronx, the Tunnel Rats transposed the ethos of Hip Hop's founding on the landscape of Los Angeles. Based on the Tunnel Rats' battle rap–tinged expositions, the Los Angeles underground was a legitimate source of Hip Hop authenticity, an unmatched one according to them. It is not surprising then, that Tunnel Rat members such as Raphi (Lee 2016), became regulars at Los Angeles underground bastions like Project Blowed. Distinct resonances had converged on the Hip Hop Shop, and the scene was reinventing itself (Image C.2).

Image C.2 Tunnel Rats, at a reunion performance, 2023. L to R, Peace 586, Zane, Elsie, Dax, Macho, Propaganda, Sojourn, Raphi. (Reproduced courtesy of Raphael Henley)

Ava Duvernay's (2008) documentary *This Is the Life*, depicting one of Los Angeles's monumental underground Hip Hop spots, The Good Life Cafe, captures a glimpse of various worlds—The LA underground scene, Brown Los Angeles, and the Christian Hip Hop scene—intersecting. The documentary momentarily spotlights the crew, Of Mexican Descent, consisting of Xololanxinxo and 2Mex, as they gained acceptance in the predominantly Black American scene. 2Mex describes his first visits to the Good Life and how he was initially struck by the messages of Black empowerment he encountered there. He was inspired by these messages, despite not being Black. He and Xololanxinxo gained notoriety for representing their Mexican cultures through their catchy and intricate rhyme styles, eventually winning over the crowds there. Subsequently, the documentary introduces Pigeon John, who identified as a Christian rapper. Pigeon John also succeeded at winning over the crowd, even if some questioned his message. Word on the street was that his stage presence and style influenced many. Both 2Mex and Pigeon John belonged to crews that visited Hex's Hip Hop shop. These seemingly disconnected worlds influenced each other in creative ways.

Inspiration

It was May 2023. As the sun was setting, I struggled to find parking in the bustling MacArthur Park area en route to an event. I drove by as sidewalk vendors selling clothing and toys closed down shop and a whole new set of food vendors fired up grills and set up folding chairs. After paying to park at an overpriced corner lot, I was reminded that in this area of Los Angeles, one of the most densely populated neighborhoods in the country, space was at a premium. The event I was going to, called Graffitinspire, was a couple blocks from where the Radiotron building once stood. The event spotlighted the art of some of the earliest graffiti writers who helped build the Los Angeles scene. Few people understood, in as visceral a fashion as these artists (Bloch 2019), processes of place-making; for decades, they had claimed and reclaimed the thoroughfares and neighborhoods intersecting this area of the city, marking places with personal monikers and ubiquitous crew tags. As Hex emphasized, the art of these creatives cried out, "I am somebody," in the face of segregation, surveillance, violence, and disinvestment. The event was hosted at the Goethe Institut, in art gallery fashion. Approaching the building, I saw through its windows walls teeming with creative life. The featured artists previously created their masterpieces directly on walls. Now, these works of art were largely painted on canvases, with three-dimensional art pieces interspersed.

As I meandered through the gallery, captivated by the vivid movements of paint on canvas, I began spotting familiar faces. The primary host that night was Carmelo Alvarez. I caught up with him eventually. Initially, he took to the mic and welcomed guests, while a DJ spun mostly Hip Hop music in the background. The gallery was already near capacity, and visitors continued to file in. Amid a crowd of strangers, it felt great to recognize and be recognized. "Hey, how's it going bro! It's been years!" John "Zender" Estrada called out, as he stretched out his hand. Zender was among the featured artists. He milled around a table selling prints of his art. Nearby, I spotted Mike "Iceman" Rivera. He too came over to greet me. Later, he would take part in a dance cypher, featuring mostly old school B-boys and B-girls, and some poppers. As I walked further into the gallery I bumped into Hex. He was excited to learn about how my book was going and offered to share some of his photos for the project. As we spoke, he introduced me to another writer, Jeronimo "Jero One," who shared a history with those who moved from New York to Los Angeles as a child and helped birth the movement; he was a reminder of the creative exchange across coasts.

Resonances of Radiotron and the Hip Hop Shop surfaced throughout the event's flow, in the art, the conversations, and the references made from the mic. Many of the artists whose art was on display had been part of the original batch of Radiotron artists who were mentored by Carmelo. Artists like Crime "RickOne" Gonzalez still had photos from some of his pieces that decorated the facade of the Radiotron building. Many of these artists remained in contact with each other, especially on social media, communicating publicly and privately and sustaining art worlds online (Gault 2022). Many maintained personal collaborations, working on projects together and sharing in business endeavors. At the event, some carried around black books, sketching out their pieces and inviting other writers to grace their pages with their signature scripts. The event was a time of reminiscing, but it was much more than that.

In one sense, Graffitinspire approximated writer, producer, and filmmaker dream hampton's (Wolf 2022) observation that Hip Hop is now entering into its "museum phase." The works of these graffiti writers were on display in museum fashion. And while graffiti has long been exhibited in galleries, many of the works at this exhibit were period pieces that pointed back to specific, distant moments in time. Most pieces were fresh, in the fullest sense of the word, but the memories they conjured for some were fleeting. References to Radiotron or to Hex's Hip Hop shop brought forth a sense of nostalgia, even for someone like me who did not have the opportunity to visit these sites when they were up and running. I could hear the joy of memorialization in some of the conversations. Still, this event pointed to other possibilities as well. A museum phase might further legitimize these artforms. Indeed, for some of these artists it was already happening; many of them worked in art-related fields and made a living from their creative knowledge. Furthermore, as hinted at within the name of the event, the event was intended to inspire others, young and old.

A cluster of creatives, some who were present that evening, many who were not, had helped to forge a channel of resonance rooted in those early days of West Coast Hip Hop. The Hip Hop iterations most prominent in Brown Los Angeles especially drew from resonance channels linked to the Caribbean, to the Borderlands, and to Black funk culture. Yet, the energies present were now their own channel of resonance, one rooted in the soil, sounds, and aromas of neighborhoods like Westlake and Pico Union surrounding MacArthur Park. When forging this channel forty years ago, creatives looked to New York City, and combined their native and local knowledge with the translocal forms they caught, to establish a new Hip Hop outpost in Los Angeles. Now, many looked to Los Angeles as its own hub of creative resonance, rife with a unique aesthetic and deep networks of creative production.

This channel of resonance was not a dying echo, but a continued dialogue with the next generation. As I watched a dance cypher initiating, I noticed that nearly all of the dancers were veteran B-boys, such as Iceman and Wilpower, active since forty years ago when the scene was taking off. It was evident that across the decades they had persisted in their craft, and still made impressive moves on the floor. As the cypher progressed, a teenaged poplocker by the name of Nikko Motion jumped in. "Rapper's Delight" blared through the speakers, and Nikko treated the audience to an impromptu popping performance with crisp movements, precise poses, and fluid transitions, his body descending toward the ground, then moving back up like a machine. Nikko was a testament to how the older funk frequency resonated with and continued to be innovated by a younger generation. Behind the cypher, I spotted the work of Deity, a Chicana graffiti writer whose work depicted stylish women surrounded by classic cars, and lush floral arrangements. Her work blended motifs of Chicana aesthetics, with backdrops highlighting her women subjects in subtle iconic, perhaps deified fashion. Her pieces conveyed a strength and beauty that defied urban change.

When I reconnected with Zender, he introduced me to a writer named Ronek. He and Ronek had teamed up on a community-based arts project. Ronek hosts a podcast, "Got No Control," where guest graffiti writers share their stories; several of his guests were present that evening, their art featured in the gallery. Ronek shared how he had already lived in other parts of the country and had continued to develop his craft as a graffiti writer. He was doing the work of preserving history through his podcast, but he continued to innovate and to develop the craft as well. His work had a community-based element to it, as he hoped to give back to communities such as the one he grew up in. Hailing from a neighborhood in Dominguez, between Compton, Long Beach, and Carson, Ronek drew on his creative skills to get ahead in life. Now, he was organizing with others, such as Zender, to create opportunities for youth to explore and develop their own talents.

I was encouraged to hear about how so many of these artists were in fact giving back to their communities through their artforms. Preserving history was important, because it was a history of struggle and of resistance, and they recognized that these histories could be a source of education and inspiration. Moreover, these creatives had found ways to harness this history—this resonance—toward reinventing and reconceptualizing an ongoing movement. To be fair, the movement had now sprouted many branches, and not all identified with this particular core group of artists. Yet, even for those who did not see themselves in this scene, there was an uncanny connection to the forms and expressions that developed into the Los Angeles/West Coast scene, underground and commercial. This was the lineage, alive, and on full display that evening.

Sky-Rhyming the Future

The stories of the graffiti writers at Graffitinspire had much in common with the sky-rhyming tales I heard from Dax and Zane. Sky-rhyming, like the writing of early graffiti writers, was a responsive act, and one marking a transitional phase in West Coast creative culture. The time of sky-rhyming describes the period during which Hip Hop was received on the West Coast; it was a period during which the prospects and the practices of West Coast Hip Hop were being defined. And for many creatives in this period, Hip Hop was not passively absorbed, but rather actively adapted. Thus, sky-rhyming was envisioning and refashioning a movement within a new context. The time of sky-rhyming was a moment of translation. For many creatives within Brown Los Angeles, this moment was life-changing.

I was struck by how creatives encountered Hip Hop with a sense of awe. As they began to identify with it, they were taken aback by what it embodied. Before seeing themselves in it, creatives described being overwhelmed by it, by the artistic possibilities it contained. Soon, they were drawn to identify with it, as if they had no choice (Rosa 2019); Hip Hop resonated with them. And yet, as personal as identification with Hip Hop was, it was a deeply social process. Creatives drew from the cultural resources that surrounded them in order to fashion their Hip Hop identities; these were the channels of resonance that made Hip Hop intelligible to Los Angeles creatives (Khabeer 2016). Likewise, they drew on the communities around them to shape their performative possibilities. As Hip Hop resonated in collective ways, it became that much more ingrained within individuals. In Brown Los Angeles, many creatives made sense of their surroundings through Hip Hop, building communities of refuge and resonance.

Nevertheless, I was especially surprised by how the time of sky-rhyming was only a brief window. The period lasted less than three years total, quashed by legal injunctions on creative expressions like street dancing, the crack epidemic, the proliferation of street gangs, and perhaps the ebb and flow of creative evolution. Certainly, Hip Hop found life down new avenues, and many creatives adapted to these new flows of artistry; others did not and found themselves in precarious situations. Creatives from Brown Los Angeles especially encountered shifts related to how their racial identities positioned them in their creative fields.

I suspect the mythologizing of the time of sky-rhyming is valued and contested because something was lost after that brief period of time. Certainly, creatives may experience nostalgia tied to the joys of their youths, yet something deeper seems to be amiss. The time of sky-rhyming represents a moment of purity and authenticity. It was a time when a popular movement felt less commercialized, as mainstream media lost little time to commodify it. Soon, the movement would be swept up, ever expected to perform the realities of urban life, especially Black urban life (Rivera 2003), while still producing an ever-marketable product. Commercial incursions into the culture expanded in the time of sky-rhyming, even as naivete about those opportunities remained among some creatives. Creatives from Brown Los Angeles rode this wave as well. Moreover, when it comes to questions of Hip Hop authenticity, artistic participation in the time of sky-rhyming offers a special claim for creatives from Brown Los Angeles. To have been there, or to trace a direct lineage to those that were there, adds a layer of clout, of street credibility, to many from Brown Los Angeles. Forty years later, the sky-rhyming era experiences that took place at sites like the Radio Club, Radiotron, backyard parties, and street cyphers, represent a resonance channel unto themselves.

Hip Hop memorialization requires, in my estimation, honoring of its Black American and Afrodiasporic roots, of the struggle and creativity uniquely intersecting in the Bronx. The collaborators I spoke with largely affirmed this. Likewise, the Africanist aesthetics, the dark matter that Imani Kai Johnson (2022) names, these resonances are ever present in the movement whether unconsciously conjured or intentionally performed; and they are remembered whether creatives allude to a Bronx origin story or to a perceived primordial source (Mailla-Pozo 2018). Simultaneously, collaborators from Brown Los Angeles made sense of Hip Hop through channels of resonance tied to localized sources and extended ethnoracial histories, from indigenous pasts, to colonial outgrowths, to civil rights struggles (McFarland 2013; Villegas 2021). The localized connections remain an ever-present foundation to the legitimacy that many creatives from Brown Los Angeles appealed to regarding their place within Hip Hop.

Some creatives memorialized the streets of the Westlake neighborhood as their primary source of Hip Hop resonance. For others, resonances were rooted in South Central, Pico Union, East Los Angeles, Pico Rivera, West Covina, the San Fernando Valley, Wilmington, Santa Ana, Pomona, San Bernardino, and even my own childhood stomping grounds of Fullerton and Buena Park. In these places, where the movement first touched down, where the struggles to keep it real first happened, where resonance was first felt and resulted in deeply embodied action and reaction, there too are Hip Hop origin stories. The underground stream of the movement will survive for as long as creatives can sky-rhyme what they perceive from their surroundings, projecting in deeply spiritual ways onto a wall, record, or cypher their existential reality; it will continue as long as Hip Hop creatives reflect, as Jon Gill (2020:141) describes, "the greatest possibilities for the beauty of humanity available to their particular epoch." And as the movement continues to create space for people and performativities on the margins, even those once left out of the movement, while sustaining resonances of its beginnings, it will inadvertently evolve and perhaps experience multiple rebirths.

APPENDIX

Samples and Sampling

In this volume I interweave data from four general sources to generate a story of Hip Hop beginnings in Brown Los Angeles: oral history interviews, autoethnographic observations, analysis of print, material, and sonic culture, and review of public user-generated information found on social media platforms. In-depth oral history interviews of participants in the early West Coast scene are the empirical foundation of this project. The primary question I asked of interview collaborators was, "How did you get started in Hip Hop?" From there, interviews were free flowing and conversational in nature. I sought to uncover the ways that Hip Hop resonated within Brown Los Angeles through documenting the processes of creative production that collaborators testified to. The project was intentionally emplaced, tracking stories across the cartographies of the greater Los Angeles area with the understanding that Hip Hop manifested as a deeply local movement (Forman 2002). Simultaneously, I recognized that resonant experiences were not contained solely within the confines of civic, state, and national borders.

Analog, Digital, and Social Waves

I interspersed segments of my own story throughout this volume to orient readers as to the particular ethnographic sensibilities I drew from, in keeping with a hiphopography approach (Alim 2009:104; see also Alim and Hi-Tek 2006; Durham 2014; Spady et al. 2006). Drawing from my own recollections also mitigated a practical limitation: The COVID-19 pandemic initially restricted in-person events that would have provided participant observation opportunities. My own engagement in the field, especially in the 1990s, helped me to articulate the scene from a lived perspective. Likewise, the experience of a pandemic compelled me to think about how movements spread.

My own experience in a creative field shaped how I crafted a larger story from collaborators' individual stories: My junior year in high school, 1994–1995, I struck gold when my parents agreed to buy me a computer so that I could complete my school projects. It was a major sacrifice for them, yet it was a critical decision during one of the most strenuous seasons of my educational journey. The computer came with an unexpected creative benefit. As I explored different applications, I found that it contained a program called Creative Wave Studio. The program both allowed users to record sounds via built in CD player or analog input and allowed users to manipulate sounds. The application provided visual representations of recorded sound waves and had a zoom function for examining wave segments and wave cycles. Users could pinpoint where sounds started and ended within particular audio segments, and could chop, move, and duplicate segments along a single linear timeline. I spent hours experimenting with sound segments, and learned how to use the program's functions to produce my own beats. From sampled sounds I learned to create coherent sonic mosaics.

The application had several functions that revolutionized my understanding of sonic resonances. Most functions were easy enough to master as they mirrored commands in Microsoft Word, such as cut, copy, and paste, but pertained to audio segments on a linear soundtrack. Two unique functions were "Loop" and "Paste Mix." Loop allowed users to duplicate audio segments in sequential fashion; I would select a segment, and clone it back-to-back multiple times over. I created extended breakbeat tracks, for example, by looping a breakbeat segment over and over. Paste Mix allowed me to blend one segment with another, generating a new sound from multiple segments blended together on the same track. I began to sample from a variety of sound sources and learned to make song length beats to rap over. I found jazz or classical music tracks that easily mixed with drum breaks. However, if I sequenced wave segments at points where their wave cycles did not match up, sonic artifacts, usually clicking sounds, emerged. These artifacts taught me to measure and splice wave segments at places where wave cycles matched up. Likewise, in terms of blending sounds, I learned to be attentive to musical keys and wave cycles, so that intersecting sounds could function in resonant fashion, rather than clashing in dissonant fashion. Through hours of experimentation with these basic audio functions, I learned about resonance, harmony, musical sequencing, and other principles.

My process of weaving stories together for this book has been similar to the processes I learned in the mid-1990s of fashioning sonic resonances—samples—over a linear timeline. Sampling, as Abdul Khabeer (2016) notes, can function in similar fashion to the academic practice of citation. This resonates with Blackwell's analogy of the work of oral historians as DJs. According to Blackwell (2011:38), "Oral historians spin the historical record by sampling new voices and cutting and mixing the established soundscape to allow listeners to hear something different, even in grooves they thought they knew." This too, resonates with Flores's (2000:49) description of "putting-on-record, the gathering and sorting of materials from the past in accordance with the needs and interests of the present." The analogy of curating oral histories as musical performance is thus not altogether new in my work. More importantly, this act of curation generates something new, that offers possibilities for the present and future (Khabeer 2016; Villegas 2021). As I learned early on in my beat production experiments, much of this comes about through attentively managing the consonance and dissonance of samples.

Some sampled stories worked well when juxtaposed side by side, as if they were on a similar wave cycle, a similar "wavelength." Such samples resonated with each other. Sometimes samples did not easily fit, either in terms of mixing or in terms of sequencing. I sometimes resolved that by zooming in and cutting down samples to find aspects that blended into existing arrangements. At other times, samples were not congruent, and their proximate juxtapositions marked a rupture (Rose 1994), a point of distinction or contrast. When collecting accounts, I recognized that it was not my job to artificially blend accounts. At times, it was best to allow ruptures to remain, especially when particular experiences distinguished themselves in such ways that merited a track of their own. Such cases did not necessarily mean that the voices I selected were the most famous or prestigious, but rather that the voices illustrated a particular resonance. In this way, the voices that I selected were illustrative in nature. They captured a particular experience that, even if embedded in only one person's story, represented a broader resonance within the creative ecology.

Sampling Sources

In sampling sources for this project, I began with familiar voices and sounds, similar to my first days of experimenting with beat production on my computer. As someone with past connections to particular underground Hip Hop scenes, I had ties to creatives in the field whose stories I could sample from, or who could connect me to others whose stories I could sample from. In my early attempts of beat production, I discovered I could borrow CDs from friends and find samples there. In similar fashion, I began to inquire of friends with ties to underground scenes about whom they suggested I talk to. If I was not able to connect with creatives within particular areas of creativity, my last resort was to attempt to make cold contacts through social media or other channels. Some cold contacts rendered surprisingly fruitful results, with creatives willing to participate in interviews because they believed in the project.

Alongside my own primary data collection, the process of sampling involved deliberate mapping of the creative field by reviewing existing accounts of the early scene. I looked for the earliest media productions of the West Coast scene, including songs and film; news reports of the early scene, including newspaper publications, television news reports, and early documentaries; and archival images of event flyers or advertisements, in university archives or social media. Recently produced secondary sources, which often relied on oral history interviews, included research publications, documentaries, and podcasts featuring interviews of early scene creatives. As I argue from the beginning of this volume, most recent accounts favor rappers as the primary drivers of the scene. Some recent work has brought to light the role of DJs and DJ crews in driving West Coast Hip Hop. I worked to sample from creatives involved in various spheres of cultural production, and my assessment of the scene helped me to identify participants' fields beyond those typically emphasized.

My collaborators participated across the four elements of Hip Hop, emceeing, B-boying/B-girling, DJing, and graffiti writing. I sampled from these and related spheres. Furthermore, I worked to sample from creatives who helped build platforms of cultural production. Such individuals exercised creativity in shaping cultural scenes. Likewise, they were often creators of art in their own rights, whether or not they were known as such in the scenes they helped to develop. Within these particular elements, I attempted to sample from people from distinct backgrounds in terms of ethnoracial identities, national origins, and gender identities. The scene tended to heavily favor men, but I did seek the stories of women as well. As when I produced music, I sometimes felt strong impressions regarding certain types of samples that I needed to draw from, and I would do my best to "dig in the crates" for this type of sample. I sometimes had to put in extra work to gain a particular type of interview to sample from.

Finally, on various occasions, I visited sites of West Coast Hip Hop performance to engage early creatives still active in the field. The Radiotron anniversary, and B-boy Summit, for example, proved to be helpful in this regard. I also visited smaller-scale events, such as some in my old stomping grounds of Santa Ana, California. I was able to have follow-up conversations with some creatives I had already interviewed who were still active in the field. At the Radiotron anniversary, months before the pandemic started, I was able to identify some of the initial creatives I hoped to interview and scheduled follow-up conversations with them. More than scheduling and interviewing, though, these were opportunities to reconnect to the scene. The underground ethos was alive and well, accompanied by a healthy dose of nostalgia and preservationism. Still, I could observe how innovation was taking place, and how resonances were being transmitted across generations (Khabeer 2016). Older creatives were present, but so were young ones—children, teens, and young adults—who were engaging in the elements. Sampling these moments helped to confirm the processes that were at work in a previous era, albeit now in more democratized fashion, with the advent of social media and other technologies.

Technology

I employed several technological mechanisms in the process of data collection. I was especially reliant on my computer and my phone for purposes of communicating and recording interviews. Two potential limitations were turned into an opportunity with the help of technology. My residence on the East Coast, and early pandemic lockdowns would appear to limit the project, but I found that they motivated the project. Using Zoom and other virtual platforms, I was able to conduct numerous interviews remotely. Particularly at the start of the pandemic, I found that creatives were open to conversation. I knew that I was experiencing a degree of social isolation, and I suspect others were as well. The conversations we had were nourishing and energizing. Through digital technologies, and with permission from collaborators, I recorded and transcribed conversations. I typically used transcription software, such as Otter.ai or Zoom's built-in transcription functions. I reviewed interviews for accuracy and made corrections.

Cell phones and computers also proved to be exceedingly effective in documenting visual and sonic artifacts of the nascent West Coast scene. I found Google Keep a surprisingly adept application for storing and organizing observation notes. Having the application accessible both on my phone and on my computer proved especially efficient. Perusing social media accounts belonging to creatives involved in the early scene or who document the early scene presented a variety of helpful details regarding the scene. Social media, in fact, proved to be a treasure trove for leads on the development of the West Coast scene. Instagram and Facebook were especially helpful for this. Youtube was helpful for listening to a variety of sonic samples. User-generated interactions on these sites also provided helpful details about the scene. Often, I reached out to those who posted material and let them know about my project. If I used their material I cited them. In various cases such interactions resulted in my gaining a collaborator for the project.

Google Keep became more than a storage archive; it became a living repository within which to organize my interview data, my observations of visual and sonic culture, and to catalog existing secondary sources. Through creating Google Keep "notes," I was able to organize individual "samples" of data. Individual Keep notes represented samples of selected data. Google Keep became like my digital audio workstation (DAW), with which I chopped, structured, and organized particular tracks. Carrying it in my pocket added incredible freedom, in terms of being able to jot down notes and add multimedia observations. It also required my commitment to personal boundaries, as digital production was always at my fingertips. Working across a variety of media forms for this project required that I code data in resonant fashion. That is, I examined how distinct media sources, including my interview transcripts, resonated with each other. Resonances were not always self-evident, and coding with intellectual precision and emotional awareness mattered.

Google Keep was central to my process of coding data. Within Keep, I coded data using hashtags. Whenever I recognized an important theme within the data I collected,

I created a hashtag, and wrote it into the individual Keep note that contained the archived data. Within Google Keep, the creation of hashtags allows for efficient search functions. Keep can search for individual hashtags, or can search for multiple hashtags, indicating which notes contain the selected hashtag/s. Including multiple hashtags within individual Keep notes allowed me to identify what data points, documented in individual notes, shared resonance with other data points documented in their respective notes. As such, I organized most of my data on Google Keep.

On the Go, Standing Still

In conducting a hiphopograpy of brown creatives in the early West Coast scene, I was faced with the dilemma of tracing a movement on the go (Zanfagna 2017), while being restricted in movement due to pandemic lockdowns. In many ways, this served as an analogy for the predicament of the West Coast scene I was studying. The creatives I spoke to were deeply invested in the movement. Their investment was often accompanied with more than a tinge of nostalgia. They hoped to see the movement continue moving, yet were also committed to a level of preservation. They often articulated themselves as keepers of the culture. They helped the movement's global adaptation, and held that in tension with their preservationist commitments. I was reminded of when I layered sounds that were old, with sounds that were new, in my old production suite. Sometimes such sounds resonated beautifully, mystically so. When I watched some of these creatives at work, I realized that they too were working to layer (Rose 1994) their worlds with the old and the new. Sampling can be a work of innovation, and one which I hope inspires care for the original sources.

References

Abe, Marié. 2018. *Resonances of Chindon-Ya: Sounding Space and Sociality in Contemporary Japan*. Middleton, CT: Wesleyan University Press.

Abrams, Jonathan. 2022. *The Come Up: An Oral History of the Rise of Hip-Hop*. New York: Crown.

Ali, Lorraine. 1993. "Latin Class: Kid Frost and the Chicano Rap School." *Option: Music ALternatives* 53:66–72.

Alim, H. Samy. 2008. "Straight Outta Compton, Straight Aus München: Global Linguistic Flows, Identities, and the Politics of Language in a Global Hip Hop Nation." Pp. 1–22 in *Global Linguistic Flows: Hip Hop Cultures, Youth Identities, and the Politics of Language*, edited by H. S. Alim, A. Ibrahim, and A. Pennycook. New York: Routledge.

Alim, H. Samy. 2009. "Translocal Style Communities: Hip Hop Youth as Cultural Theorists of Style, Language, and Globalization." *Pragmatics* 19(1):103–27.

Alim, H. Samy, and Hi-Tek. 2006. "'The Natti Ain't No Punk City': Emic Views of Hip Hop Cultures." *Callaloo* 29(3):969–90. https://doi.org/10.1353/cal.2006.0129.

Alonso, Alex. 2020. "Street TV—Greg Mack and 1580 KDAY: Hip-Hop, Radio and the Mack Attack." *Google Podcasts*. Retrieved July 25, 2023 (https://podcasts.google.com).

Alvarez, Luis. 2007. "From Zoot Suits to Hip Hop: Towards a Relational Chicana/o Studies1." *Latino Studies; London* 5:53–75. https://doi.org/10.1057/palgrave.lst.8600237

Alvarez, Tony. 2019. *Roadium Radio—Ernie G. (Proper Dos)*. Vol. 4. Roadium Radio.

Alvarez, Tony. 2020a. *Chris "the Glove" Taylor*. Vol. 39. JE Visual Studios Production.

Alvarez, Tony. 2020b. "Mellow Man Ace—Episode 1—Roadium Radio—Tony Vision—Hosted by Tony A."

Alvarez, Tony. 2020c. "Roadium Radio—Cli-n-tel." Vol. 27. JE Visual Studios Production.

Anzaldúa, Gloria. 1999. *Borderlands*. San Francisco: Aunt Lute Books.

Arellano, Gustavo. 2013. "Whatever Happened to Jonny Chingas?" *OC Weekly*, January 24.

Arellano, Gustavo. 2018. "Column: Of Course Latinos Can Assimilate into American Society: Just Look at Whittier." *Los Angeles Times*, August 1.

Armendariz, Alice. 2015. "Trudie Arguelles-Barrett." *Alice Bag*. Retrieved October 8, 2020 (https://alicebag.com/women-in-la-punk/2015/10/27/trudie-arguelles-barrett).

Armstrong, Andrew B. 2019. *24 Bars to Kill: Hip Hop, Aspiration, and Japan's Social Margins*. New York: Berghahn Books.

Aversa, Guy. 2011. "You Found That Eastside Sound: Eastside Legends—The Carlos Brothers (AKA The Shadows)." *You Found That Eastside Sound*. Retrieved June 24, 2021 (https://wwwyoufoundthateastsidesoundcom.blogspot.com/2011/08/eastside-legends-carlos-brothers-aka.html).

Bailey Jr., Ralph. 1987. "Run D.M.C., Barry White Try To 'Rap' Gangs Away." *Los Angeles Sentinel (1934-)*, June 25, A1.

Barker, George C. 1958. *Pachuco: An American-Spanish Argot and Its Social Functions in Tucson, Arizona*. Tucson: University of Arizona Press.

BBC. 1989. "Bridlington Graffiti Event 1989—BBC TV." *Youtube*, uploaded by The Cold Krush, September 5, 2020. https://www.youtube.com/watch?v=XJ74-ayZAHM

Becker, Howard Saul. 1984. *Art Worlds*. Berkeley: University of California Press.

Belhoste, Gregoire. 2015. "Alex Jordanov Est Le plus Grand Reporter Français Vivant." *Vice*. July 27. Retrieved October 2, 2021 (https://www.vice.com/fr/article/exeqpm/alex-jordanov-est-le-plus-grand-reporter-francais-vivant-191)

Blackwell, Maylie. 2011. *¡Chicana Power!: Contested Histories of Feminism in the Chicano Movement*. Austin: University of Texas Press.

Bloch, Stefano. 2019. *Going All City: Struggle and Survival in LA's Graffiti Subculture*. Chicago: University of Chicago Press.

Borha, Imade Nibokun. 2013. *Battle Rap Gospel: The Story of the Tunnel Rats*. Los Angeles: University of Southern California.

Bourdieu, Pierre. 1990. *In Other Words: Essays Towards a Reflexive Sociology*. Redwood City, CA: Stanford University Press.

Boyer, Edward J. 1986. "Celebrities Use Airwaves to Take on Street Violence: [Home Edition]." *Los Angeles Times (Pre-1997 Fulltext)*, October 10, 1.

Brewster, Bill, and Frank Broughton. 2011. *The Record Players: DJ Revolutionaries*. Grove/Atlantic, Inc.

Brown, August. 2020. "Whodini Rapper John 'Ecstasy' Fletcher, Hip-Hop Pioneer, Dies at 56." *Los Angeles Times*, December 24.

Brown, Brandon. 2019. *Outlaw Radio Live—Outlaw Radio 12/27/19 & DJ Antron Interview*.

Busey, Christopher L., and Carolyn Silva. 2021. "Troubling the Essentialist Discourse of Brown in Education: The Anti-Black Sociopolitical and Sociohistorical Etymology of Latinxs as a Brown Monolith." *Educational Researcher* 50(3):176–86. https://doi.org/10.3102/0013189X20963582.

Carew, Topper. 1983. *Breakin' 'N' Enterin'*. Rainbow TV Works.

Castillo Planas, Melissa. 2020. *A Mexican State of Mind: New York City and the New Borderlands of Culture*. New Brunswick, NJ: Rutgers University Press.

Castillo-Garsow, Melissa, and Jason Nichols, eds. 2016. *La Verdad: An International Dialogue on Hip Hop Latinidades*. Columbus: Ohio State University Press.

Castro, Alan Leal. 2014. *Kobra—Blue City Strutters/Boo-Yaa Tribe (Interview Part 1)*.

Chang, Jeff. 2005. *Can't Stop Won't Stop: A History of the Hip-Hop Generation*. New York: St. Martin's Press.

Chang, Jeff, and Michael Nardone. 1994. "Reminiscing on Uncle Jam's Army, LAs Old School, and the Godfather of the Jheri-Curl." *Rap Pages*, December.

Chicago Street TV. 2020. *Mellow Man Ace Address Big Pun Situation! Dissing Eazy-E! NWA Having a Mexican Rapper!* https://www.youtube.com/watch?v=wnDd6diNwQ4.

Chow, James. 2023. "How a Legendary LA Dance Crew Helped Spark Korea's B-Boy Scene." *LAist*, May 16.

Cizmar, Martin. 2010. "Krazy D: What Happened after N.W.A. and the Posse?" *Phoenix New Times*.

Coddington, Amy. 2021. "A 'Fresh New Music Mix' for the 1980s: Broadcasting Multiculturalism on Crossover Radio." *Journal of the Society for American Music* 15(1):30–59. https://doi.org/10.1017/S1752196320000462.

Coleman, Brian. 2016. "1580 KDAY—And the Beat Goes On." *Medium*. Retrieved October 8, 2020 (https://medium.com/@briancoleman/1580-kday-and-the-beat-goes-on-9dab5b6c55e6).

Contreras, Frank. n.d. "Saving Soul Records Bio." *Saving Soul*. Retrieved November 30, 2022 (https://www.savingsoul.com/bio.html).

Cooper, Christopher. 2013. *Through My Windows*. Pomona, CA: Dimlights.

Cross, Brian. 1993. *It's Not about a Salary . . .: Rap, Race and Resistance in Los Angeles*. London: Verso.

Cummings, Laura L. 2003. "Cloth-Wrapped People, Trouble, and Power: Pachuco Culture in the Greater Southwest." *Journal of the Southwest* 45(3):329–48.

Davis, Mike. 1995. "Beyond Blade Runner: Urban Control (1)." *Mediamatic Magazine*, January 1.

Davis, Mike. 2006. *City of Quartz: Excavating the Future in Los Angeles*. New York: Verso Books.

Day, Keri. 2022. *Azusa Reimagined: A Radical Vision of Religious and Democratic Belonging*. Stanford, CA: Stanford University Press.

Del Barco, Mandalit. 1996. "Rap's Latino Sabor." Pp. 63–84 in *Droppin' Science: Critical Essays on Rap Music and Hip Hop Culture*, edited by W. E. Perkins. Philadelphia, PA: Temple University Press.

Delgado, Fernando Pedro. 1998. "Chicano Ideology Revisited: Rap Music and the (Re) Articulation of Chicanismo." *Western Journal of Communication* 62(2):95–113. https://doi.org/10.1080/10570319809374601.

Diaz, Angel. 2015. "Are You Down? Darlene Ortiz Talks Her Years with Ice-T and What Her Family Thought of the 'Power' Cover." *Complex*, December 3.

Dublab. 2020. *Metro Art and Dublab Present: DEEP ROUTES Episode #1—Downtown L.A., Punk's Edge*, July 7.

Durán, Javier. 2002. "Nation and Translation: The 'Pachuco' in Mexican Popular Culture: Germán Valdéz's Tin Tan." *Journal of the Midwest Modern Language Association* 35(2):41–49. https://doi.org/10.2307/1315165.

Durham, Aisha S. 2014. *Home with Hip Hop Feminism*. New York: Peter Lang.

DuVernay, Ava, dir. 2008. *This Is the Life*. The DuVernay Agency.

Ellsberg, Daniel. 2003. *Secrets: A Memoir of Vietnam and the Pentagon Papers*. New York: Penguin.

Emdin, Christopher. 2017. "On Innervisions and Becoming in Urban Education: Pentecostal Hip-Hop Pedagogies in the Key of Life." *Review of Education, Pedagogy, and Cultural Studies* 39(1):106–19. https://doi.org/10.1080/10714413.2017.1262170.

Espinosa, Gastón. 2014. *Latino Pentecostals in America: Faith and Politics in Action*. Cambridge, MA: Harvard University Press.

Ewoodzie, Joseph C., Jr. 2017. *Break Beats in the Bronx: Rediscovering Hip-Hop's Early Years*. Chapel Hill: University of North Carolina Press.

Fernandes, Sujatha. 2011. *Close to the Edge: In Search of the Global Hip Hop Generation*. New York: Verso.

Fernandes, Sujatha. 2018. "Black Aesthetics and Afro-Latinx Hip Hop." *ReVista* 17(2):71–74.

Flores, Edward. 2014. *God's Gangs: Barrio Ministry, Masculinity, and Gang Recovery*. New York: New York University Press.

Flores, Juan. 2000. *From Bomba to Hip-Hop: Puerto Rican Culture and Latino Identity*. New York: Columbia University Press.

Forman, Murray. 2002. *The 'Hood Comes First: Race, Space, and Place in Rap and Hip-Hop*. Middletown, CT: Wesleyan University Press.

Fujita, Ryo. 2013. "Interview with L.A. Graffiti Pioneer Graff1." *L.A. TACO*, March 11. Retrieved February 11, 2021 (https://www.lataco.com/interview-with-l-a-graffiti-pioneer-graff1/).

Garcia, Ignacio M. 1997. *Chicanismo: The Forging of a Militant Ethos among Mexican Americans*. Tucson: University of Arizona Press.

Garcia, MaryEllen. 2009. "Pachucos, Chicano Homeboys and Gypsy Caló: Transmission of a Speech Style." *Ethnic Studies Review* 32(2):24–51.

Garay, Gary. 2022. "He Is One of L.A.'s Greatest Musical Enigmas. Who, Exactly, Was Jonny Chingas?" *Los Angeles Times*, March 17.

Gary, Kevin. 2010. "Ahmad—The Death of Me." *HipHopDX*, August 19.

Gault, Erika D. 2022. *Networking the Black Church: Digital Black Christians and Hip Hop*. New York: New York University Press.

Gault, Erika D., and Travis Harris. 2019. *Beyond Christian Hip Hop: A Move towards Christians and Hip Hop*. New York: Routledge.

Gill, Jon Ivan. 2020. *Underground Rap as Religion: A Theopoetic Examination of a Process Aesthetic Religion*. New York: Routledge.

Glaser, Gary. 1991. *Bombing L.A.* Beefbone Music, Glaser Productions.

Gold, Jonathan. 1990. "Kid Frost: Political Rap for Chicano Solidarity: Pop Music: His Hit 'La Raza' Is the First Popular East L.A. Anthem in Years." *Los Angeles Times (1923–1995)*, August 20, F2.

Goldstein, Patrick. 1984. "Shrimp and Crew: Street-Wise Boogaloo." *Los Angeles Times (1923–1995)*, March 25, 15.

Gollner, Philip. 1985. "Inner-City Youths Seek a Place to 'Break' Away." *Los Angeles Times*, August 15.

Golonka, Taylor. 2021. *Exclusive Interview with Michael Chambers AKA "Turbo" and Bruno Falcon AKA "Poppin Taco."*

Grody, Steve. 2006. *Graffiti L.A.: Street Styles and Art*. New York: Abrams.

Grody, Steve. 2007. "Early Influences and L.A. Starts Up." *Graffiti LA*. Retrieved September 19, 2020 (http://graffitila.com/text-cuts-from-graffiti-la).

Guerrero, Mark. 2020. *Mark Guerrero Radio—Gilbert Rocha.*

Guzman-Sanchez, Thomas. 2012. *Underground Dance Masters: Final History of a Forgotten Era*. Santa Barbara, CA: ABC-CLIO.

Hall, Haven. 2015. "DubCNN Exclusive Interview: Myka 9." *DubCNN*. Retrieved October 7, 2020 (http://www.dubcnn.com/2015/10/06/dubcnn-exclusive-interview-myka-9/).

Hamilton, Denise. 1990a. "Artists Plan to Take Can in Hand for a Wall-to-Wall Showdown." *Los Angeles Times (1923–1995)*, January 4, WSJ15.

Hamilton, Denise. 1990b. "Dueling Spray Cans: Graffiti Artists in Showdown on Furniture Warehouse Wall." *Los Angeles Times*, January 6.

Hamilton, Denise. 1990c. "Rival Spray Paint Artists Plan Legal Wall-to-Wall Showdown." *Los Angeles Times (1923–1995)*, January 5, SBB10.

Hansen, Helena. 2018. *Addicted to Christ: Remaking Men in Puerto Rican Pentecostal Drug Ministries*. Oakland: University of California Press.

Harkness, Geoff. 2013. "Gangs and Gangsta Rap in Chicago: A Microscenes Perspective." *Poetics* 41(2):151–76. https://doi.org/10.1016/j.poetic.2013.01.001.

Harris, Basil. 2012. *Ana Lollipop Sanchez Dance Mogul Magazine Exclusive Pt.1. Dance Mogul Magazine*. August, 21. Retrieved March 22, 2020 (https://www.youtube.com/watch?v=wg4naTncDwg)

Harrison, Anthony Kwame. 2009. *Hip Hop Underground: The Integrity and Ethics of Racial Identification*. Philadelphia, PA: Temple University Press.

Harrison, Anthony Kwame. 2015a. "Hip Hop and Race." Pp. 191–99 in *The Routledge Reader on the Sociology of Music*, edited by J. Shepherd and K. Devine. London: Routledge.

Harrison, Anthony Kwame. 2015b. "Hip-Hop and Racial Identification: An (Auto) Ethnographic Perspective." Pp. 152–67 in *The Cambridge Companion to Hip Hop*, edited by J. A. Williams. Cambridge: Cambridge University Press.

Harrison, Anthony Kwame, and Craig E. Arthur. 2019. "Hip-Hop Ethos." *Humanities* 8(1):39. https://doi.org/10.3390/h8010039.

Henderson, April K. 2006. "Dancing between Islands: Hip Hop and the Samoan Diaspora." Pp. 180–99 in *The Vinyl Ain't Final: Hip Hop and the Globalization of Black Popular Culture*, edited by D. Basu and S. J. Lemelle. New York: Pluto Press.

Hernandez, Jillian. 2020. *Aesthetics of Excess: The Art and Politics of Black and Latina Embodiment*. Durham, NC: Duke University Press.

Hess, Mickey. 2009. *Hip Hop in America: A Regional Guide*. Santa Barbara, CA: ABC-CLIO.

Hochman, Steve. 1990a. "Kid Frost Raps to La Raza: Critics Denounce the Gang References, but the Rapper Says His Music Is a Reflection of Chicano Culture in East L.A." *Los Angeles Times*, August 26.

Hochman, Steve. 1990b. "Rappers Go to the Source for Anti-Gang Video: Pop: They Tape 'All in the Same Gang' and Hold a No-More-Wars Summit at the Nickerson Gardens Housing Project: Some Onlookers Doubt the Effort Will Do Any Good." *Los Angeles Times (1923–1995)*, April 19, NaN-NaN.

Hochman, Steve. 1991. "Alliance Forms to Counter Image of Latino Pap Rap." *Los Angeles Times*, October 12.

Hodge, Daniel White. 2010. *The Soul of Hip Hop: Rims, Timbs and a Cultural Theology*. Downers Grove, IL: InterVarsity Press.

Hodge, Daniel White. 2016. *Hip Hop's Hostile Gospel: A Post-Soul Theological Exploration*. Boston, MA: Brill.

Holland, Jahmal. 2015. *Spanish FLY*. Los Angeles: USC School of Cinematic Arts.

Hondagneu-Sotelo, Pierrette, and Manuel Pastor. 2021. *South Central Dreams: Finding Home and Building Community in South L.A.* New York: New York University Press.

Hooker, Juliet. 2014. "Hybrid Subjectivities, Latin American Mestizaje, and Latino Political Thought on Race." *Politics, Groups, and Identities* 2:188–201. https://doi.org/10.1080/21565503.2014.904798.

Jeffries, Michael P. 2011. *Thug Life: Race, Gender, and the Meaning of Hip-Hop*. Chicago: University of Chicago Press.

Jiménez, Gabriela. 2011. "'Something 2 Dance 2': Electro Hop in 1980s Los Angeles and Its Afrofuturist Link." *Black Music Research Journal* 31(1):131–44. https://doi.org/10.5406/blacmusiresej.31.1.0131.

Johnson, Gaye Theresa. 2013. *Spaces of Conflict, Sounds of Solidarity: Music, Race, and Spatial Entitlement in Los Angeles*. Berkeley: University of California Press.

Johnson, Imani Kai. 2022. *Dark Matter in Breaking Cyphers: The Life of Africanist Aesthetics in Global Hip Hop*. New York: Oxford University Press.

Johnson, Nate. 2016. "Lockin' with Hip-Hop's Own Fred Astaire: Shabba-Doo (Aka 'Ozone' from Breakin')." *Shea Magazine*, February 19.

Jones, Scott. 1995. "Santiago Gets Big Second Half from Carbajal." *Los Angeles Times*, September 23.

Jones, Von. 1985. "Street Kids Create a New Attitude." *Los Angeles Sentinel (1934–)*, September 26, D1.

Jordanov, Alex. 2017. *The Game: From the Street to Wall Street*. Paris: Brainworks.

Kelly, Raegan. 1993. "Hip-Hop Chicano: A Separate but Parallel Story." Pp. 65–76 in *It's Not about a Salary…: Rap, Race and Resistance in Los Angeles*, edited by B. Cross. London: Verso.

Kelly, Raegan. 2004. "Hip-Hop Chicano: A Separate but Parallel Story." Pp. 95–103 in *That's the Joint! The Hip-Hop Studies Reader*, edited by M. Forman and M. A. Neal. New York: Routledge.

Keogh, Tom. 2021. "Marcus 'Kutfather' Tufono, a DJ Who Was a Major Influence on Seattle's Hip-Hop Scene, Dies at 48 | The Seattle Times." *Seattle Times*, January 11. Retrieved October 7, 2023 (https://www.seattletimes.com/entertainment/music/marcus-kutfather-tufono-a-dj-who-was-a-major-influence-on-seattles-hip-hop-scene-dies-at-48/)

Khabeer, Su'ad Abdul. 2016. *Muslim Cool: Race, Religion, and Hip Hop in the United States*. New York: New York University Press.

Khalfani, Michael. 2017a. "Disco Daddys' Wide World of Hip-Hop—Chris the Glove." November 25, in *Disco Daddy's Wide World of Hip-Hop and RnB*, 31:56. https://podcasters.spotify.com/pod/show/disco-daddy/episodes/DISCO-DADDYS-WIDE-WORLD-OF-HIP-HOP--CHRIS-THE-GLOVE-e2inmh

Khalfani, Michael. 2017b. "Disco Daddy's Wide World of Hip Hop—Michael "Boogaloo Shrimp" Chambers." December 2, in *Disco Daddy's Wide World of Hip-Hop and RnB*, 1:19:06. https://podcasters.spotify.com/pod/show/disco-daddy/episodes/DISCO-DADDYS-WIDE-WORLD-OF-HIP-HOP---MICHAEL-BOOGALOO-SHRIMP-CHAMBERS-e2inmg

Khalfani, Michael. 2017c. "Disco Daddys' Wide World of Hip-Hop and RnB—OG Kid Frost." 12/23/2017 in *Disco Daddy's Wide World of Hip-Hop and RnB*, 1:20:29. https://podcasters.spotify.com/pod/show/disco-daddy/episodes/DISCO-DADDYS-WIDE-WORLD-OF-HIP-HOP-AND-RnB--OG-Kid-Frost-e2inmd

Kitwana, Bakari. 2002. *The Hip Hop Generation: Young Blacks and the Crisis in African American Culture*. New York: Basic Civitas.

Kun, Josh. 2005. *Audiotopia: Music, Race, and America*. Berkeley: University of California Press.

Kun, Josh, and Laura Pulido. 2013. *Black and Brown in Los Angeles: Beyond Conflict and Coalition*. Berkeley: University of California Press.

Lakewood, Vanessa Fleet. 2022. "The Camera in the Cypher: High Times and Hypervisibility in Early Hip Hop Dance." Pp. 32–57 in *The Oxford Handbook of Hip Hop Dance Studies, Oxford Handbooks*, edited by E. by M. Fogarty and I. K. Johnson. Oxford; New York: Oxford University Press.

Lannert, John. 1990. "Yo! Homeboy! Now It's Rap 'En Español.'" *Sun Sentinel*, July 15. Retrieved October 19, 2022 (https://www.sun-sentinel.com/1990/07/15/yo-homeboy-now-its-rap-en-espanol/).

Last.fm. n.d. "THE RADIO CREW Lineup, Biography." *Last.Fm*. Retrieved June 8, 2021 (https://www.last.fm/music/THE+RADIO+CREW/+wiki).

LA Times. 1992. "Raul M. Garcia; Musician." March 18.

Latorre, Guisela. 2008. *Walls of Empowerment: Chicana/o Indigenist Murals of California*. Austin: University of Texas Press.

Le Flambeur, Bob. 2019. "Le journalisme total selon Alex Jordanov." *Gonzaï*, February 7.

Lee, Grace Jahng. 2015. "Seoul-Born, Bogotá-Raised, L.A.-Grown, Brooklyn-Aged: Profile of Chino." *KoreanAmericanStory.Org*. Retrieved June 7, 2021 (http://koreanamericanstory.org/written/profile-of-chino/).

Lee, Jooyoung. 2016. *Blowin' Up: Rap Dreams in South Central*. Chicago: University of Chicago Press.

Lena, Jennifer C. 2012. *Banding Together: How Communities Create Genres in Popular Music*. Princeton, NJ: Princeton University Press.

León, Luis D. 2004. *La Llorona's Children: Religion, Life, and Death in the U.S.–Mexican Borderlands*. Berkeley: University of California Press.

Lin, Jan. 2019. *Taking Back the Boulevard: Art, Activism, and Gentrification in Los Angeles*. New York: New York University Press.

Lindsey, Jamil. 2018. "Mellowman Ace Talks Latin Hip-Hop and Moving to L.A. from Cuba." *The Real Gully TV*, July 18. Retrieved July 27, 2023 (https://www.youtube.com/watch?v=5ip6sYl1huU).

Lomelí, Francisco A. 2017. "Introduction: Revisiting the Vision of Aztlan." Pp. 1–26 in *Aztlán: Essays on the Chicano Homeland: Revised and Expanded Edition*, edited by R. Anaya, F. A. Lomelí, and E. R. Lamadrid. Albuquerque: University of New Mexico Press.

Lordi, Emily J. 2013. *Black Resonance: Iconic Women Singers and African American Literature*. New Brunswick, NJ: Rutgers University Press.

Loza, Steven Joseph. 1993. *Barrio Rhythm: Mexican American Music in Los Angeles*. Chicago: University of Illinois Press.

Macías, Anthony. 2008. *Mexican American Mojo: Popular Music, Dance, and Urban Culture in Los Angeles, 1935–1968*. Durham, NC: Duke University Press.

Macías, Anthony. 2014. "Black and Brown Get Down: Cultural Politics, Chicano Music, and Hip Hop in Racialized Los Angeles." Pp. 55–75 in *Sounds and the City: Popular Music, Place, and Globalization, Leisure Studies in a Global Era*, edited by B. Lashua, K. Spracklen, and S. Wagg. London: Palgrave Macmillan.

Mackey, Danielle. 2018. "El Salvador's 'Iron Fist' Crackdown on Gangs: A Lethal Policy with U.S. Origins." Retrieved June 10, 2019 (https://www.worldpoliticsreview.com/articles/24136/el-salvador-s-iron-fist-crackdown-on-gangs-a-lethal-policy-with-u-s-origins).

MacWeeney, India. 2008. *Imagining the Real: Chicano Youth, Hip Hop, Race, Space and Authenticity*. London; Goldsmiths: University of London.

Magaña, Maurice Rafael. 2020. *Cartographies of Youth Resistance: Hip-Hop, Punk, and Urban Autonomy in Mexico*. Berkeley: University of California Press.

Magaña, Maurice Rafael. 2022. "The Politics of Black and Brown Solidarities: Race, Space, and Hip-Hop Cultural Production in Los Angeles." *Ethnic and Racial Studies* 45(2):942–65. https://doi.org/10.1080/01419870.2021.1896016.

Maillo-Pozo, Sharina. 2018. "Reconstructing Dominican Latinidad." *Small Axe: A Caribbean Journal of Criticism* 22(2):85–98.

Manzella, John. 2017. *A Little History on DJ J SCRATCH*, February 7. Retrieved July 21, 2021 (https://www.youtube.com/watch?v=DTUI6pI4AKs)

Mao, Jeff. 2006. "Cut Chemist & Hymnal." *Redbullmusicacademy.Com*. Retrieved October 7, 2020 (https://www.redbullmusicacademy.com/lectures/cut-chemist-and-hymnal-bring-the-funky-sermon).

Marquez, Jessica. 2016. "Pioneers of New York City Graffiti Scene Weigh in On Its Past, Present and Future." *Llero.Net*. Retrieved July 23, 2021 (https://llero.net/pioneers-of-new-york-city-graffiti-scene-weigh-in-on-its-past-present-and-future/2/).

Marrow, Tracy, and Douglas Century. 2011. *Ice: A Memoir of Gangster Life and Redemption—from South Central to Hollywood*. New York: Random House.

Martinez, Cid, and Victor M. Rios. 2011. "Conflict, Cooperation, and Avoidance." Pp. 343–62 in *Just Neighbors? Research on African American and Latino Relations in the United States*, edited by C. Martinez, V. M. Rios, E. E. Telles, M. Q. Sawyer, and G. Rivera-Salgado. New York: Russell Sage Foundation.

Martínez, Ruben. 1993. *The Other Side: Notes from the New L.A., Mexico City, and Beyond*. New York: Vintage Books.

Martinez-Morrison, Amanda. 2014. "Black and Tan Realities: Chicanos in the Borderlands of the Hip-Hop Nation." *Alter/Nativas* Spring(2):1–24.

Mausfeld, Dianne Violeta. 2019. "'These Stories Have to Be Told': Chicano Rap as Historical Source." *Popular Music History* 12(2):174–93. https://doi.org/10.1558/pomh.39209.

McFarland, Pancho. 2006. "Chicano Rap Roots: Black-Brown Cultural Exchange and the Making of a Genre." *Callaloo* 29(3):939–55.

McFarland, Pancho. 2008. *Chicano Rap: Gender and Violence in the Postindustrial Barrio*. Austin: University of Texas Press.

McFarland, Pancho. 2013. *The Chican@ Hip Hop Nation: Politics of a New Millennial Mestizaje*. East Lansing: Michigan State University Press.

McFarland, Pancho. 2018. *Toward a Chican@ Hip Hop Anti-Colonialism*. New York: Routledge.

McKenna, Kristine. 1984. "Pop Beat." *Los Angeles Times*, June 16, 77, 80.

McLuhan, Marshall. 1964. *Understanding Media: The Extensions of Man*. New York: McGraw-Hill.

McMains, Juliet. 2015. *Spinning Mambo into Salsa: Caribbean Dance in Global Commerce*. New York: Oxford University Press.

Medina, Cruz. 2014. "'(Who Discovered) America': Ozomatli and the Mestiz@ Rhetoric of Hip Hop." *Alter/Nativas* Spring(2):1–24.

Medina, Sal. 1992. "In Memory of Jonny Chingas." *Firme Magazine*.

Mendoza-Denton, Norma, and Bryan Gordon. 2015. "Language and Social Meaning in Bilingual Mexico and the United States." Pp. 553–78 in *The Handbook of Hispanic Sociolinguistics*, edited by M. Diaz-Campos. Hoboken, NJ: John Wiley & Sons.

Meraz, Gerard. 2008. "1980s | East L.A.'s DJ Culture." *KCET*. Retrieved April 27, 2020 (https://www.kcet.org/history-society/backyard-parties-1980s-east-las-dj-culture).

Miller, Monica R. 2012. *Religion and Hip Hop*. New York: Routledge.

Ming, Tu Ying, and Lark Corbeil. 1991. *The History of Break Dance (Mr. Animation, Oz Rock and Flat Top—Stories)*. Tularco Enterprises. Retrieved February 5, 2021 (https://www.youtube.com/watch?v=IlezgUmyBTs)

Miranda, Carolina. 2023. "Zoot Suit: How the Bold Look Made History and Continues to Influence Fashion." *Los Angeles Times*, June 13. Retrieved June 19, 2023 (https://www.latimes.com/entertainment-arts/story/2023-06-13/zoot-suit-how-the-bold-look-made-history-and-continues-to-influence-fashion)

Morgan, Marcyliena. 2009. *The Real Hiphop: Battling for Knowledge, Power, and Respect in the LA Underground*. Durham, NC: Duke University Press.

Morgan, Marcyliena, and Dionne Bennett. 2011. "Hip-Hop and the Global Imprint of a Black Cultural Form." *Daedalus* 140(2):176–96. https://doi.org/10.1162/DAED_a_00086.

Mullen, Brendan. 2000. "Down for the Good Life." *LA Weekly*, June 21.

Muñoz, Matt. 2015. "It'll Be 4/4 on the Dance Floor with DJ Sidney Perry." *Bakersfield Californian*, August 19.

Murch, Donna. 2015. "Crack in Los Angeles: Crisis, Militarization, and Black Response to the Late Twentieth-Century War on Drugs." *Journal of American History* 102(1):162–73. https://doi.org/10.1093/jahist/jav260.

NARA. 1952. "Texas, El Paso Alien Arrivals, 1924–1952."

Nava, Alejandro. 2022. *Street Scriptures: Between God and Hip-Hop*. Chicago: University of Chicago Press.

Nibokun, Imade. 2013. "The Best West Coast Christian Rappers in History." *LA Weekly*, April 25.

Nibokun, Imade. 2014. *Battle Rap Gospel: The Story of the Tunnel Rats*. Retrieved September 12, 2021 (https://www.youtube.com/watch?v=J-2Qedfib6Q).

Ogbar, Jeffrey Ogbonna Green. 2007. *Hip-Hop Revolution: The Culture and Politics of Rap*. Lawrence: University Press of Kansas.

Oliver, Myrna. 1996. "C. Bernard Jackson; Creator, Director of the Inner City Cultural Center." *Los Angeles Times*, July 19.

Oro, Paul Joseph López. 2020. "Garifunizando Ambas Américas: Hemispheric Entanglements of Blackness/Indigeneity/AfroLatinidad." *Postmodern Culture* 31(1):1–18. https://doi.org/10.1353/pmc.2020.0025.

Orsi, Robert A. 1999. *Gods of the City: Religion and the American Urban Landscape*. Bloomington, IN: Indiana University Press.

Ortiz, Darlene, and Heidi Siegmund Cuda. 2015. *Definition of Down: My Life with Ice T and the Birth of Hip Hop*. Los Angeles: Over the Edge.

Ossé, Reggie, 2015. *The Combat Jack Show: The Ty Dolla Sign and Darlene Ortiz Episode (LSN Podcast)*. Retrieved June 14, 2022. https://www.youtube.com/watch?v=RNbLLJ6ercU.

Osumare, H. 2007. *The Africanist Aesthetic in Global Hip-Hop: Power Moves*. New York: Springer.

Osuna, Steven. 2019. "The Psycho Realm Blues: The Violence of Policing, Disordering Practices, and Rap Criticism in Los Angeles." *Chiricu* 4(1):76–100.

Pabon, Jorge. 2006. "Physical Graffiti: The History of Hip-Hop Dance." Pp. 18–26 in *Total Chaos: The Art and Aesthetics of Hip-Hop*, edited by J. Chang. New York: Basic Books.

Patrin, Nate. 2020. *Bring That Beat Back: How Sampling Built Hip-Hop*. Minneapolis: University of Minnesota Press.

Patterson, Orlando. 1982. *Slavery and Social Death*. Cambridge, MA: Harvard University Press.

Pennycook, Alastair. 2007. *Global Englishes and Transcultural Flows*. New York: Routledge.

Perry, Marc D. 2015. *Negro Soy Yo: Hip Hop and Raced Citizenship in Neoliberal Cuba*. Durham, NC: Duke University Press.

Pinn, Anthony B. 2003. *Noise and Spirit: The Religious and Spiritual Sensibilities of Rap Music*. New York: New York University Press.

Pinn, Anthony B. 2007. "Bling and Blessings: Thoughts on the Intersections of Rap Music and Religious Meaning." *CrossCurrents* 57(2):289–95.

Porter, Mark. 2020. *Ecologies of Resonance in Christian Musicking*. New York: Oxford University Press.

Prinz, Jesse J. 2012. *The Conscious Brain*. New York: Oxford University Press.

Quijano, Hiyasmin. 2014. "Empire of Funk Shows Influence of Fil-Ams on US Hip Hop Culture." *Inquirer*, February 18.

RadiotronEvent. 2009. "Radiotron New Report 1." *Youtube web site*. Retrieved July 3, 2023 (https://www.youtube.com/watch?v=shQgQ7GiZH8)

Ramirez, Andres. 2019. "Kid Frost and DJ Ralph M (Funkdoobiest) Interview at Radiotron 2019."

Ramírez, Catherine S. 2009. *The Woman in the Zoot Suit: Gender, Nationalism, and the Cultural Politics of Memory*. Durham, NC: Duke University Press.

Ramírez, Daniel. 2015. *Migrating Faith: Pentecostalism in the United States and Mexico in the Twentieth Century.* Chapel Hill, NC: University of North Carolina Press.

Recinos, Harold J. 2010. "Transforming Ecclesiology: Hip-Hop Matters." Pp. 155–70 in *In Our Own Voices: Latino/a Renditions of Theology,* edited by B. Valentín. Maryknoll, NY: Orbis Books.

Reyes, Patrick B. 2016. *Nobody Cries When We Die: God, Community, and Surviving to Adulthood.* St. Louis, MO: Chalice Press.

Reznowski, Gabriella. 2014. "Hip-Hop Mundial: Latino Voices, Global Hip-Hop, and the Academy." Pp. 85–94 in *Popular Culture: Arts and Social Change in Latin America,* edited by L. Shirey. New Orleans, LA: SALALM, Inc.

Rios, Hector. 2018. *LA Times Festival of Books 2018: Hip-Hop as Storytelling: The Four Elemen…*

Rivera, Raquel Z. 2001. "Hip-Hop, Puerto Ricans, and Ethnoracial Identities in New York." Pp. 235–62 in *Mambo Montage, the Latinization of New York City,* edited by A. Laó-Montes and A. Dávila. New York: Columbia University Press.

Rivera, Raquel Z. 2002. "Hip Hop and New York Puerto Ricans." In *Latino/a Popular Culture,* edited by M. Habell-Pallan and M. Romero. New York: New York University Press.

Rivera, Raquel Z. 2003. *New York Ricans from the Hip Hop Zone.* London: Palgrave Macmillan.

Rivera-Rideau, Petra R. 2016. "From Panama to the Bay: Los Rakas' Expressions of Afrolatinidad." Pp. 63–79 in *La Verdad: A Reader of Hip-Hop Latinidades,* edited by Melissa Castillo-Garsow and Jason Nichols. Columbus: Ohio State University Press.

Robinson, Jerald, and Mario Robinson. 2020. "Supadopefresh Podcast 001 | Bboy Orko." Retrieved October 8, 2020. (https://www.youtube.com/watch?v=4H-zSBggqnk&t=191s)

Rodríguez, Richard T. 2009. *Next of Kin: The Family in Chicano/a Cultural Politics.* Durham, NC: Duke University Press.

Rodríguez, Richard T. 2016. "The Verse of the Godfather." Pp. 107–22 in *Velvet Barrios: Popular Culture and Chicana/o Sexualities,* edited by A. G. D. Alba. New York: Springer.

Román, Miriam Jiménez. 2009. "Looking at That Middle Ground: Racial Mixing as Panacea?" Pp. 325–36 in *A Companion to Latina/o Studies,* edited by J. Flores and R. Rosaldo. Hoboken, NJ: John Wiley & Sons.

Rosa, Hartmut. 2019. *Resonance: A Sociology of Our Relationship to the World.* Hoboken, NJ: John Wiley & Sons.

Rose, Tricia. 1994. *Black Noise: Rap Music and Black Culture in Contemporary America.* Middletown, CT: Wesleyan University Press.

Rose, Tricia. 2008. *The Hip Hop Wars: What We Talk about When We Talk about Hip Hop—and Why It Matters.* New York: Basic Books.

Sahagun, Louis. 1990. "Gang Homicides Increase 69% in L.A. County Areas: Violence: Authorities Blame Heavy Firepower, Impact of Poverty and Appeal of a 'Trendy' Image." *Los Angeles Times,* August 21.

Saldívar, José David. 1997. *Border Matters: Remapping American Cultural Studies.* Berkeley: University of California Press.

Sanchez-Walsh, Arlene. 2003. *Latino Pentecostal Identity: Evangelical Faith, Self, and Society.* New York: Columbia University Press.

Shake City Bboys. 2023. "Eye on LA Episode #2." *Youtube* web site. Retrieved July 19, 23 (https://www.youtube.com/watch?v=-sodLAZmdKc).

Sharma, Nitasha Tamar. 2010. *Hip Hop Desis: South Asian Americans, Blackness, and a Global Race Consciousness.* Durham, NC: Duke University Press.

Silver, Kane. 2020. *The Ins and Outs—Episode #122—Popin Pete.* Vol. 122.

Small, Mark. 2008. "Berklee Today: The Laboriel Legacy." Retrieved May 13, 2023 (https://college.berklee.edu/news/1286/berklee-today-the-laboriel-legacy).

Smith, Harrison. 2021. "Adolfo 'Shabba-Doo' Quiñones, Street-Dance Star of 'Breakin'" Movies, Dies at 65." *Washington Post,* January 15.

Snowden, Don. 1984. "Latino Bands." *Los Angeles Times,* January 8.

Snowden, Don. 1985. "Do-It-Yourself Way in Pop Music World." *Los Angeles Times (1923–1995)*, March 1, oc_e2.

Sonksen, Mike. 2012. "Beats and Rhymes: Revisiting Wisdom and Knowledge." *KCET*. Retrieved October 7, 2020 (https://www.kcet.org/history-society/beats-rhymes-revisiting-wisdom-and-knowledge).

Sonksen, Mike. 2015. "Something in the Water: Hip Hop History in Cerritos." *KCET*. Retrieved October 7, 2020 (https://www.kcet.org/history-society/something-in-the-water-hip-hop-history-in-cerritos).

Spady, James G., Samir Meghelli, and H. Samy Alim. 2006. *Tha Global Cipha: Hip Hop Culture and Consciousness*. Philadelphia, PA: Black History Museum Press.

Sperling, Matthew. 1985. "Boogie, Don't Fight, Film Dancer Says." *San Bernardino County Sun*, January 20, B-3.

Spurrier, Jeff. 1983. "Pop Music: L.A. Rockers' Summer Cry: Let's Dance Pop Music Dance Fever Dance Fever." *Los Angeles Times (1923–1995)*, August 14, u68.

Stewart, Addi. 2019. "Myka Nyne: Nynth Wonder of the World." *HubPages*. Retrieved October 7, 2020 (https://hubpages.com/entertainment/Myka-Nyne-Nynth-Wonder-of-the-World-of-Rhymes).

Sullivan, Arnold. 2019a. "Dusty Vision Radio Presents: Mellow Man Ace Mr. Schick." *Dusty Vision Radio*, September 12. Retrieved April 2, 20. (https://www.youtube.com/watch?v=M-Sdz2l1dkU&t=823s)

Sullivan, Arnold. 2019b. "Kid Frost Used To Battle Ice T - Dusty Vision Radio - ALT Interview Part 2." *Dusty Vision Radio*, September 20. Retrieved November 30, 2022. (https://www.youtube.com/watch?v=X6GjMQK4VSE)

Tate, Imani. 2013. "Music and Dance Help Couple in Surviving Terrors of Native El Salvador." *Daily Bulletin*, February 14.

Tatum, Charles M. 2011. *Lowriders in Chicano Culture: From Low to Slow to Show*. Santa Barbara, CA: ABC-CLIO.

Taylor, Christopher. 2018. "Radiotron—A Hip Hop History Lesson on the Movie Breakin." *Steemit*. Retrieved October 18, 2020 (https://steemit.com/steemit/@christheglove/the-movie-breakin-was-based-off-of-club-radio).

The Radio Crew. 1983. *Breaking and Entering*. Rayco Music and Rainbow TV Music, vinyl record.

Thompson-Hernandez, Walter. 2017. "If You're Latino Then Chances Are You Remember the Rapper Who Took the World by Storm in 1990." *We Are Mitú—Business and Entertainment, Culture and Sport, Movies and Music*, September 29.

Thornton, Sarah. 1994. "Moral Panic, the Media and British Rave Culture." Pp. 176–92 in *Microphone fiends: Youth music and youth culture*, edited by A. Ross and T. Rose. New York: Routledge.

Tinajero, Robert. 2016. "Borderland Hip Hop Rhetoric: Identity and Counterhegemony." Pp. 17–40 in *La Verdad: An International Dialogue on Hip Hop Latinidades*, edited by M. Castillo-Garsow and J. Nichols. Columbus: Ohio State University Press.

Viator, Felicia A. 2019. "West Coast Originals: A Case for Reassessing the 'Bronx West' Story of Black Youth Culture in 1980s Los Angeles." *American Studies* 58(3):87–105. https://doi.org/10.1353/ams.2019.0042.

Viator, Felicia Angeja. 2020. *To Live and Defy in LA: How Gangsta Rap Changed America*. Cambridge, MA: Harvard University Press.

Viesca, Victor Hugo. 2004. "The Battle of Los Angeles: The Cultural Politics of Chicana/o Music in the Greater Eastside." *American Quarterly* 56(3):719–39.

Vigil, James Diego. 1982. "Human Revitalization: The Six Tasks of Victory Outreach." *Drew Gateway* 52(3):49–59.

Villegas, Mark R. 2021. *Manifest Technique: Hip Hop, Empire, and Visionary Filipino American Culture*. Champaign: University of Illinois Press.

Vincent, Rickey. 2014. *Funk: The Music, the People, and the Rhythm of the One*. New York: St. Martin's Press.

Vito, Christopher. 2019. *The Values of Independent Hip-Hop in the Post-Golden Era: Hip-Hop's Rebels*. New York: Palgrave Pivot.

Waksman, Steve. 2022. *Live Music in America: A History from Jenny Lind to Beyoncé*. New York: Oxford University Press.

Wang, Oliver. 2010. "The Journey of 'Viva Tirado': A Musical Conversation within Afro-Chicano Los Angeles." *Journal of Popular Music Studies* 22(4):348–66. https://doi.org/10.1111/j.1533-1598.2010.01250.x.

Westhoff, Ben. 2016. *Original Gangstas: The Untold Story of Dr. Dre, Eazy-E, Ice Cube, Tupac Shakur, and the Birth of West Coast Rap*. New York: Hachette Books.

Whitaker, Bill. 1986. "1986 News on Gang Violence at Run D.M.C. Concerts." *CBS News*.

Wilkerson, David R., John L. Sherrill, and Elizabeth Sherrill. 1963. *The Cross and the Switchblade*. New York: Bernard Geis Associates.

Wilson, Greg. 2003. "Electro-Funk—What Did It All Mean?: Dance Culture's Missing Link." *Electrofunkroots.Co.Uk*, November.

Wilson, William. 1992. "Commentary: A Look at the Real American Graffiti." *LA Times*, May 27.

Wolf, Jessica. 2022. "UCLA Poised to Become a World Leader in Hip-Hop Studies." *UCLA Newsroom*. Retrieved July 20, 2023 (https://newsroom.ucla.edu/releases/ucla-launches-hip-hop-initiative).

Xhaferi, Erduan. 2020. "HHI Albania on Instagram: Julio 'lilCesar' Rivas." *Instagram*. Retrieved February 28, 2024 (https://www.instagram.com/tv/CBd3X_8gQRB/).

Yang, Benjamin. 2020. "Ep 60: Ice T." *Behind the Baller Podcast with Ben Baller*, March 5. Retrieved February 6, 2021 (https://www.youtube.com/watch?v=bPFgwn5COJw)

Zanfagna, Christina. 2017. *Holy Hip Hop in the City of Angels*. Berkeley: University of California Press.

Index

For the benefit of digital users, indexed terms that span two pages (e.g., 52–53) may, on occasion, appear on only one of those pages.

Figures are indicated by an italic *f* following the page number.

1200 Technics turntables, 187
12th Tribe, 192
2 Live Crew, 176
2Mex, 208, 213
360 Degrees, 173

Aceves, Robert "Ace Rock," 72–73, 75–77, 81–83, 125, 126–27, 130–31, 151, 196
Aceyalone, 191
Adam Ant, 124
Afrika Bambaataa, 81, 90, 119, 121–23
Afrika Islam, 125, 129–30, 144–45
Afrocentric Hip Hop, 199
Afrodiasporic, 178
Aguilar, Carlos, 115–16
Ahmad, 173–74
    4th Avenue Jones, 115–16
Air Force Crew, 137–38, 149–50, 175–76
Akida and Ray (emcees), 115–16
Akwid, 148
Alim, Samy, 115–16
alternative families, 116
Alvarez, Adolfo; "Oz Rock," 119–20, 123, 135, 146–47, 161, 175–76
Alvarez, Carmelo, 70, 134–45, 146–47, 149–53, 201, 205–6, 214
Alvarez, Cynthia, 141
Alvarez, Sofia; "Mama Breaker," 143–44
Alvarez, Tony; DJ Tony A Da Wizard, 83, 125, 148, 157–58, 160–61
Anaheim, California, 86
Anti–Drug Abuse Act of 1986, 196–97
Argüelles, Trudie, 122
Arguinzoni, Julie and Sonny, 178, 179, 186
Asgard Records, 204
Asia One, 113
Assemblies of God, 178
authenticity, 199
Aztlan, 182–83
Azusa Street Revival, 177–78, 192

B-Boy Summit, 72, 113

B-Boys, 96–97, 99, 102, 109, 111, 113
B-Girls, 109, 111, 113, 214, 215
B-Real, 201–2
Baby New York, 161
Back in the Day, 173
Backyard parties, East Los Angeles, 88, 89
Baker, Arthur, 90
Barnsdall Junior Arts Center, 137–38
Barrett, KK, 121, 122, 123–24, 131
Basil, Toni, 30, 75
Bay Area, California, 111–12, 160
Beat Junkies, 148
Beat Street (Film), 102–3, 111, 145
Beatboxing, 103
Bell (California), 200
Belmont Tunnel, the, 121
Berry, Fred "Mr. Penguin"; Rerun, 35–36, 75
Bible Study, 150
Big John's Hall, 160
Biola University, 115
biting, 99
Black American and Afrodiasporic roots, 1–2, 19–20, 178, 217–18
Black American gangs, 169
Black Americans, 81–82, 117–18, 126, 177
Black Americans and brown communities, 126, 131, 164–65, 171–72, 201–2
Black Los Angeles, 157–58, 164–65
Bloods (gang), 118, 167–68, 201–2
Bloods and Crips, 77, 149–50, 169
Blue City Crew; Blue City Strutters, 127, 128, 157–58, 159–60
Body Rock (film), 120–21
Bojorquez, Charles "Chaz," 49–50
Bombing L.A. (1989 documentary), 205
Bonnie Brae Street, 177–78
Boo-Yaa Tribe, 11, 157–58, 160–61
boogaloo (dance), 160
Boogie Down Productions (BDP), 199–200
Boogie Motion Productions (BMP), 84–85
Booker T, 125
Boone, Pat, 179

Borderlands life, 47–49
Borha, Imade Nibokun, 191–92
Boundary crossing (race, geography, and genre), 157–59, 164–65, 171–72
Breakin', 161
Breakin' films, 127, 128–29, 131, 144, 168
Breakin' 2: Electric Boogaloo, 127, 151, 196
Breakin' 'N' Enterin', 126–27, 133
  Breakin' 'N' Enterin' music, 126–27
Breaking, 72–73, 119–21, 124, 126, 128–29, 159–64, 189–90, 198–99
  Breaking (Los Angeles), 134, 135–36, 137, 143, 146–47, 148–50
Broadway (producer), 202–3
Broadway, street in Los Angeles, 90
Bronx, New York, 95, 117, 119, 178, 203
Broussard, Greg, 126–27
brown and Black, 72–73, 74, 76–77, 160–61
brown creative, 89, 90, 91, 158, 160
brown identity, 19–20
Brown Los Angeles, 2, 72, 75–76, 138, 152, 158, 170–71, 173, 192, 195, 199
Brown Los Angeles Hip Hop, 215, 216–18
Buchanan, Hines, 148
Buena Park, California, 104–5, 218
Buena Park High School, 104–5, 115
Buffalo Gals by Malcolm McLaren, 102
Byron "Crase" Marquez, 116–17, 118–20, 121, 126, 128, 131

California Academy of Performing Arts, 141, 143
California Department of Corrections, 197
California Youth Authority, 169–70
Caló, 157
Calvario, Arnel, 148
Calvary Chapel churches, 175
Cambodian American, 72
Cameo, 195
Campbell, Don; "Campbellock," 34–35, 75
Canaan Fellowship church, 173–74
Cannon Films, 38–39, 127–28, 142–43, 144, 151
Captain EO at Disneyland, 128–29
Captain Rapp, 1 n.2, 79
Carew, Topper, 126–27
Carson, California, 157–60, 215–16
Carson Twin Cinema, 160–61
Casa Camino Real, 108–9, 171, 195
Cazals, 110
Celluloid Records, 121–22
Central American diaspora, 136–37, 150
Central American/ "Little Central American," 123
Central valley of California, 75

Chaka Khan, 124
Chambers, Michael "Boogaloo Shrimp," 37–38, 70, 81–82, 108–9, 127, 160–61
Chang, Jeff, 82
channels of resonance, 84–85, 178, 215, 216–17, 218
Chevy Shank, 125, 126, 131
Chicanos, 85
  aesthetics, 72, 77, 115, 133, 182–84, 215
  Chicano rap, 157, 159, 182–84
  community, 111–12
  culture, 76–77, 181, 182
  gang members, 140–41
Cholos, 97–98, 199
Christian Hip Hop, 174, 176–77, 182, 191–93, 210, 212
Christian music, 173
Christian Rapper, 176, 189
Claremont, California, 73, 74
Click the Supah Latin, 77–78, 103, 106, 115–16, 148, 150, 171
Club Elements, 173–74
Club Metro, 175–76
Club Nouveau, 195
Club Unity, 173–74
cocaine and crack, 199–200
Coddington, Amy, 195
Cold Crush Brothers, 123
Coldest Rap, Cold Wind Madness, 124
Colors, film, 126–27
Community Youth Gang Services (CYGS), 168–69
Compton, 81, 215–16
Contreras, Frank; DJ Tricks, 157, 159, 167
Cooley, Joe, 170
Coolio, 89
Cooper, Chris "Super C"; Sup the Chemist, 176–77, 186, 188, 192
CoPacabana, 79
Cordova, David; West Grim, 167–68
crack epidemic, 217
crewism, 196
Crime, 148–49
Crips (gang), 118, 167–68, 202
  Crips and Bloods, 77
Cross, Brian, 86–87, 168
cross-racial tension, 115, 167–68
Cross and the Switchblade, the, 179, 183
Cross Colours, 197, 207
crossover radio stations, 195
Cruz, Nicky, 179, 183
Cuba Gooding Jr., 150, 189
Cuban American, 120–21

INDEX

Cudahy, California, 39–40
Cut Chemist, 148
cypher, 214, 215, 217, 218
Cypress Hill, 10, 41, 201–2
Cypress Street, 201–2

Dacio, Isaiah "Icy Ice," 157–58
Daly City, California, 159
dance battle, 160
dance cypher, 163–64, 173–74, 196
Davis, Mike, 135–36
    Day of Peace, 168–69
De La Cruz, Jeff, 160–61
De la Luz, Greg "Coco," 126–27
Debbie Deb, 195–96
Def Jef, 202
Deity, 215
Delicious Vinyl, 200–1
Denver, Colorado, 110–11
Devoux, Donald, 128–29, 160–61
diasporas, 171–72
dickies pants, 72, 77
Digital Underground, 202
Dilated Peoples, 208
disco, 79, 85–86, 88–89, 161, 194–96
Disco Daddy, 1 n.2, 79, 149–50
DJ Aladdin, 170–71
DJ Antron, 145
DJ Babu, 208
DJ Battle Cat, 170–71
DJ Captain Rock, 145
DJ Dove, Eddie Valenciano, 184–85, 187–88
DJ Freak Daddy, 84–85
DJ Fuego, 202–3
DJ Hazze, 137–38
DJ M–Walk, 170–71
DJ Muggs, 201
DJ Nasty Nes, 159
DJ Pebo Rodriguez, 195
DJ Rhettmatic, 148
DJ Roman Gallegos, 173–74
DJ Romeo, 170–71
DJ Scratchmatic, 148
Dj Soluz, 47
DJ Tray Ski, 170–71
DJ Tropical, 89
DJ Yella, 86, 170
DJs, DJing, 113, 159
Dolphin Park, 160
Dominguez, 215–16
Dominguez High School, 76
Double Dutch Bus, 72
    Doves, the, 167–68

Dr Dre, 77, 81, 86, 148, 157–58, 159, 170, 189, 202
drugs, 194–95, 197
Dublab Podcast, 122
Duke of Earl (play), 181, 182, 190–91
DVX (Devastating Vocal Excellence), 201–2
Dynamic Rockers, 120–21
Dynamic Twins, 177, 186, 191–92

East Coast Hip Hop, 81, 199, 203
East Los Angeles, 12, 74, 76–77, 89–90, 95, 183, 218
Eazy-E, 202
Egyptian Lover, 82, 83, 84–85, 91, 125–27
Eighteen with a Bullet, 157
El Rancho High School, 97
El Salvador, 137–38
Electric Boogaloos, 75, 119–20, 127
Electric Boogie, 119–20
Electro music, 30–31, 84, 86–87, 90, 142, 161
ElectroBeat Records, 31–32, 84, 130–31
Elysian Park, 108–9
emceeing/rapping, 113, 200
Erule (artist), 191
Escape from Havana, 200–1
Estrada, Billy Starr, 37–38
Estrada, Eric, 179
Estrada, John "Zender," 49–51, 79, 145, 146, 149, 196, 214
Eve After Dark, 81
Everett, Gregory "G-Bone," 87–88
Evidence (artist), 208
Evil E, 39–40, 125
Ewoodzie, Joseph C, 79
Exposé (artists), 195
Eye on LA (ABC), 128–29

F–Troop (gang), 167–68
Fab 5, 122
Fairfax High School, 116, 208
Falcon, Bruno "Pop N Taco," 37–38, 39f, 75–76, 81–83, 127, 128
Fame (TV Show), 111
fashion, 111
Fat Cap (brand), 207
Ferguson, Aaron; Graff1, 121, 125, 132
Fila, 110
Filipino and Samoan crews, 161
First Baptist Church of Santa Ana, 134
Fisherman's Wharf (San Francisco), 110–11
Flashdance (film), 120–21
Floor Patrol, 161–64
Florentine Gardens, 108–9

Fluky Luke, 35
Fontana, California, 186
FoosGoneWild, 72
Forman, Murray, 165
Foundation Funkollective, 173–74
Frame, 205–6
Frank, Andrew, 36–37
Freestyle Fellowship, 191, 208
freestyle music, 30–31, 195–96
freestyle Rapping, 109, 173–74
Fresno, 75
Fuego (DJ), 204
Fullerton, California, 102–3, 199, 218
Funk, 72, 74, 75, 85–86, 104–5, 124, 125, 159–60, 161
  Funk and soul culture in Northern California's Bay Area, 110–11
Funk Freaks, 72
Funkdoobiest, 77–78, 201–2
futurism, 90

gangs
  gang banging, 161, 189, 190
  gang "colors" and "insignia," 165–66
  gang culture, 74, 77
  gang intervention, 169
  gang violence in Los Angeles, 165–66, 167–69, 196–97, 199, 202
  gangbanging music, 74
  gangbangers, 166
  gangs and migration, 202
  proliferation of gangs, 217
Gangsta Rap, 129, 164–65, 199, 205
Garcia, Henry "Hen Gee," 39–43, 125
Garcia, Raul "Jonny Chingas"; Rulie Garcia, 55–71
Garifuna, 40
gateway cities, 200
Gemini, 89
gender and musical genres, 194–96
Generation One (dance crew), 104–5
Gesuden, Liza, 115–16
Ghetto blasters, 73–74
Giant Casting Shadows (GCS), 47
Gigolo Rap, 79
Gill, Jon, 218
Gino's, 79
Gladys Knight and the Pips, 102
Glaser, Gary, 205
Goethe Institut, 213
Goff, Arthur, 37
Gonzales, Delilah "Lilah," 199, 200
Gonzales, Neecee, 108–9, 195–96, 197–98

Gonzales, Paul, 168–69
Gonzalez, Julio; DJ Julio G, 170–71, 182, 201
Gonzalez, Tony; DJ Tony G, 89, 145, 148, 170, 182, 195, 200–1
Good Life Cafe, the, 116, 173–74, 213
Gory (B-boy), 162, 163–64
Got No Control (podcast), 215–16
Graff Lab, 113
graffiti, 194–95, 197, 205, 207, 213, 215
graffiti convention, 205–7
graffiti writers, 116–17, 118, 119, 121, 131
graffiti writing, 101, 109, 113–14
  New York City graffiti, 51
Graffitinspire, 213, 214–15, 216
Grandmixer DST, 121–22, 123
Grody, Steve, 148–49
Groovatrons, 73, 74, 75–76
Guadalajara, Jalisco, 163–64
Guatemala, 117, 118
Guevara, Ruben "Funkahuatl," 64, 86–87
Gutierrez, Ernie (DJ), 83
Gutierrez, Miguel (DJ), 148
Guzman, David, 144–46, 149–50, 151, 175–77, 185–86, 191–92
Guzman-Sanchez, Thomas, 75–76
gymnastics, 198–99

Hahn, James, 169–70
Hamilton, Denise, 206
Handyman (B-boy), 135
Harbor Area, 157–61, 171–72
Harrison, Anthony Kwame, 174
Harvest Christian Fellowship, 175
Hawaii, 119–20, 177–78
Heckle and Jeckle, 135
Henderson, Andre, 186–88
Henderson, April, 119–20, 159–60
Hernandez, Carlos, 85
Hi-C (artist), 148, 157–58
Hi-NRG music, 32
Hip Hop and the Black American experience, 200
Hip Hop as Public Outreach, 179–80, 181
Hip Hop elements, 96
Hip Hop Fashion, 109
Hip Hop School of the Arts (Pomona, California), 134
Hip Hop Shop, the, 161, 207–9, 212, 213, 214–15
Hip Hop's reputation in middle America, 165
Hip Hop's resonance, 95–96, 160–61, 164, 175, 178
hiphopography, 17

Hisatake, Jack and Charlie, 160–61
Hispanic Causing Panic, 112
Hispanic Zone, 201–2
Holguin, Albert "Jurny," 8–9, 173, 185–86, 191–92, 210
Hollywood, 73–74, 117–18, 120–21, 128, 131, 150
Hollywood Boulevard and Highland Ave, 73–74
Hollywood High School, 117–18, 174, 185–86, 188, 192
Holy Terra Records, 185
Homestyle, 116
Honduras, 117
Honey Rockwell, 126
house party scene, 201
Huizar, Hugo "Mr Smooth Huizar," 37–38, 128–29
Hungry Breakers, 143
Huntington Park, 200
Huntsberger, Jack, 135, 141, 142–43, 151

I.D.O.L. King, 115–16
Ice Cube, 77, 86
Ice-T (artist), 31, 68, 77, 89, 104, 129–30, 142, 159–60, 180–81, 202
Iceman; Mike Rivera, 81–83, 161–65, 168, 194, 196, 197, 207–8, 214, 215
Immigration, Migration in Los Angeles, 136–37
incarceration, 164–65, 196
Indigenous communities, 162–63
Inland Empire (IE), 175–76, 203
Inner City Cultural Arts Center, 138
International Foursquare Church, 175

Jackson, Bernard, 138
Jackson, Michael, 108, 124, 128–29
Jammin Gemini, 170
Jammin' James, 170–71
Jarre, Jean Michel, 90
Jazzy J Boog Soulfire, 128–29
JC and the Boyz, 177, 185–86, 191–92
JDC records, 29, 83
Jeronimo "Jero One," 214
Jesus Christ, 175, 177
Jesus Movement, 175
Jewish diaspora, 177
Jimenez, Jose "J–Vibe," 68–69, 90, 91
Jimmy Jam, 126
J.J. Fad, 202
Johnee Blaze, 72
Johnny J, 70
Johnson, Imani Kai, 217–18
Juratovac, Rigel "Crayone," 205

K2S, 148–49
Kangols, 110
Kato, 108, 112
Kaufman, Rory, 150
KDAY, 91, 106, 145, 150, 168–72, 195
   mixmasters, 170–71, 201
Kelly, Raegan, 86–87
Khabeer, Su'ad Abdul, 4–5, 6–7, 43, 216–17, 220, 221–22
Khalfani, Michael, 89, 124
   Disco Daddy, 79
Kid Frost; Arturo Molina, 31, 42, 84, 89, 104, 112, 130–31, 152, 168, 177
   La Raza (song), 112, 200–1
Kiedis, Anthony; Red Hot Chili Peppers, 124
King Tee, 202
Kirby, Ed (KDAY), 168–69
Knott's Berry Farm (Buena Park, California), 34–35
Koine Greek, 177
Kool Hec Si, Hector Castro, 202–4
Koolski, 102–3, 199
Kraftwerk, 90
KRS1, 199, 204
Kun, Josh, 86–88
Kung Fu flicks, 160–61

LA '81, '82, '83, 73–74
L.A. Bomb Squad, 149
LA Breakers, 149–50
LA Dream Team, 84, 169–70
LA graffiti, 143, 148–49
LA Photo Center, 205
La Puente, California, 178
LA Street Scene Festival, 149–50, 168–69
LA Symphony, 115–16
Laboriel family, 40
Lakota Nation, 201–2
Lara, Danny, 180–84, 188–89, 190–92
Latin Alliance, 104
Latin American Bible Institute (LABI), 178, 179
Latin Kings; Puerto Roc Posse, 184, 202–4
Latinas and Hip Hop, 200
LAtino Hip Hop, 202–3, 204
Latino Pentecostal churches, 173–74
Latino Pentecostalism, 178
Latinos, 117–18, 126
Lauper, Cyndi, 195
Laurie, Greg, 175
legal injunctions on creative expressions like street dancing, 217
Legg Lake in Whittier, 73–74
Leimert Park, 191

Levitt Pavilion, MacArthur Park, 152
Lighter Shade of Brown (Artist), 10
Lil Coco, 161
Lisa Lisa, 195–96
Lisa Miss Rockberry Love, 84
Little Luis, 137–38
　Lockers, the, 75
locking, 80, 127–28, 130, 142, 160
Long Beach, 75–76, 108–9, 157, 167–68, 215–16
Long Beach Arena, 165
Long Beach concert, 165–66
Long Beach Insanes, 166–67
Lonzo Williams, 81
Look out Weekend, 195–96
Lord's Personal Gangsters (LPG), 185–86
Los Angeles, 206
Los Angeles City Hall, 135
Los Angeles County Jail, 197
Los Angeles County Youth Gang Services, 168–69, 202
Los Angeles Hip Hop, 158, 174, 201
Los Angeles Memorial Coliseum, 149–50
Los Angeles Popping Scene, 108–9
Los Angeles River, 206
Los Angeles underground, 212–13
Los Angeles uprisings, 115
Loveland Church, 186
lowriders, 10, 11, 47, 77, 85, 112, 182
LPG, the Lord's Personal Gangsters, 9–10, 9f, 191–92, 210
　LPG (Dax and Jurny), 173–74
Lynwood, 200
Lyrical Engineer Genius G/Tony/Lyrical G, 164

Mabin, Anthony; "DJ Antron," 148
MacArthur Park, 121, 123, 135–37, 141–43, 145, 146, 149, 151, 152, 207–8, 213, 215
Mack, Greg, 170–71, 195
Madonna, 124–25, 142, 195
Malcom McLaren, 124
Manzella, John; DJ J Scratch, 84
martial arts films, 160–61
Martin, Gid, 84–85
Mas Pingon (song by Mellow Man Ace), 200–1
Mass Media, 109, 110
Mata, Michael (pastor), 144, 150
Matt Groening, 124
Mavericks Flat, 35–36
Mayorga, Dino, 101–2, 104–5
Maywood, city, 145–46
MC Hammer, 202
MC Peace, 186
MC Ren, 202

MC Scroller, 177
　MC Sin, 175, 176
McFarland, Pancho, 12–13, 182
Medina, Teddy, 104–5
Medrano, Ralph (DJ); "The Mixican," 77–78, 148, 170–71, 201–2
Medusa, 75–76, 152
Mejia, Gerardo, 126–27
Mellow Man Ace, Ase Kool, Ulpiano Sergio Reyes, 10, 44–45, 148, 200–2
Melrose Avenue, 207, 208
mental health, 196–97
Mentirosa (song by Mellow Man Ace), 200–1
Meraz, Gerard, 88, 89
mestizaje–Joseph Paul Lopez Oro on mestizaje, 43
Mexicali, Mexico, 161–63
Mexican American, 138–40, 177
Mexican American DJs, 83
Mexico City, 162–63
Miami, Florida, 111–12, 120–21, 176
Michael Concepcion, 202, 203, 204
Michel'le, 202
microscenes, 116
Midnite Lockers, 160
mobile DJ crews, 80, 106, 129–31, 157–58
Montenegro, Jose; Pastor Peps, 184, 188–89
MSK, 113
Murch, Donna, 196–97
　Music Commission, the, 85
Music industry, 195, 198
mutual recognition, 115–19, 121–22, 127–28, 133
Myka 9, 148, 152, 189, 191
Mytar, Jason, 116

N.W.A, 86, 183–84, 201
Nardone, Michael, 82
Nava, Alex, 175
New Mexico, 26
New York City, 111–12
New York City B-boys, 111, 126
New York City Breakers, 111
　New York City Carmelo, 140–41
New York City Hip Hop Culture, 110–11, 117, 118–22, 123, 127, 159–60
New York Hip Hop Scene, 197–98, 205, 208–9
　NY Hip Hop Elements/Scene, 96–97, 100, 102
New Zealand, 119–20, 159–60
Newport Beach, California, 176
Nicholas, Fayard, 138
Nike Corporation, 120–21

Nikko Motion, 215
No Bone Tyrone, 76
Normandy Ave, 118
nu wave music, 85–86, 125, 161
NWA, 77, 191

Oakland, 75
    Observatory theater (Santa Ana), 72
OG Chino, 121
    Old English lettering, 72, 73–74, 77, 118
Oldies, 182
Olympics, 1984, 149–50
Orange County, California, 85, 86
Orange Pavilion, 165–66
Orsi, Robert, 179
Ortiz, Darlene, 146–47
Osseé, Reggie, 146–47
Osumare, Halifu, 135–36
Osuna, Steven, 12–13

Pacheco, Tyrone; "T–Tuff/Tomahawk Funk," 201–2
pachuca and pachuco aesthetics, 47, 48–49
Paez, Jorge; Maromero Paez, 162
Panic Zone (song by NWA), 201–2
Pareles, 195
Parliament Funkadelic, 73
Pasadena, 82, 191, 202–3
Pasifika People, 119–20
Patrulla del Piso, 162–63
Peace 586, 191–92
Pentecostal, Pentecostalism, 173, 174, 175, 177–78, 179–80
    Pentecost in the Bible, 192
Pentecostalism and Hip Hop, 178
Philippines, 120–21
Pico Rivera, 95, 96, 97, 112, 164, 218
Pico Union, 105–6, 215, 218
Pigeon John, 152, 213
place-making, 213
Planet Patrol, 90
Planet Rock (song by Afrika Bambaata), 30–31, 90–91
Policing, militarization, 164–65
Political Rap/Hip Hop, 199–200
pommel horse, 198–99
Pomona, California, 73–74, 76, 81–82, 218
    Pomona Fairgrounds, 82
Pop-Break, 85–86
Pope, Greg "Cambellock Jr," 35–36, 75
popping, 99, 108, 127–28, 130, 135, 142, 160, 190–91, 214
Popping Pete (Filipino American), 80

Port of Los Angeles, 157
Power 106 (radio station), 195
Power album cover, 146–47
power moves, 135–36
Primo Dee, 149
Prince, 124
    Procussions, the, 115–16
Project Blowed, 116, 173–74, 208, 212
Propaganda (emcee), 115–16, 190–91
Proper Dos (Hip Hop artists), 83
Providence, Rhode Island, 120–21
Psycho Realm, 45
Public Enemy, 204
Puente Hills Mall, 73–74
Puerto Ricans, 27–28, 177–78
    Nuyorican, 95
Punk Music/Punk Movement, 85–86, 122, 123, 131
    Punk Rock Scene (NYC), 123
Punking and Whacking, 36–37

Quiñones, Adolfo; "Shabbadoo," 35, 37–38, 43, 75–76, 80, 127, 128

racial conflicts in Los Angeles, 115, 116–18, 121, 124, 128, 131
racial stereotypes and Hip Hop, 165–66
Radio Club, The Radio, The Radio Club, 32, 116–17, 119–33, 141–42, 144–46, 168, 217
Radio Crew, 126–27
Radio Shack, 90
Radiotron, 79, 132–33, 168, 175–76, 177–78, 189–90, 201, 205, 213, 214–15, 217
Radiotron Wizards, 149–50
Rakaa (artist), 208
Ralph Bailey Jr. (1987) of the Los Angeles Sentinel, 169–70
Ralph Medrano/DJ Ralph M, 201–2
Rampart Scandal or Rampart Division of the LAPD, 135–36
Rap-Sures, the, 176
rap for God, 176
Rap Pages, 166
Raphi, 152, 212
Rapper's Delight, 215
Rashaun, 199
record collections, 159
Red Shield Community Center run by the Salvation Army, 140–41
resonance, 4–7, 86–87, 96
Reyes brothers, 201–2
Reynosa, Dax, 1, 173, 185–86, 188–89, 191–92, 210–12
    "Just Schoolin," 7

Reynosa, Zane, 47, 191–92, 210, 216
Rhyme Syndicate, 42–43, 129–30, 159–60
Rich Roc/ Ese Rich Roc, 157
Rico Suave (song by Gerardo), 126–27
Rifleman, 152
Rios, Hector; Hex, 51–52, 194–95, 197, 205, 206–9, 210, 213–14
Risk, 206
Rivas, "Lil" Cesar, 79, 134, 135, 137–38, 147f, 148–49, 152, 175–76, 207–8
Rivera, Danny; Mr. Schick, 44–45, 200–1
Riverside, 175–76
Riverside area, 176
Roadium Mixtapes, 148, 157–58
Roadium Swap Meet, 170
Robie, Jon, 90
Robot style of Poplocking, 76
robotin, 127–28, 160
　robotin and struttin, 111
Rock of the '80s (music festival), 188–89
Rock Steady Crew, 110, 111, 119–21, 199, 208–9
　Rock Steady Crew, West Coast branch, 103
Rockberry Jam (song by the LA Dream Team), 84
Rocksteady, 119
Rodger Clayton, 80, 82, 83–85, 166, 167–68, 170
Rodriguez, Jose; DJ Pebo, 25–33, 83, 130–31
Rodriguez, Lizette, 84
Rodriguez, Richard, 84
Rodriguez, Vidal "Lil Coco," 128
Roger "Orko" Romero, 124, 125, 126
Roland TR-808, 90, 91
Romero, Roger; Orko, 137–38, 148–49, 175–76, 207–8
Ronald Reagan, 196–97
Ronek, 215–16
Rosa, Hartmut, 4–5, 16–17, 216–17
Rosa, Shawndel "Jazzy D," 146–47, 148
Rose, Tricia, 4–5, 116, 194
Rosemead, 106
Roth, David Lee, 124
Roxy, The (New York City), 121–22, 123, 145
Roybal, Pat; Lil Blitz, 110–12
Roybal, Steven; "Gremz," "Zulu Gremlin," 110–12, 113, 195–96, 198–99, 207–8
Roybal, Steve Sr., 110–11
Run DMC, 84, 123, 166, 167, 168–70
　"Raising Hell" tour, 165
Russell Simmons, 166

Saint City Session, 134
Salsa, Cha Cha, and the Mambo, 33
Same Gang, 202–3, 205

Samerika Hall, 160
Samoan, 119–20, 128, 131, 157–58, 159–60
San Bernardino, California, 82–83, 175, 203, 218
San Diego, 159
San Fernando Valley, 75–76, 116, 218
San Gabriel Valley, 89
　San Gabriel Valley area of Los Angeles County, 108, 112
San Pedro, 157
Sanchez-Walsh, Arlene, 181
Sanchez, Ana "Lollipop," 33–39, 127
Santa Ana, California, 47, 84–85, 134, 167–68, 218
Santa Monica, 83
Santiago, Mark; "Freeze Rockin Markski," 95, 96–102, 105, 106–8, 110, 117–18, 164, 198, 207–8
Satele, Fao, 160
Satele, Teleso, 160
Saturday Night Fever, 79
Scott Park, 160
Seattle, Washington, 159
Segregation, 200
Sen Dog; Reyes, Senen; Sen Stiff, 201–2
　Sen Dog and Mellow, 41, 201–2
Sevilla, "B-boy Don," 102, 148
Seymour, William, 177–78
Shake City Rockers, 125, 126, 131, 149–50
Shandu, 121, 149
Sick Jacken, 45
Siempre en Domingo, 162–63
Singleton, Chuck (pastor), 186
Skate Junction (West Covina), 73–74
Skateland (Compton), 73–74
Skatemaster Tate, 11
Skeeter Rabbit, 128–29
Skip hoppers, 100–1
Sky-rhyming, 1, 174, 178, 194, 210, 216–17
Slick, 206
Smith, Chuck (pastor), 175
Snoop Dogg, 77
social death, 196–97, 198–99
Sola Soul, 115–16
Soldiers for Christ, 177
Solomon, "Boogaloo Sam," 75
Solomon, Timothy; Popin Pete, 37–38, 75, 80, 127–29
Soul Drop One, 210
Soul Train, 34, 80, 119–20
South Bronx, 144–45
South Central Los Angeles, 218
South Gate, 200, 201

INDEX

South Los Angeles County, 82
Southern California, 75
Southsiders (gang), 167–68, 169
Spanish F.L.Y. (Foolish Loco Youngsters), 157, 159, 167
Spin Masters, 41
Spot, the, 173–74
Spray Can 88, 205
Star Wars, 79
Stewart, Gio, 116
Storrs, Dave, 30, 130–31
Straight to the Bank (song by Latin Alliance), 112
street dance, 33, 73, 74, 76–77
strutting, 160
Suave (DJ), 125
Suga Pop, 119–20, 123, 127, 128, 159–60
Sugar Style, 148
Sullivan, Arnold, 104
Sup the Chemist, 191–92
Super Def Creators, 159
Surf Fetish, 197, 207
synthesizer, 90

Tangerine Dream, 90
Taylor, Chris; "the Glove," 32, 124, 125–27, 130–31
Techno Hop Records, 148
technological aspects of music, 90
Teen Challenge, 179
TGO, 148–49
That's Incredible (TV Show), 102
The Dream Team Is in the House! (song by the LA Dream Team), 84
The Pilot, 120–21
The Unknown DJ, 148
This Is the Life, documentary, 213
Thrasher Magazine, 207–8
Tic Tac, 108–9
Tinker Toy, 37
Topophobia, 136–37
Traffic Jam radio mix format, 170
translocal, 215
translocal associations, 95–96
Translocal Brokers, 110–11, 119–22
Trivette, Alvin; ALT, 104
Trujillo, Damon; Krazy D, 201–2
Tufono, Marcus "Kutfather" (DJ & Rapper), 159–60
Tumba La Casa (song by the Latin Kings), 202–3, 204
Tunnel Rats, 3, 191–92, 210–12
tuttin (dance), 160

UCLA, 121–22
Umana, Norma, 134, 152
Uncle Jamm's Army (UJA), 80–83, 84–85, 86–87, 88, 130–31, 157–58, 166
underground, 18–19, 152–53, 210
underground Hip Hop, 174, 194, 196, 204, 209
underground Hip Hop heads, 173–74
underground scene, 115–16, 122, 123, 128
underground scene (Los Angeles), 208, 209
Unique Dreams Entertainment in 1978, 80
Unique St. Rockers, 161
United We Stand (UWS), 105–6
Universal Zulu Nation (UZN), 110, 119–20, 144–45, 208–9
Urbina, Wilber; Wilpower, 137, 148–49, 207–8, 215
UTI (Graffiti crew), 113, 148–49
UWS, 112–13

Valdivia, Steve, 169, 202
Vasquez, Jason; Son Doobie, 201–2
Vault, the (Long Beach), 108–9
Venice Beach, 73–74, 180–81
VHS cassettes, 85
Viator, Felicia, 81, 129
Victory Outreach Church, 178–93
Viktor Manoel, 128
Villaseñor, Manny, 84–85
VIP Records (South Central Los Angeles), 124
VSF, 91

Wack Girl, 148
Wake Up Show, 173
War on Drugs, 196–97
Warner Brothers record, 204
Watkins, Leon, 168–70
We're All in the Same Gang, 202
West Coast Funk Elements, 72–73, 77–78
West Coast Hip Hop, 116–17, 125, 126, 129, 134–35, 174, 191–92
West Coast Hip Hop commemorated sacred sites, 153
West Coast Hip Hop culture, 181–82
West Coast Hip Hop Elements, 72–73, 74, 76, 117, 126–27, 128
West Coast Rap All-Stars, 202–3
West Coast scene's resonance, 159
West Covina, California, 218
West Palm Beach Florida, 165, 166, 167
Westhoff, Ben, 202
Westlake neighborhood, 137, 218
Whacking, 127–28
White Lines, 104–5

White, Barry, 168–69
Whitmore, Chester, 138
Whittier Blvd, 108–9
Whittier, California, 173–74
Wild Style, film, 100, 113
Wilkerson, David (pastor), 179
Wilkes, Jamaal, 169–70
Will.I.Am/Will One X, 208
Williams, Bill "Slim The Robot," 75
Williams, Dianne; Queen Boogaloo, 161
Wilmington, California, 157, 161, 218
World Class Wreckin' Cru, 81, 170, 189
World on Wheels (South Central Los Angeles), 73–74

World War III (song by LPG and Ahmad), 173

Xololanxinxo, 148, 213

Yano, Steve, 157–58
Young MC, 202
Youth Break Center, 122–23, 124–30, 134–40

Zanfagna, Christina, 174, 182, 192–93, 210
Zekri, Bernard, 121–22
Zodie's (Montebello), 90
Zoot suits, 11, 14, 54, 56, 64, 77
Zulu Beads, 119